Anthropometry is the measurement of human morphology and is used in a wide range of applied and research contexts. In this volume, distinguished contributors including anthropologists, human biologists, physiologists, nutritionists and clinical scientists describe many of the ways in which anthropometry is used, and discuss problems associated with different methods of assessment. Topics include measurement error and statistical issues in anthropometry, and the construction and use of growth charts in growth monitoring. In addition, the use of anthropometry in assessments of body composition, physical performance and fitness is discussed.

This book will be of interest to graduates and researchers in human biology, anthropology, and nutrition. It will also be useful to workers in sports medicine, ergonomics, orthopaedics and paediatrics.

Cambridge Studies in Biological Anthropology 14

Anthropometry: the individual and the population

Cambridge Studies in Biological Anthropology

Series Editors

G.W. Lasker
Department of Anatomy & Cell Biology,
Wayne State University,
Detroit, Michigan, USA

C.G.N. Mascie-Taylor
Department of Biological Anthropology,
University of Cambridge

D.F. Roberts
Department of Human Genetics,
University of Newcastle-upon-Tyne

R.A. Foley
Department of Biological Anthropology,
University of Cambridge

Also in the series

G.W. Lasker *Surnames and Genetic Structure*

C.G.N. Mascie-Taylor and G.W. Lasker (editors) *Biological Aspects of Human Migration*

Barry Bogin *Patterns of Human Growth*

Julius A. Kieser *Human Adult Odontometrics – The study of variation in adult tooth size*

J.E. Lindsay Carter and Barbara Honeyman Heath *Somatotyping – Development and applications*

Roy J. Shephard *Body Composition in Biological Anthropology*

Ashley H. Robins *Biological Perspectives on Human Pigmentation*

C.G.N. Mascie-Taylor and G.W. Lasker (editors) *Applications of Biological Anthropology to Human Affairs*

Alex F. Roche *Growth, Maturation, and Body Composition – The Fels Longitudinal Study 1929–1991*

Eric J. Devor (editor) *Molecular Applications in Biological Anthropology*

Kenneth M. Weiss *The Genetic Causes of Human Disease – Principles and evolutionary approaches*

Duane Quiatt and Vernon Reynolds *Primate Behaviour – Information, social knowledge, and the evolution of culture*

G.W. Lasker and C.G.N. Mascie-Taylor *Research Strategies in Biological Anthropology – Field and survey studies*

Anthropometry: the individual and the population

EDITED BY

S.J. ULIJASZEK

Lecturer in Biological Anthropology,
Department of Biological Anthropology,
University of Cambridge, Cambridge, UK

AND

C.G.N. MASCIE-TAYLOR

Reader in Biological Anthropology,
Department of Biological Anthropology,
University of Cambridge, Cambridge, UK

CAMBRIDGE
UNIVERSITY PRESS

Published by the Press Syndicate of the University of Cambridge
The Pitt Building, Trumpington Street, Cambridge CB2 1RP
40 West 20th Street, New York, NY 10011-4211, USA
10 Stamford Road, Oakleigh, Melbourne 3166, Australia

First published 1994

Printed in Great Britain at the University Press, Cambridge

A catalogue record for this book is available from the British Library

Library of Congress cataloguing in publication data

Anthropometry: the individual and the population/edited by S.J. Ulijaszek and
C.G.N. Mascie-Taylor.
    p.   cm. – (Cambridge studies in biological anthropology)
   Includes bibliographical references and index.
   ISBN 0-521-41798-8 (hardback)
   1. Anthropometry. 2. Human growth. 3. Anthropometry –
Methodology. I. Ulijaszek, Stanley J. II. Mascie-Taylor, C.G.N.
III. Series.
GN51.A59 1994
573'.6 – dc20 93-7332 CIP

ISBN 0 521 41798 8 hardback

PN

Contents

Contributors

Dr T.J. Cole
Dunn Nutritional Laboratory, Downhams Lane, Cambridge CB4 1XJ,
UK

Dr P.H. Dangerfield
Departments of Human Anatomy and Cell Biology, and Orthopaedic
Surgery, University of Liverpool, PO Box 147, Liverpool L69 3BX,
UK

Dr P.S.W. Davies
Dunn Nutritional Laboratory, Downhams Lane, Cambridge CB4 1XJ,
UK

Dr K.E. Friedl
US Army Research Institute of Environmental Medicine, Natick,
Massachusetts 01760-5020, USA

Dr C.C. Gordon
Behavioral Sciences Division, US Army Natick Research,
Development and Engineering Center, Natick, Massachusetts 01760-
5020, USA

Dr C.J.K. Henry
School of Biological Sciences, Oxford Brookes University, Gipsy Lane,
Headington, Oxford OX3 0BP, UK

Professor G.W. Lasker
Department of Anatomy and Cell Biology, Wayne State University,
School of Medicine, 504 East Canfield Avenue, Detroit, Michigan
48201, USA

Professor J.A. Lourie
Department of Orthopaedic Surgery, Milton Keynes Hospital, Milton
Keynes MK19 6EQ, UK

Professor R.M. Malina
Department of Kinesiology and Health Education, University of
Texas, Austin, Texas 78712, USA

Dr C.G.N. Mascie-Taylor
Department of Biological Anthropology, University of Cambridge,
Downing Street, Cambridge CB2 3DZ, UK

Dr N.G. Norgan
Department of Human Sciences, Loughborough University,
Loughborough, Leicestershire LE11 3TU, UK

Professor A.M. Tomkins
Centre for International Child Health, Institute of Child Health,
30 Guilford Street, London WC1N 1EH, UK

Dr S.J. Ulijaszek
Department of Biological Anthropology, University of Cambridge,
Downing Street, Cambridge CB2 3DZ, UK

Preface

This book examines the various ways in which anthropometric measurements are used and interpreted in a range of disciplines, including biological anthropology, human biology, clinical medicine, applied physiology, health sciences and ergonomics. Anthropometry can be used to define population characteristics or to assess individuals with respect to some physical parameter, and the dual nature of this methodology is addressed by many of the authors.

The introductory chapter by G.W. Lasker discusses the role that anthropometry plays in studies of human biology, and examines the history of anthropometric measurement. The use of anthropometry in discriminating the pathological from the normal is a theme which appears in the first chapter, and is developed further by P.H. Dangerfield, who considers asymmetry in human growth, and why it is important to define what is 'normal' asymmetry. Accurate measurement is important in any science, and S.J. Ulijaszek and J.A Lourie review what is known about measurement error in anthropometry and put forward references for maximum acceptable error. In the chapter which follows, C.G.N. Mascie-Taylor considers statistical issues and approaches when analysing cross-sectional anthropometric characters in groups or populations.

Growth charts are widely used for growth monitoring in both developed and developing countries, and the next three chapters consider different aspects of monitoring. In the first of these, T.J. Cole describes different types of growth chart and the principles underlying them, and elaborates on new types of conditional height charts which he has developed. In the subsequent chapter, S.J. Ulijaszek considers the importance of understanding human growth cyclicities in relation to accurate growth monitoring in Western nations, while in the third of these, A.M. Tomkins discusses the problems associated with growth monitoring, screening and surveillance in developing countries.

Anthropometry has been widely used in the assessment of nutritional status of children in developing countries. Only recently has it been considered for the assessment of undernutrition in adults. The chapter by C.J.K. Henry considers the use of body mass index (BMI) in such assessment, and goes on to show that BMI can be used to define the limits of human survival. The BMI is a proxy for body size and, less directly, of body composition; anthropometry has been used to assess body composition in adults, but it has been little used for such assessment in children. The problems associated with this type of work are raised in the chapter by P.S.W. Davies. The following chapters by N.G. Norgan and R.M. Malina consider anthropometry and physical performance, and anthropometry and physical fitness, respectively. In an extensive review of the anthropometric concerns of scientists in the US Armed Forces, C.C. Gordon describes some approaches which may be of value to workers in other areas.

Collectively, this volume shows the many ways in which anthropometry is used. More specifically, authors address problems associated with the use and interpretation of this methodology in different areas of study.

Cambridge

Stanley J. Ulijaszek
C.G.N. Mascie-Taylor

Acknowledgements

We thank Kabi Pharmacia for their financial support of the one day anthropometry workshop held at the Department of Biological Anthropology, University of Cambridge, at which most of the chapters in this book were presented.

1 The place of anthropometry in human biology

G. W. LASKER

The chief point about anthropometrics is that any aspect of physiological function depends on the underlying morphology, and the objective way of evaluating and comparing aspects of morphology is measurement. In the human that is anthropometry. The anatomical sciences were long plagued and continue to be beset with a technical problem: descriptive anatomy necessarily leads to comparisons of categories with arbitrary inter-category boundaries. The categorizations therefore tend to be subjective and their artificiality leads to analyses which are typological. However, the human body does not work that way. Most structures vary continuously and their functioning is according to tendencies which are best described by what might be called 'vectors'. Understanding such vectors must come from analyses of the relationships between measurements of the functions and measurements of the underlying anatomical structures.

All this may seem self-evident, but a surprising amount of anatomy and pathology is still presented in typological terms. The very concepts of 'normal' and 'pathological' imply that one can determine the boundary and that it has an invariant significance for disease. But the boundary is not fixed. This can be illustrated using as an example the torus palatinus, a benign protuberance on the hard palate of some individuals. One individual does not even know that he or she has a torus palatinus, another individual has one that affects speech, and a third is worried silly that he or she has a cancerous growth of the hard palate. These differences relate in part to the *size* of the torus. Just saying 'big' or 'small', even if by reference to standard photographs or casts, is not very satisfactory; the best way to express size is by measurement, and the measurements should be made in a standardized way. Such a way may be difficult to establish and follow; the example of palatine torus exemplifies some aspects of the difference between observation and measurement. A

1

careful description of each case reveals fine details. It is virtually impossible to make a systematic comparison of a large series of descriptions of tori of various shapes and sizes, however. On the other hand a measurement, for instance of the height of the torus (the extent of maximum protrusion downward at right angles from the plane of the floor of the hard palate measured with coordinate callipers) may not well represent the overall size.

Although the methods for such measurements may be hard to design in a standardized way relevant to the problem, they permit objective statements about one or more dimensions of the structure in relation to presence or absence of problems of speech or mistake as a tumour. Whereas descriptions of individuals and their palatine tori may tell one more about their individual problems, it takes measurements to deal with problems of this kind in populations.

When serious anthropometry began and for what purposes, I do not know. Certainly by the Renaissance, Leonardo, Dürer and other artists were concerned about body proportions. In the eighteenth century examples of anthropometric measurements begin to appear in the literature. The stature of soldiers and members of the militia were sometimes recorded. Scammon (1927) ascribes the first cross-sectional studies of growth to a study of birth weights and physical properties of newborns by J. G. Roederer in 1753.

For longitudinal studies Scammon (1927) gives the priority to (and numerous authorities cite) the semiannual height measurements of a single individual, his son, by Philibert Gueneau de Montbeillard between April 11, 1759, and January 30, 1777.

Throughout the nineteenth century examples of systematic anthropometric studies steadily increased in numbers. Anthropological and ethnological societies were organized in various countries. By 1875, for instance, the British Association for the Advancement of Science had a standing Anthropometric Committee that published regular reports. In 1860 Anders Retzius, a Swedish anatomist, published on the cephalic index, the ratio of length to the breadth of the head. Efforts were made to standardize methods and before the end of the century an international meeting at Frankfurt-am-Main in Germany agreed on the way to position skulls for measurement in a horizontal plane formed by the lowest point on the inferior margin of the left orbit and the highest points of the two external auditory meati. Standardization was a major concern. Rudolf Martin published the first edition of his *Lehrbuch* in 1914. The expanded second edition (1928) remained the source for descriptions of the ways to make hundreds of anthropometric measurements both of the skeleton and of the living. The methods remained standard, at least in German-speaking countries. At present a fourth edition with dozens of different authors is in preparation.

The purposes of all these measurements were often taken for granted. Those who devised new measurements no doubt sometimes had special questions in mind, but the issue of better ways to approach a specific question as against better ways to make the measurements repeatable was seldom expressed, so intense was the attention to the need for reliability.

In the United States, there was a sharp reversal of interest. In 1941 H. L. Shapiro became the founding editor of a tiny new journal, *Anthropological Briefs*, which was to be dedicated to methodological issues. In it Morris Steggerda published the results of a survey he had conducted. He had visited a score of anthropologists and asked them to measure his wife, who accompanied him. The results were very diverse: in measuring biiliac diameter, for instance, some anthropometrists had squeezed down to the bone and others apparently had barely dented the skin; perhaps they did not even have the same conception of what constitutes the iliac crests, the measurements varied so widely.

In the same journal Sherwood Washburn wrote an article in three parts that attacked what some were doing with anthropometrics. He took as example the reporting of inter-orbital diameter. This measurement, he argued, has no real meaning in itself. Rather, species with well-developed ethmoid sinuses tend to space the orbits farther apart. The burden of his message was that if you want to study sinuses, design methods to measure sinuses. Either because of the decreasing interest in measurements for their own sake or as a result of Second World War, the little journal only survived for the three issues which contained the Washburn article. Washburn himself, however, kept up the attack on routine anthropometry. He returned to his theme at the Viking Fund Summer Seminars in Physical Anthropology held for a number of years in New York, and reported in proceedings by Bernice Kaplan in the first few volumes of the *Yearbook of Physical Anthropology* (for 1945–1951).

Washburn (1946, 1947) was then engaged in experimental morphology studies on rats and rabbits. In these experiments he showed that the bony parts for muscular attachments were much smaller if the muscle was paralysed. He had already demonstrated that a bony capsule (the orbit) is greatly reduced in size if the contents (the eye) are removed (Washburn & Detwiler, 1943).

In a very influential paper that has been widely reprinted ('The new physical anthropology', 1951) Washburn chose the example of the mandible to make his point. There are three functionally important regions of the mandible, he noted: (i) the part for attachment of the teeth (the alveolar process); (ii) the parts for attachment of the muscles of mastication (the coronoid process and adjacent parts of the ascending ramus for the temporalis and the gonial angle for the masseter and internal pterygoid); and (iii) the basic bone running from the articulations with the temporal bones to the symphysis. The previously developed standardized measurements of the mandible have only indirect relationships to the functionally important sizes of these three parts.

Washburn (1953) returned to his main theme again, and in commenting on it I wrote:

> From subsequent publications in physical anthropology one might think that Washburn and [T.D.] McCown were prophetic. It is well to remember, however, that these prophets had their forerunners. The so-called 'New Physical Anthropology,' a phrase used by Washburn (1951) to characterize a decreased emphasis on traditional methods of measurement and a preponderant emphasis on heredity, process, and functional anatomy, was by no means new. Washburn's writings, however, have disseminated these concepts widely, and his teachings have put to use in anthropology approaches first clearly stated by others many years earlier.
>
> (Lasker, 1964)

Looked at functionally, the body is forced to balance a series of vectors: thus conservation of material dictates that as organs enlarge they should tend to become more spherical (as in the brain case of hydrocephalics or the abdomen of the obese) but the attachment of large muscles requires larger areas of bone (as in the sagittal crests of the gorilla skull and the high nuchal lines on the occiputs of Neanderthals). Washburn challenged his readers to find appropriate ways to conceptualize and measure vectors such as these; standardization of anthropometry seemed very old-fashioned. In addition, these methods had not escaped misuse by Nazi racists despite the assumption that anthropometry was objective and neutral. Whatever the functional meaning of anthropometric differences, and despite the evidence adduced by Boas (1928) and others of their susceptibility to environmental modification, they were often erroneously treated as essential, inborn and racial.

Thus, after the Second World War, there was a paradigm shift in physical anthropology – at least in the United States – away from the routine taking of standardized measurements for racial typology to 'designer' tests for each new study. Then in the 1960s, when the International Biological Program organized a massive Human Adaptability

Project, it was necessary again to put the emphasis on what useful measurements could be collected throughout the world by individuals trained in various disciplines and traditions, and some minimum requirements for comparability were laid out (see Weiner & Lourie, 1981). Thus standardization was then viewed not as an end in itself, but to be used for specific purposes. Development of methods continues; always, one hopes, in a context that permits comparisons with previous studies as well as to attack new questions in greater detail.

Many textbooks on applied statistics select anthropometric measurements for some of their first examples. The reason seems to be that those learning statistics can easily understand anthropometry and grasp the value of statistics about such variable as stature. Methods which can be widely appreciated and relatively easily learned allow the results of anthropometric studies to influence health and welfare professionals and the behaviours of non-experts in the public at large.

The properties which make any anthropometric dimension appealing to the scientific mind, however, are first, its usefulness, and secondly that it can be readily repeated with little likelihood of large differences due to methodological error.

Some measurements, especially those that span bony structures, remain relatively constant from minute to minute and from day to day. Therefore remeasurement is possible as a check on reliability. Because of both their reliability and their accuracy, anthropometric measurements, if appropriate for the intended purposes, represent the human morphology well. Measured in this way human variation is a property of the object, not a subjective narrative of some post-modernist philosopher, although, of course, interpretation can be subject to distortions.

Given the accurate and objective nature of anthropometric measurements, it is hardly surprising that they lend themselves to debunking unscientific assertions about human biology. For instance, at a time when William H. Sheldon was proclaiming that somatotypes were an immutable aspect of human personality, Ancel Keys, Josef Brožek and others conducted a partial starvation experiment on volunteers. Anthropometric measurements taken on before-and-after nude photographs of the volunteers showed that, by one of Sheldon's somatotype methods, six months of the starvation phase of the experiment had produced enormous changes in the rating of each somatotype component (Lasker, 1947). Whatever it was that Sheldon alleged to be unchanging, it could not have been the physique as measured by Sheldon's measurement somatotype method. Many issues in human biology that remain contentious could best be resolved by appropriate objective measurement.

Thus, despite reservations about past uses and abuses of anthropometrics, it can be seen that they are suitable and adaptable to many scientific and applied problems about human biology including changes over time in respect to growth or evolution, human factors in design of clothing and equipment, applications to forensic identifications, objective signs of physical fitness or illnesses, and the relative genetic and environmental components of various aspects of human physique under various circumstances including nutritional and other stresses. The trick is to adapt or design appropriate measurements that bear on the evolving issues; use existing methods only if they are the most suitable or if they aid by permitting further use of already available information.

References
Boas, F. (1928). *Materials for the Study of Inheritance in Man.* New York: Columbia University Press.

Lasker, G. W. (1947). The effect of partial starvation on somatotype. An analysis of material from the Minnesota Starvation Experiment. *American Journal of Physical Anthropology* (n.s.) **5**, 323–41.

Lasker, G. W. (1964). Comment. In: *Physical Anthropology 1953–1961 (Yearbook of Physical Anthropology,* vol. 9), ed. G. W. Lasker, p. 1.

Martin, R. (1914). *Lehrbuch der Anthropologie in Systematischer Darstellung.* Jena: Gustav Fischer.

Martin, R. (1928). *Lehrbuch der Anthropologie.* (3 vols.) Jena: Gustav Fischer.

Retzius, A. A. (1860). De brachycephaliska och dolichocephaliska folkskagens geografiska utbrednik forklaring til attoljande karta. *Kungliga Vetenskaps Akademiet Forkaringar* no. 2, pp. 99–101.

Scammon, R. E. (1927). The first seriatim study of human growth. *American Journal of Physical Anthropology* **10**, 329–36.

Washburn, S. L. (1946). The effect of partial paralysis on the growth of the skull of rat and rabbit. *Anatomical Record* **94**, 163–8.

Washburn, S. L. (1947). The relation of the temporal muscle to the form of the skull. *Anatomical Record* **99**, 239–48.

Washburn, S. L. (1951). The new physical anthropology. *Transactions of the New York Academy of Science* (II) **13**, 298–304.

Washburn, S. L. (1953). The strategy of physical anthropology. In: *Anthropology Today*, ed. A. L. Kroeber, pp. 714–27. Chicago: University of Chicago Press.

Washburn, S. L. & Detwiler, S. R. (1943). An experiment bearing on the problems of physical anthropology. *American Journal of Physical Anthropology* (n.s.) **1**, 171–90.

Weiner, J. S. & Lourie, J. A. (1981). *Practical Human Biology.* London: Academic Press.

2 Asymmetry and growth

PETER H. DANGERFIELD

Complete body symmetry may be regarded as the norm in the animal kingdom, with a history dating back to the earliest animals to evolve on the planet. In contrast, asymmetry in nature is fairly rare. Examples include the male narwhal with its elongated tusk, formed from a left spiralling overgrown tooth, male fiddler crabs with an enlarged right claw and the New Zealand wrybill, with a beak which bends to the right. Consistent right–left differences within the individual, termed handed asymmetry, are also present in many vertebrates (Brown & Wolpert, 1990). Examples of this are the dextral looping of the heart during embryological development, and the variations in the lobes of the lungs between right and left. Minor limb asymmetry, which may be measured using careful anthropometry, is the norm and common in the human. In contrast, gross asymmetry, which is at once detectable by the human eye, is rare.

Limb asymmetry has been described in normal subjects and associated with pathological conditions. It is closely related to laterality (frequently referred to as handedness) and has been shown to be associated with a wide range of musculoskeletal diseases and malignancies. It may also occur spontaneously and have no known pathological cause.

The development of the right and left limbs depends on a similar morphogenesis for the right and left sides of the body and is a consequence of the development of mirror symmetry, the plane of the symmetry being the midline of the embryo. However, this is in contrast to the development of the asymmetrical visceral organs such as the liver, heart and pancreas, which must arise out of the intrinsic handedness within the embryo (Brown et al., 1989). The presence of this handed asymmetry implies the existence of a mechanism in the embryo which enables it to tell its right from its left and interpret this positional information in morphogenesis. The factors which control handed asymmetry are complex and as yet ill understood.

7

Laterality and asymmetry
Asymmetry of the skull

The human cerebral cortex is characterized by certain functional asymmetries from which no clear homologue is known in non-human primates. These asymmetries are due in part to the presence, in the left cerebral cortex, of mechanisms developed to mediate language and skilled manipulative activities. Skull asymmetries and, by inference, dominance by one of the hemispheres appear in the fossil record (Geschwind, 1985). Studies on normal and neurological patients have shown that the right and left hemispheres display various functional asymmetries and these are accompanied by regional morphological asymmetries (Blinkov & Glezer, 1968; Geschwind, 1985; Crow, 1990; Steinmetz *et al.*, 1990). Right–left asymmetries have been identified in the temporal speech cortex and in the length and slope of the lateral sulcus as well as the inferior frontal gyrus. The posterior portion of the left hemisphere is commonly wider and protrudes further on the right, while the anterior portion of the right hemisphere is wider and protrudes further forward than the left (Henery & Mayhew, 1989). This protrusion of one hemisphere beyond the other is known as 'petalia', and can be detected by using computerized tomography (CT) scanning. Furthermore, since the shape of the skull is considered to be determined mainly by the shape of the underlying brain, such brain asymmetries may also mirror the overlying shape of the skull, producing plagiocephaly.

The skull itself has been reported to be asymmetrical, particularly in the context of the face. Liebreich, a pioneer in investigations of skull and face asymmetry, concluded that this was a constant and characteristic feature of humans (Liebreich, 1908). The left side of the face and mandible are larger than the right and plagiocephaly is not uncommon in the normal population (Halperin, 1931). However, it has also been reported that there is no systematic tendency for one side of the mandible to be larger than the other in the context of mesiodistal tooth diameter, even though larger teeth have a greater side-to-side asymmetry (Garn, Lewis & Kerewsky, 1966).

Facial asymmetry

Facial asymmetry has been reported for children (Mullick, 1965; Burke, 1971). This asymmetry is small and its proportion does not change with growth. It can also be demonstrated that, by using stereophotogrammetry or computer-acquired images of the face, the joining together of a reversed half with the same normal half results in a facial representation quite dissimilar to the original. This trick is frequently used to demonstrate the normal asymmetry of the face, the maxillary area being larger on the left than the right (Burke, 1971). The use of image processing techniques permits skull reconstructions; these are used in orthodontics, where asymmetries may be encountered (Georgiou & Forsyth, 1991). Unilateral facial hypertrophy is a rare condition, but has been reported affecting both the skeletal and muscular tissue of the face (Gordin, Gabriele & Higgins, 1989; Khanna & Andrade, 1989). Hemifacial microsomia is a progressive asymmetry in the mandible which involves the skeletal and soft tissue derived from the first and second pharyngeal arches. Growth failure occurs in the midline, leading to a progressive disfiguration of the lower face. Other examples of facial asymmetries are hypoplasia of the first branchial arch, which is more common on the right, and cleft lip, which is more common on the left (Burke, 1971).

Thus mild degrees of facial asymmetry are the norm, representing natural conditions which overlap gradually with the clinically pathological. However, quantitative evaluation of the degree of asymmetry is required if pathology is suspected.

Handedness

Humans have shown a preference for the use of the right hand in performing unimanual tasks for at least 17 000 years, on the basis of study of historic and prehistoric drawing, painting and sculpture (Coren & Porac, 1977). The lateralized representation in the left cortex of mechanisms for language mediation and object manipulation are likely to be a consequence of the requirement of the asymmetric employment of the forelimbs in the making and use of tools during hominid evolution. Such tool use has been described in the fossil record dating back to 2.6 million years ago and is probably unique to human evolution (Potts & Shipman, 1981; Johanson & Shreeve, 1990).

The ubiquitous occurrence of stone tools associated with various different fossil hominids must attest to the vital role which the manufacture and use of such artifacts played in human evolution. The development of tool use in turn must imply asymmetrical use of the limbs in such a way that the left hand was used to steady the object being manipulated while the right hand was used to perform the skilled manipulation. The emergence of right-handedness is therefore closely related to asymmetry of the cortex, which in turn must be closely related to the need for asymmetrical use of the forelimb. The adaptiveness of this asymmetrical development and arrangement must follow from a few assumptions of brain organization and evolution. The colateralization of language mechanisms in present day *Homo sapiens* to the left hemisphere is therefore held to be a consequence of the coupling of these linguistic mechanisms to the motor mechanisms already lateralized to the left hemisphere at an earlier point in hominid evolution. The evolution of laterality can therefore be accounted for within current concepts of human evolution.

Laterality of fractures

Does the presence of laterality in the brain and its effect on the limbs have any clinical manifestations in the context of accidental damage to the limbs, such as by fractures? Although clinicians consider the musculo-skeletal system to be symmetrical, it is certainly clear from reports that the sides of the body are not equally at risk from injury and disease. The dominant limb is frequently more involved than the non-dominant limb in carpal tunnel syndrome (Phillips, 1965), osteoarthritis of the hand (Acheson, Chan & Clemett, 1970) and Dupuytren's Contracture (Boyes, 1954).

Since Truesdell (1921) observed that overgrowth occurred following fractures, there have been a number of reports showing that the femur in particular grows on average about 1 cm in children, following trauma (Aitkin, Blackett & Cincotti, 1939; Griffin & Green, 1972; Staheli, 1967; Meals, 1979b). It has been suggested that the overgrowth is due either to cerebral asymmetrical influences or to functional hypertrophy (Meals, 1979b). However, information relating to the side preference for frac-tures is sparse, possibly because of the likelihood that injuries are random events. Investigation of the incidence of fractures of the appendicular skeleton has demonstrated that there is a tendency for one side to be involved more than the other (Meals, 1979a). The majority of upper limb fractures proximal to the wrist affect the left side while those distal to the wrist appear to affect the right limb. For right-handed people, the affected limb is on the non-dominant side, possibly because falls on that side are more awkward (Williams & Heather, 1973).

Bone asymmetries in the limbs

The limbs may be regarded as mirror images of each other, possessing complete symmetry about the midline axis, and thus being completely symmetrical (Brown & Wolpert, 1990). The developmental processes for the two sides of this midline axis with respect to limb development must therefore be identical. However, asymmetry in limb bones is known to exist. Notably, the right humerus and forearm may be longer than the left; there may also be crossed asymmetry, with the left femur being longer than the right. In addition the upper limb may display a greater degree of asymmetry than the lower limb.

Many late nineteenth and early twentieth century studies relating to asymmetry were undertaken, primarily in France and Germany, using disarticulated skeletal material. In France, Rollet (1902) found inequality in the length of the upper limbs in 99 of 100 subjects studied, with the right humerus being longer than the left. Garson (1879) noted the inequality in length of the lower limbs with the right being shorter than the left in 54.3% of cases.

Normally, asymmetry studies were undertaken on prepared cadeveric material, measuring the lengths and weights of the long bones of the body (Ingalls, 1931; Hrdlicka, 1932; Ludwig, 1932; Schultz, 1937; Trotter & Gleser, 1952; Jolicoer, 1963; Schulter-Ellis, 1979) or alternatively utilizing archaeological material (Munter, 1936; Ruff, 1979). Other studies were undertaken using careful anthropometric measurement of the living subject (Ingelmark, 1942). Similar conclusions were reached in all studies, despite differences in methods. The human upper limbs are more bilaterally asymmetrical in length and weight than the lower limb bones, and the right upper limb is significantly longer (1–3%) and heavier (2–4%) than the left limb. Conversely, the left lower limb bones, particularly the femur, are slightly longer and heavier than the right (less than 1%) (Ruff & Jones, 1981). Laubach & McConville (1967) employed anthropometric methodology to establish whether right-side to left-side differences existed in different body measurements. They found statistically significant differences for 8 of 21 different measurements, most of them being in the forelimb. Malina & Buschang (1984) reported left–right asymmetries in normal males and a mentally retarded population, with the latter group displaying greater asymmetry.

Radiographic techniques have also been employed to study asymmetry of the limbs (Ingelmark, 1946; Buskirk, Anderson & Brozek, 1956; Garn, Mayor & Shaw, 1976). Other studies, concentrating on the relation between bone dimensions and physical activity, have revealed that athletes frequently display asymmetries not present in non-athletic controls (Buskirk, Anderson & Brozek, 1956; King, Brelsford & Tullos, 1969; Jones *et al.*, 1977). For example, Buskirk *et al.* (1956) compared anthropometric measurements taken on the surface of the arms of soldiers and tennis players with X-rays of the same limb, finding that tennis playing led to an increase in length of the radius and ulna in the arm used to swing the tennis racket. Such investigations suggest a relationship between activity and bone growth.

However, not all studies of bilateral asymmetry support a pure environmental and exercise-related explanation for asymmetry. Schultz (1926) reported marked asymmetry in the lengths of the femur and foot of the human foetus as early as the sixteenth week. A study of bone area, cortical area (bone mass) and percentage cortical area in patients suffering from chronic renal failure showed significant right–left asymmetries in the metacarpus, with an individual direction of the asymmetry which was independent of natural laterality (Garn, Mayor & Shaw, 1976). Other asymmetries independent of activity levels have also been reported by Montoye *et al.* (1976). Limb asymmetry has also been shown to decrease with age (Ruff & Jones, 1981). Anthropometric studies undertaken in Liverpool show asymmetry in the normal neonate and growing child, as well as associated with spinal curvature (scoliosis), club foot and Wilms' tumour.

Asymmetry in the lower limb

In orthopaedic practice, asymmetry in the lower limb is frequently a cause of patient referral to hospital, either as the primary problem or discovered as a result of some other condition. It is a common orthopaedic problem in the child (Vogel, 1984). Ingelmark (1942) discussed physiological asymmetry in the lower limbs, commenting that after the age of two years the right lower limb was often longer than the left. Between the ages of 10 and 15 years, the asymmetry disappeared but in the adult the left limb was often longer than the right. There is radiological evidence that the adult right limb is shorter than the left (Rush & Steiner, 1964; Ingelmark & Lindstrom, 1963).

Radiological measurement of the legs is presently the most accurate method available clinically for assessing leg length discrepancy and is used in timing surgical growth arrest procedures and predicting the expected degree of inequality at maturity in cases of infantile congenital growth defects. Standards are available for radiological leg length measurement (Anderson, Green & Messner, 1963). Femoral and tibial growth has also been used as a method to calculate the remaining growth in the bones at any skeletal age (Tupman, 1962). In neither instance are normal values for right and left limbs quoted.

Inequality in lower limb length is often a source of painful self-consciousness to the adolescent or young adult. It may result from fractures or infection stimulating growth in the epiphysis, or from hemihypertrophy, or it may be idiopathic. Decreased growth may result from a congenital malformation, particularly of the femur, after diseases such as poliomyelitis or as a result of damage to the epiphysis. All these conditions may require surgical correction of the inequality by leg lengthening, epiphyseal arrest or shortening of the normal limb. Untreated, minor inequalities of the lower limb can lead to lumbar back pain and arthritis or to pelvic tilt and spinal deformities such as scoliosis, itself an asymmetry of a midline structure. They may also lead to increased risk of injury in recreational running and jogging (Brunet *et al.*, 1990). Limb length asymmetries will also affect the gait pattern and will in turn affect the pelvis (causing pelvic tilt), hip joints and lumbar spine, leading to increased risk of arthritic change in the spine. However, pelvic tilt itself can arise as a result of asymmetry of the pelvis, scoliosis or hip joint malposition (Wagner, 1990).

Lower limb asymmetries have also been reported associated with femoral anteversion (torsion) (Upadhyay, Burwell & Moulton, 1986; Upadhyay *et al.*, 1990). Using B-mode ultrasound the femoral anteversion was measured on the right and left sides; marked degrees of asymmetry of more than 10° were found, related to age, side and tibia:foot length ratio.

Congenital short femur is an uncommon lower limb shortening condition, which may range from the rare complete absence of the bone, associated with an abnormal development of the pelvis, to the commoner form of a unilateral small femur (Grill & Dungl, 1991). Its incidence has been estimated to be 1 in 50 000 (Rogala *et al.*, 1974). Nine different types have been described (Pappas, 1983). At birth, the exact characteristics of the shortening cannot be defined, but by two years of age, classification by clinical and radiological examination is possible (Fixen & Lloyd-Roberts, 1974; Hamanishi, 1980). By careful measurement during growth, it has been shown that the relative lengths of the bones in the involved limb retain almost unchanged (Ring, 1959; Amstutz, 1969; Westin, Sakai & Wood, 1976; Pappas, 1983). Thus prediction of the final discrepancy is possible from early anthropometric measurements; such growth data enable the correct treatment to be undertaken.

Tibial agenesis is a rare anomaly of the lower limb (De Santis *et al.*, 1990). First described by Otto in 1841, there are considered to be four types of tibial agenesis (Otto, 1841; Jones, Barnes & Lloyd-Roberts, 1978). The condition is considered to be a genetic mutation caused by external factors such as drugs, or to be due to familial inheritance (De Santis *et al.*, 1990). The asymmetry of the lower limbs is often gross and may require amputation of the affected tibia.

Hemihypertrophy and other asymmetries of the skeleton

Tissue overgrowth is encountered in a wide range of rare congenital and late-developing conditions which collectively form an important group of syndromes. Reports of this overgrowth of one part of the body are not uncommon. The clinical entity of hemihypertrophy or overgrowth or hemiatrophy or undergrowth of the body apply clinically when the normal minor asymmetry of the body becomes pronounced or obvious to the untrained eye. This situation is, probably rightly, considered pathological. Other variants of over- and undergrowth are macrodactyly and micromelia. Congenital overgrowth of the whole body may also be encountered in conditions such as Soto's Syndrome, Wiedemann–Beckwith syndrome and neurocutaneous syndromes such as tuberous sclerosis, Lindau-von-Hippel disease and Sturge–Wever disease. These conditions can all be associated with growth asymmetry.

Asymmetry pathology arises through overgrowth or undergrowth of a part or a whole side of the body compared with the normal values for the particular body region. These growth abnormalities will consequently determine clinical hemihypertrophy or hemiatrophy. The pathogeneses of these asymmetries are not known, although they may be due to abnormalities arising in early embryogenesis leading to cellular hyperplasia rather than cellular hypertrophy. In one approach to classification, the hemihypertrophy may be regarded as partial, crossed or total (Schwartzman, Grossman & Dragutsky, 1942). In the partial type, one part of the body such as the face, breast or one or both extremities of one side or a part of an organ may be involved (Barr, 1929). In the crossed type of hemihypertrophy, only a part of a side of the body is involved; in the total type, one complete half of the body is enlarged with no part of the side excluded.

A revised classification was proposed by Ward & Lerner (1947). They divided hemihypertrophy into congenital and acquired forms, subdividing congenital hemihypertrophy into 'total' types involving all systems of the body and 'limited' types where the involvement is restricted to a particular system such as the muscular or vascular system. Subsequently, Barskey (1967) developed the concept of 'true' against 'pseudo' hypertrophy, which depends on the involvement or non-involvement of bone. In the 'true' type, the skeleton and soft tissues overgrow. If only soft tissue is involved, the condition is classed as a 'pseudotype'. This classification was subsequently further extended and refined by Temtamy & McKusick (1978).

Early reports of hemihypertrophy date back to the nineteenth century; they describe cases of partial hemihypertrophy or details of preserved specimens and models in the anatomical and surgical museums such as those of Broca and Dupuytren (Devoges, 1856). Studies by Gesell (1921) and Lenstrup (1926) led to the widespread recognition of the condition;

subsequently, a number of comprehensive reviews of the subject were published (Wakefield & Hines, 1933; Ward & Lerner, 1947; Ringrose, Jabbour & Keele, 1965; Viljoen, Pearn & Beighton, 1984).

A rare sporadic syndrome with manifestations of hemihypertrophy, macrodactyly, exostoses, scoliosis, cavernous hemiangiomas, lipomas, sabaceous naevi and rugated soles of the feet is the Proteus syndrome (Wiedemann *et al.*, 1983; Viljoen *et al.*, 1987; Bialer, Riedy & Wilson, 1988; Samlaska *et al.*, 1989). The mesenchymal origins of some of the tissues involved in this syndrome implies complex embryological involvement in the causation of this and other hemihypertrophy conditions.

Hemihypertrophy is also associated with a predisposition to malignant disease, particularly Wilms' tumour (nephroblastoma), adrenocortical neoplasia, hepatoblastoma and certain growth problems and dysplasias (Miller, Fraumeni & Manning, 1964; Fraumeni, Geiser & Manning, 1967; Pendergrass, 1976; Smith, 1976). Children with hemihypertrophy, alone or associated with other syndromes such as Beckwith–Wiedemann syndrome, have been found to subsequently develop malignancy (Azouz *et al.*, 1990). Partial hemihypertrophy or anisomelia such as leg length inequality has also been reported after irradiation for childhood tumours (Butler *et al.*, 1990; Goldwein, 1991).

Hemihypertrophy and skeletal asymmetry are found in Russel–Silver dwarfism (Smith, 1976). The affected individuals are small for their gestational age at birth but the growth pattern in childhood parallels normal growth whilst remaining below the third centile. Although the asymmetry may be limited to the arms or legs, in some cases the whole of one side of the individual's head, trunk and limbs can be affected.

Asymmetry of the skeleton has been associated with neurofibromatosis, although this is rare in the face (Tsiklakis & Nikopoulou, 1990). The presence of café-au-lait spots and the development of neuromata suggest an embryological cause for the condition, involving ectodermally derived structures. The cause of asymmetry in this condition is not known. Angiodysplasias such as haemangiomata and arteriovenous malformation may also be associated with limb asymmetry, as is coarctation of the aorta (Todd *et al.*, 1983). Severe asymmetry affecting the trunk is often associated with Poland's syndrome, where there is absence of the pectoralis major muscle on one side of the body. The absence of this muscle may also be associated with breast asymmetry (Rintala & Nordstrom, 1989).

Other growth asymmetries such as macrodactyly and micromelia are localized expansions of a limb and are probably distinct conditions. Examples of localized disorders include Ollier's disease and dysplasia epiphysealis hemimelica. Reduplication of a limb is an extreme example of asymmetry probably caused by embryological developmental anomalies (Dangerfield & Cornah, 1974).

Chemical treatment of animal embryos has been shown to induce limb asymmetry in some cases of developmental abnormality (Brown *et al.*, 1989), while some pharmological preparations act asymmetrically on the brain (Geschwind, 1985). This raises the possibility of intrinsic differences in the development of the right and left limbs. The handedness of induced asymmetrical limb defects has been shown to be highly correlated with embryonic visceral status, and with the mechanism of induction connected to visceral asymmetry (Brown *et al.*, 1989). In addition, there is a high correlation between limb defects and situs both in culture and *in utero*, suggesting that the maternal environment plays no part in the development of asymmetry.

Asymmetry and anthropometry

Anthropometric investigations of asymmetry in normal Liverpool and Nottingham children have been carried out, for use as controls in studies of the growth of children with orthopaedic conditions, including scoliosis and Perthe's Disease of the hip (Burwell *et al.*, 1978; Burwell & Dangerfield, 1980; Dangerfield, 1988). Measurements were made on both sides of the body. The sample included neonates and children of all ages, including adolescents.

Neonates

The uterine environment is known to influence the ultimate size of the foetus at term. Evidence that foetal growth slows down from 34 to 36 weeks onwards is based on the mechanical influence of the uterus, whose capacity for further growth is virtually complete by this stage (Tanner, 1978). The slowing down mechanism may be controlled by either placental ageing or changes in the haemodynamics of the maternal circulation. The effects of these changes may be exaggerated in the low-birth-weight baby, who can display abnormalities of the growth of the limbs in circumference or length (Tanner, 1978).

There are few studies of limb asymmetry relating to the foetal and neonatal period. Schultz (1926) reported asymmetry in the lengths of the femur and foot in the human foetus as early as the fourth month of gestation. However, Feingold & Bossert (1975) found no statistical evidence of hand asymmetry in the neonate. Some results from the Liverpool study of 106 male and 106 female neonates of full-term normal

Table 2.1. *Neonates: limb asymmetry*

Data are lengths in millimetres.

Variable	left	right	difference
Male			
Upper arm length	84.3	84.1	−0.2
Forearm length	74.5	75.1	+0.4
Forearm and hand length	133.6	133.5	−0.1
Dorsum of hand length	62.2	61.3	−0.9
Upper leg length	103.8	103.7	−0.1
Tibial length	87.7	88.1	+0.4
Foot length	77.8	77.5	−0.2
Female			
Upper arm length	83.7	83.3	−0.4
Forearm length	72.5	73.0	+0.5
Forearm and hand length	131.8	131.7	−0.1
Dorsum of hand length	62.1	61.4	−0.7
Upper leg length	105.1	105.2	+0.1
Tibial length	87.5	87.8	+0.3
Foot length	77.3	77.3	0.0

Table 2.2. *Skeletal limb symmetry in neonates*

Wilcoxon matched pairs signed ranks test for left against right. sig, Significance: NS, not significant.

Variable	Male			Female		
	z	p	sig	z	p	sig
Upper arm length	1.92	0.05	NS −	2.16	0.03	−
Forearm length	2.49	0.01	+	2.91	0.00	+
Forearm and hand length	0.45	0.65	NS −	0.70	0.48	NS −
Dorsum of hand length	4.97	0.0001	−	3.31	0.001	−
Upper leg length	0.56	0.57	NS −	0.94	0.34	NS +
Tibial length	2.61	0.001	+	1.87	0.06	NS +
Foot length	0.94	0.35	NS −	0.26	0.79	NS =

birth (Dangerfield & Taylor, 1983, 1984) are given in Tables 2.1 and 2.2. This shows that there are small differences between right and left limb segments as measured anthropometrically. There are significant differences between the female upper arm, forearm, and hand lengths and the male forearm, hand and tibial lengths. In both sexes, the left upper arm and dorsum of hand is longer than the right, and the right forearm and

Table 2.3. *Some upper limb measurements for boys aged 3–12 years*

Data are lengths in millimetres; SE, standard error.

| | Upper arm length | | | | Forearm and hand length | | | |
| | Left limb | | Right limb | | Left limb | | Right limb | |
Age	Mean	SE	Mean	SE	Mean	SE	Mean	SE
3	173.0	2.0	173.2	2.0	246.6	2.2	244.0	2.2
4	178.5	2.5	178.0	2.6	262.2	2.1	256.3	2.4
5	193.7	2.7	194.4	3.0	279.6	3.1	276.3	3.1
6	204.4	2.8	205.3	2.8	289.4	3.2	285.8	2.8
7	215.7	1.7	216.2	2.0	303.2	2.4	299.4	2.5
8	223.2	2.6	222.8	2.8	312.6	4.4	309.4	3.9
9	238.2	3.4	237.8	3.1	330.9	3.7	328.6	3.6
10	243.5	2.8	243.9	2.8	338.2	3.4	331.9	3.0
11	253.2	3.2	253.4	3.5	352.1	4.4	345.3	4.2
12	264.5	2.5	266.5	1.5	353.0	3.2	349.0	3.0

tibial lengths are greater than the left. These results suggest that limb skeletal symmetry changes with age and growth, since other studies on older children show that the differences reverse in favour of the right for the upper arm and left for the forearm (Burwell *et al.*, 1984). The neonatal findings therefore offer support for a hypothesis of oscillating skeletal symmetry. However, the findings for the limbs cannot be interpreted without study of the asymmetry of the chest and spine, work which is currently being undertaken in Liverpool. Ossification of the vertebral arches has been shown to be asymmetrical in the foetal period, and this requires further investigation in full-term normal neonates (Taylor, 1983).

The growing child

Table 2.3 gives results for homologous body measurements for the upper arm lengths in boys aged 3–12 years, and shows minor fluctuations in mean values with age between left and right limbs, with an overall tendency for lengthening on the right. In contrast, left forearm and hand lengths are greater. Although consistent, this asymmetry is small and probably of no functional importance; its cause is still unknown.

Asymmetry in scoliosis

Scoliosis, or lateral curvature of the spine, occurs in children of all ages. Although it is often associated with congenital abnormalities within the spinal column and also accompanies many neurological and dysplastic diseases, the most common type is the so-called idiopathic scoliosis. This was classified by James (1954) into infantile, juvenile and adolescent according to the age of diagnosis or onset of the curvature.

Adolescent idiopathic scoliosis affects about one in eight hundred girls and can rapidly progress to a severe deformity of the trunk. The nature of the spinal deformity results in an acquired asymmetry of the trunk, which is manifest as a rib-hump. This is the characteristic of the hunch-back. Anthropometric studies of children and adolescents with idiopathic scoliosis have demonstrated abnormalities of their growth affecting stature; for example, scoliotic adolescent girls are taller than the normal population. Scoliotic children also have an asymmetry in their upper limbs. This asymmetry is not obvious to the untrained eye but is easily detected by anthropometry.

In children with infantile idiopathic scoliosis, asymmetry has been found in the upper limbs, related to the side and severity of the spinal curve. Children with a right-sided curve have a longer arm on the right and those with a left-sided curve have a longer arm on the left. This difference is most marked in the upper arm, represented by the humeral segment of the limb.

In adolescent girls with right-sided curves present in the thoracic, thoracolumbar or lumbar region, the right upper limb is longer than the left when compared with the normal control population (Burwell, Dangerfield & Vernon, 1977; Taylor, 1978; Dangerfield & Burwell, 1980). However, in the affected girls with a left spinal curve, the upper limb asymmetry was only significantly different for those cases with a thoracic curve. By further grouping these children according to their curve patterns, it has been found that those with right-sided thoracic curves have right upper arms proportionally longer on the side of the convexity of the curvature, which correlates with the magnitude of the spinal curve angle at the time of measurement (Burwell *et al.*, 1984).

Recently, the application of computer analysis and finite element analysis to examine the human thorax in scoliosis has shown a tendency for the rib length of patients with right thoracic scoliosis to be longer on the right side, while in left lumbar curves the ribs are longer on the left (Stokes & Laible, 1990). Rib asymmetry has been reported in other investigations (Sevastik, Aaro & Normelli, 1984; Normelli, Sevastik & Akrivos, 1986). Minor trunk asymmetries, referred to as Constitutional Back Asymmetry, are common in the normal population, and are frequently detected in school screening programmes (Willner, 1984; Dangerfield *et al.*, 1987*b*). This pattern of asymmetry has a blurred demarcation between normality, where it is of no consequence, and pathology, where it is associated with scoliosis. Rib angle asymmetries are also an important left–right difference. By examination of the segmental rib–vertebra angle (RVA) in the thorax, it has been shown that the RVA displays asymmetry, associated with bilateral drooping of the RVA in idiopathic scoliosis (Wojcik, Webb & Burwell, 1990; Wythers *et al.*, 1991; Grivas *et al.*, 1991). These findings are considered to represent a developmental abnormality in the upper thorax, affecting the rib cage and spine, due to a basic CNS central pattern generator abnormality which in turn leads to the development of the asymmetry of spine manifest clinically as scoliosis.

The asymmetry of the limbs and ribcage in scoliosis may also represent the skeletal expression of a constitutional predisposition (diathesis) to a thoracic or thoracolumbar curve in subjects who develop a 'scoliogenic lesion' from any cause. The symmetry is therefore intrinsic to the growing bones as part of the overall picture of the pathology of spinal curvatures. However, the limb asymmetry could also be explained by functional causes, similar to the overgrowth frequently observed in athletes.

The mechanisms behind control of the 'scoliogenic lesion' are still not fully clear, although there is evidence to support a concept of maldevelopment which involves the basic embryological formation of the CNS and related structures, affecting the subsequent development of central pattern generators and control mechanisms which in turn affect the development and function of the skeleton, musculature and peripheral nervous system (Burwell & Dangerfield, 1992). Cerebral lateralization has also been suggested as a possible causal factor (Goldberg & Dowling, 1991).

Asymmetry in Wilms' tumour

The advances in the treatment of nephroblastoma in the past two decades have considerably improved the survival rate of the affected child, allowing growth studies of these children to be carried out. The development of post-irradiation deformities in the ribcage and spinal deformity can be carefully monitored and attention directed towards the detection of asymmetry in the axial and appendicular skeleton in the light of the recognized association between hemihypertrophy and nephroblastoma.

In a small pilot study, the growth of 28 children was investigated, revealing minor degrees of body asymmetry (Dangerfield *et al.*, 1987*a*). Right-side left-side differences in the foot and tibia differed from the normal control population and occurred irrespective of either irradiation or chemotherapy. This suggests that the asymmetry of malignant disease is either a fundamental biological process, or a simple cause and effect arising from irradiation. Anisomelia has recently been reported after irradiation for childhood tumours; this supports the latter possibility, although it does not explain asymmetries arising from chemotherapy.

Asymmetry associated with coarctation of the aorta

An anthropometric and clinical study of children with coarctation of the aorta, treated using subclavian flap aortoplasty, found upper limb asymmetry, with a shorter limb on the side affected by the surgery (Todd *et al.*, 1983). This asymmetry could be a result of the surgery affecting the blood supply to the limb, but does not appear to be progressive with growth. Alternatively, the asymmetry could represent a developmental embryological problem, which is manifest as aortic arch anomaly and limb asymmetry.

New methods of measuring asymmetries

Anthropometric techniques employed to measure lengths and breadths on the surface of the body still use mechanical technology with a long history of development. Currently, in Liverpool and other centres, the range of equipment manufactured by Holtain Ltd (Crymmch, Dyfed, South Wales) is widely employed. For specialist applications to the spine, other equipment such as the scoliometer (OSCL Scoliometer, USA) and Formulator Body Contour Tracer are required (Dangerfield *et al.*, 1987*a*). Recently, in Liverpool, a computerized imaging system has been developed which employs projected light fringes to record images of the trunk and body surface very rapidly (in 1/50 of a second) (Dangerfield *et al.*, 1991). The image is acquired using a CCD (charge coupled device) television camera and allows for the analysis of 262 144 three-dimensional data points to an accuracy of about 1 mm. The graphical output is in the form of contour maps, three-dimensional reconstructions and other representations (Fig. 2.1). Scaling enables distances to be measured between anatomical landmarks. This system has the potential to record any surface shape and is used to measure asymmetry of the trunk and limbs. Radiographic information will also be incorporated into the system in the future.

Conclusions

This chapter reviews existing knowledge of body and limb asymmetry as found in both the normal and pathological state. There is little doubt that such asymmetries exist. Although in normal populations this asymmetry is small and is considered to be of no functional significance, its role in growth is unclear. The asymmetry of normality merges gradually with the

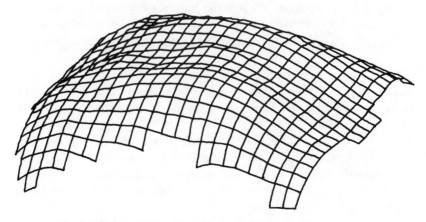

Fig. 2.1. Representation of graphical output from the Liverpool computerized imaging system.

asymmetry of pathology and thus a careful study of normality could shed considerable light on the abnormal. Asymmetry itself is unlikely to affect the results of normal anthropometric investigations. It only becomes important if the investigation is an applied study with reference to a pathological condition.

References

Acheson, R., Chan, Y. & Clemett, A. (1970) New Haven Survey of Joint Disease XII: Distribution and symptoms of osteoarthritis in the hands with reference to handedness. *Annals of Rheumatoid Disease* **29**, 275–9.

Aitkin, A. P., Blackett, C. W. & Cincotti, J. J. (1939). Overgrowth of the femoral shaft following fractures in children. *Journal of Bone and Joint Surgery* **21**, 334–8.

Amstutz, H. C. (1969). The morphology, natural history and treatment of proximal focal deficiencies. In: *Proximal Femoral Focal Deficiency, a Congenital Anomaly*, ed. G. T. Atkin, pp. 50–76. Washington, DC: National Academy of Sciences.

Anderson, M., Green, W. T. & Messner, M. B. (1963). Growth and predictions of growth in the lower extremities. *Journal of Bone and Joint Surgery* **45**A, 1–24.

Azouz, E. M., Larson, E. J., Patel, J. & Gyepes, M. T. (1990). Beckwith-Wiedemann syndrome: development of nephroblastoma during the surveillance period. *Pediatric Radiology* **20**, 550–2.

Barr, D. (1929). Congenital hemihypertrophy and partial gigantism. *Journal of the Missouri Medical Association* **26**, 298–302.

Barskey, A. J. (1967). Macrodactyly. *Journal of Bone and Joint Surgery* **49**A, 1255–66.

Bialer, M. G., Riedy, M. J. & Wilson, W. G. (1988). Proteus syndrome verses Bannayan-Zonana syndrome: a problem in differential diagnosis. *European Journal of Pediatrics* **148**, 122–5.

Blinkov, S. M. & Glezer, I. I. (1968). *The Human Brain in Figures and Tables. A Quantitative Handbook*. New York: Plenum Press.

Boyes, J. (1954). Dupuytren's contracture – notes on the age of onset and the relationship to handedness. *American Journal of Surgery* **88**, 147.

Brown, N. A., Hoyle, C. I., McCarthy, A. & Wolpert, L. (1989). The development of asymmetry: the sidedness of drug-induced limb abnormalities is reversed in situs-inversus mice. *Development* **107**, 637–42.

Brown, N. A. & Wolpert, L. (1990). The development of handedness in left/right asymmetry. *Development* **109**, 1–9.

Brunet, M. E., Cook, S. D., Brinker, M. R. & Dickinson, J. A. (1990). A survey of running injuries in 1505 competitive and recreational runners. *Journal of Sports Medicine and Physical Fitness* **30**, 307–15.

Burke, P. H. (1971). Stereophotogrammetric measurement of normal facial asymmetry. *Human Biology* **43**, 536–9.

Burwell, R. G. & Dangerfield, P. H. (1980). Skeletal measurement. In: *Scientific Foundations of Orthopaedics & Traumatology*, ed. R. Owen, J. Goodfellow & P. Bullough, pp. 317–29. London: Heinemann.

Burwell, R. G. & Dangerfield, P. H. (1992). Pathogenesis and assessment of scoliosis. In: *Surgery of the Spine: a combined neurosurgical and orthopaedic approach*, ed. G. F. G. Findley & R. Owen, pp. 365–408. London: Blackwell Scientific Publications.

Burwell, R. G., Dangerfield, P. H., Hall, D. J., Vernon, C. L. & Harrison, M. H. M. (1978). Perthes' Disease. An anthropometric study revealing impaired and disproportionate growth. *Journal of Bone Joint Surgery* **60**B, 461–9.

Burwell, R. G., Dangerfield, P. H., James, N. J., Johnson, F., Webb, J. K. & Wilson, Y. G. (1984). Anthropometric studies of normal and scoliotic children. In: *Pathogenesis of Idiopathic Scoliosis*, ed. R. R. Jacobs, pp. 27–44. Chicago: Scoliosis Research Society.

Burwell, R. G., Dangerfield, P. H. & Vernon, C. L. (1977). Anthropometry and scoliosis. In: *The Proceedings of the Fifth Symposium on Scoliosis*, ed. P. A. Zorab, pp. 123–63. London: Academic Press.

Buskirk, E. R., Anderson, K. L. & Brozek, J. (1956). Unilateral activity and bone and muscle development in the forearm. *Research Quarterly* **27**, 127–31.

Butler, M. S., Robertson, W. W., Rate, W., D'Angio, G. J. & Drummond, D. S. (1990). Skeletal sequelae of radiation therapy for malignant childhood tumours. *Clinical Orthopaedics* **251**, 235–40.

Coren, S. & Porac, C. (1977). Fifty centuries of right-handedness: the historical record. *Science* **198**, 631–2.

Crow, T. J. (1990) Temporal lobe asymmetries as the key to the etiology of schizophrenia. *Schizophrenia Bulletin* **16**, 433–43.

Dangerfield, P. H. (1988). Liverpool growth standards for children aged 3 to 11. *Proc. 5th International Auxology Congress, Exeter*, ed. J. M. Tanner, p. 58. Milton Keynes: Kabi Vitrium AB.

Dangerfield, P. H. & Burwell, R. G. (1980). Anthropometry and scoliosis. In:

Spinal Deformities, 2nd edition, ed. R. Roaf, pp. 259–80. Tunbridge Wells: Pitman.

Dangerfield, P. H. & Cornah, M. S. (1974). Reduplication of the femur. *Journal of Bone and Joint Surgery* **56B**, 744–5.

Dangerfield, P. H., Denton, J. S., Barnes, S. B. & Drake, N. B. (1987a). The assessment of rib-cage and spinal deformity in scoliosis. In: *Proceedings of the 4th International Conference on Surface Topography and Scoliosis*, ed. I. A. F. Stokes, J. R. Pekelsky & M. S. Moreland, pp. 53–65. Stuttgart: Gustav Fischer Verlag.

Dangerfield, P. H., Pearson, J. D., Nunn, N., Dorgan, J. C., Klenerman, L., Hobson, C. A. & Harvey, D. M. (1991). Measurement of the angle of trunk inclination using a computerised imaging system. In: *6th International Symposium on Surface Topography and Scoliosis*, ed. A. Alberti, B. Drerup & E. Hierholzer, Stuttgart: Gustav Fischer Verlag.

Dangerfield, P. H. & Taylor, C. J. (1983). Anthropometric standards for term neonates. *Early Human Development* **8**, 225–33.

Dangerfield, P. H. & Taylor, C. J. (1984) Liverpool growth study: neonatal anthropometric standards. In: *Human Growth and Development*, ed. J. Borms, R. Hauspie, A. Sand, C. Suzanne & M. Hebbelinck, pp. 131–7. London: Plenum Press.

Dangerfield, P. H., Tulloch, C. J., Owen, R. & Martin, J. (1987b). Spinal deformity in nephroblastoma: preliminary observations. *Annals of the Royal College of Surgeons in England* **69**, 56–9.

De Santis, N., Razzano, E., Scognamiglio, R. & Rega, A. N. (1990). Tibial agenesis; a new rationale in management of type II - report of three cases with long-term follow-up. *Journal of Pediatric Orthopedics* **10**, 198–201.

Devoges, P. M. (1856). Predominance de developpement du cote droit sur le cote gauche; developpement hypertrophique des trois premiers doights de la main et du pieds droits. *Bulletin de la Société Anatomique* **31**, 510–8.

Feingold, M. & Bossert, W. H. (1975). Normal values for selected physical parameters. *Birth Defects* **10**, 1–15.

Fixen, J. A. & Lloyd-Roberts, G. C. (1974). The natural history and early treatment of proximal femoral dysplasia. *Journal of Bone and Joint Surgery* **56B**, 86–95.

Fraumeni, J. F., Geiser, C. F. & Manning, M. D. (1967). Wilms' tumor and congenital hemihypertrophy: report of five new cases and a review of the literature. *Pediatrics* **40**, 886–9.

Garn, S. M., Lewis, A. B. & Kerewsky, R. S. (1966). The meaning of bilateral asymmetry in the permanent dentition. *The Angle Orthodontist* **36**, 55–62.

Garn, S. M., Mayor, G. H. & Shaw, H. A. (1976). Paradoxical bilateral asymmetry in bone size and bone mass in the hand. *American Journal of Physical Anthropology* **45**, 209–10.

Garson, J. G. (1879). Inequality in length of the lower limbs. *Journal of Anatomy and Physiology* **13**, 502–7.

Georgiou, S. & Forsyth, D. (1991). Scanning the headlines. *Image Processing* **3**, 27–9.

Geschwind, N. (1985). Implications for evolution, genetics and clinical syndromes. In: *Cerebral Lateralization in Non-Human Species*, ed. S. D. Glick. London: Academic Press.

Geshwind, N. & Levitsky, W. (1968). Left–right asymmetries in temporal speech region. *Science*, **161** 186–7.

Gesell, A. (1921). Hemihypertrophy and mental defect. *Archives of Neurology and Psychiatry* **6**, 400.

Goldberg, C. J. & Dowling, F. E. (1991). Idiopathic scoliosis and asymmetry of form and function. *Spine* **16**, 84–7.

Goldwein, J. W. (1991). Effects of radiation therapy on skeletal growth in childhood. *Clinical Orthopaedics* **262**, 101–7.

Gordin, S. J., Gabriele, O. F. & Higgins, W. L. (1989). MRI of unilateral facial asymmetry. *Magnetic Resonance Imaging* **7**, 565–6.

Griffin, P. P. & Green, W. T. (1972). Fractures of the shaft of the femur in children. Treatment and results. *Orthopedic Clinics North America* **3**, 213–24.

Grill, F. & Dungl, P. (1991). Lengthening for congenital short femur. *Journal of Bone and Joint Surgery* **73B**, 439–47.

Grivas, T. B., Burwell, R. G., Purdue, M., Webb, J. K. & Moulton, A. (1991). The rib cage deformity in infantile idiopathic scoliosis – the funnel shaped chest in relation to specific rotation as a prognostic factor. In: *6th International Symposium on Surface Topography and Scoliosis*, ed. A. Alberti, B. Drerup & E. Hierholzer, pp. 93–109. Stuttgart: Gustav Fischer Verlag.

Halperin, G. (1931). Normal asymmetry and unilateral hypertrophy. *Archives of Internal Medicine* **48**, 676–82.

Hamanishi, C. (1980). Congenital short femur. Clinical, genetic and epidemiological comparison of the naturally occurring with that caused by thalidomide. *Journal of Bone and Joint Surgery* **62B**, 307–20.

Henery, C. C. & Mayhew, T. M. (1989). The cerebrum and cerebellum of the fixed human brain: efficient and unbiased estimates of volumes and cortical surface areas. *Journal of Anatomy* **167**, 167–80.

Hrdlicka, A. (1932). The principal dimensions, absolute and relative, of the humerus in the white race. *American Journal of Physical Anthropology* **16**, 431–50.

Ingalls, N. W. (1931). Observations on bone weights. *American Journal of Anatomy* **48**, 45–98.

Ingelmark, B. E. (1942). Der Zusammenhang zwischen der Händigkeit und den Asymmetrien und Belastungsverhaltnissen der Extremitäten sowie des Rückgrats. *Upsala Låkareforening Forhandlinger* **48**, 227–391.

Ingelmark, B. E. (1946). Uber die Längenasymmetrien der Extremitäten und ihren Zusammenhang mit der Rechts-Linkshändigkeit. Eine neue röntgenologische Registriermethode nebst erhaltenen Resultaten. *Upsala Låkareforening Forhandlinger* **52**, 17–82.

Ingelmark, B. E. & Lindstrom, J. (1963). Asymmetries of the lower extremities and pelvis and their relations to lumbar scoliosis. *Acta Morphologia Neerlando-Scandinavica* **5**, 221–34.

James, J. I. P. (1954). Idiopathic scoliosis: the prognosis, diagnosis and operative indications related to curve patterns and age of onset. *Journal of Bone and Joint Surgery* **36**B, 36.

Johanson, D. & Shreeve, J. (1990). *Lucy's Child. The Discovery of a Human Ancestor.* London: Viking.

Jolicoer, P. (1963). Bilateral asymmetry and asymmetry in limb bones of Martes Americana and man. *Reviews of Canadian Biology* **22**, 409–32.

Jones, D., Barnes, J. & Lloyd-Roberts, P. (1978). Congenital aplasia and dysplasia of the tibia with intact fibula. *Journal of Bone and Joint Surgery* **60**B, 31–9.

Jones, H. H., Priest, J. D., Hayes, W. C., Tichenor, C. C. & Nagel, D. A. (1977). Humeral hypertrophy in response to exercise. *Journal of Bone and Joint Surgery* **59**A, 204–8.

Khana, J. N. & Andrade, N. N. (1989). Hemifacial hypertrophy. Report of two cases. *International Journal of Oral Maxillofacial Surgery* **18**, 294–7.

King, J. W., Brelsford, H. J. & Tullos, H. S. (1969). Analysis of the pitching arm of the professional baseball pitcher. *Clinical Orthopedics* **67**, 116–23.

Laubach, L. L. & McConville, J. T. (1967). Notes on anthropometric technique: anthropometric measurements – right and left sides. *American Journal of Physical Anthropology* **26**, 367–70.

Lenstrup, E. (1926). Eight cases of hemihypertrophy. *Acta Paediatrica* **6**, 205.

Liebreich, R. (1908). *L'asymetrie de la Figure et son Origin.* Paris: Masson.

Ludwig, W. (1932). *Das Rechts-Links-Problem im Tierreich und beim Menschen.* Berlin: Springer Verlag.

Malina, R. M. & Buschang, P. H. (1984). Anthropometric asymmetry in normal and mentally retarded males. *Annals of Human Biology* **11**(6), 515–32.

Meals, R. A. (1979a). The laterality of fractures and dislocations with respect to handedness. *Clinical Orthopedics* **143**, 158–61.

Meals, R. A. (1979b). Overgrowth of the femur following fractures in children: influence of handedness. *Journal of Bone and Joint Surgery* **61**A, 381–4.

Miller, R. W., Fraumeni, J. F. & Manning, M. D. (1964). Association of Wilms' tumor with aniridia, hemihypertrophy and other congenital malformations. *New England Journal of Medicine* **270**, 922–7.

Montoye, H. J., McCabe, J. F., Metzner, H. L. & Garn, S. M. (1976) Physical activity and bone density. *Human Biology* **48**, 599–610.

Mullick, J. F. (1965). An investigation of cranio-facial asymmetry using the serial twin study method. *American Journal of Orthodontics* **51**, 112–29.

Munter, A. H. (1936). A study of the lengths of the long bones of the arms and legs in man with special reference to Anglo-Saxon skeletons. *Biometrika* **28**, 258–94.

Normelli, H., Sevastik, J. A. & Akrivos, J. (1986). The length and ash weight of the ribs of normal and scoliotic persons. *Spine* **10**, 590–2.

Otto, A. W. (1841). *Monstrorum Sexeentorum Descripto Anatomica Sumptibis.* Breslau: Ferdinandi Hirt.

Pappas, A. M. (1983). Congenital abnormalities of the femur and related lower extremity malformations. *Journal of Pediatric Orthopedics* **3**, 45–60.

Pendergrass, T. W. (1976). Congenital anomalies in children with Wilms' tumor. *Cancer* **37**, 403–8.

Phillips, R. (1965). Carpal tunnel syndrome as a manifestation of systemic disease. *Annals of Rheumatic Diseases* **26**, 59.

Potts, R. & Shipman, P. (1981). Cutmarks made by stone tools on bones from the Olduvai Gorge, Tanzania. *Nature* **291**, 577–80.

Ring, P. A. (1959) Congenital short femur; simple femoral hypoplasia. *Journal of Bone and Joint Surgery* **41B**, 73–9.

Ringrose, R. E., Jabbour, J. T. & Keele, D. K. (1965). Hemihypertrophy. *Pediatrics* **36**, 434–48.

Rintala, A. E. & Nordstrom, R. E. (1989). Treatment of severe asymmetry of the female breast. *Scandinavian Journal of Plastic Reconstructive Surgery and Hand Surgery* **23**, 231–5.

Rogala, E. J., Wynne-Davies, R., Littlejohn, A. & Gormley, J. (1974). Congenital limb anomalies: frequency and aetiological factors. *Journal of Medical Genetics* **11**, 221–33.

Rollet, E. (1902). L'homme droit et l'homme gauche. Discours d'ouverture a la Societe d'Anthropologie de Lyon. *Archives d'Anthropologie Criminal* **17**, 177–204.

Ruff, C. B. (1979). Right-left asymmetry in long bones of Californian Indians. *American Journal of Physical Anthropology* **50**, 477–8.

Ruff, C. B. & Jones, H. H. (1981). Bilateral asymmetry in cortical bone of the humerus and tibia – sex and age factors. *Human Biology* **53**, 69–86.

Rush, W. A. & Steiner, H. A. (1946). A study of lower extremity length inequality. *American Journal of Roentgenology* **56**, 616–20.

Samlaska, C. P., Levin, S. W., James, W. D., Benson, P. M., Walker, J. C. & Perlik, P. C. (1989). Proteus syndrome. *Archives of Dermatology* **125**, 1109–14.

Schulter-Ellis, F. P. (1979). The glenoid fossa on skeletons of known handedness. *American Journal of Physical Anthropology* **50**, 479.

Schultz, A. H. (1926). Fetal growth of man and other primates. *Quarterly Review of Biology* **1**, 465–521.

Schultz, A. H. (1937). Proportions, variability and asymmetries of the long bones of the limbs and clavicles in man and apes. *Human Biology* **9**, 281–328.

Schwartzman, J., Grossman, L. & Dragutsky, D. (1942). True total hemihypertrophy. *Archives of Pediatrics* **59**, 637–45.

Sevastik, A. B., Aaro, S. & Normelli, H. (1984). Scoliosis: experimental and clinical studies. *Clinical Orthopedics* **191**, 27–34.

Smith, D. W. (1976). *Recognisable Patterns of Human Malformations.* (*Major Problems in Clinical Pediatrics,* 2nd edition, Vol. 7.) Philadelphia: WB Saunders.

Staheli, L. T. (1967). Femoral and tibial growth following femoral shaft fractures in childhood. *Clinical Orthopaedics* **55**, 159–63.

Steinmetz, H., Rademacher, J., Jancke, L., Huang, Y. X., Thron, A. & Zilles, K. (1990). Total surface of temporal intersylvian cortex: diverging left-right asymmetries. *Brain Language* **39**, 357–72.

Stokes, I. A. F. & Laible, J. P. (1990). Three-dimensional osseo-ligamentous model of the thorax representing initiation of scoliosis by asymmetrical growth. *Journal of Biomechanics* **23**, 589–95.

Tanner, J. M. (1978). Physical growth and development. In: *Textbook of*

Paediatrics, ed. J. O. Forfar & C. Arneil, pp. 249–303. London: Churchill-Livingstone.

Taylor, J. R. (1978). Genesis of Scoliosis. *Journal of Anatomy* **126**, 434.

Taylor, J. R. (1983). Scoliosis and growth: patterns of asymmetry in normal vertebral growth. *Acta Orthopaediatrica Scandinavica* **54**, 596–602.

Temtamy, S. & McKusick, V. (1978). Macrodactaly as an isolated anomaly. *Birth Defects* **14**, 507–23.

Todd, P. J., Dangerfield, P. H., Hamilton, D. I. & Wilkinson, J. I. (1983). Late effects on the upper limb of subclavian flap aortoplasty. *Journal of Thoracic Cardiovascular Surgery* **85**, 678–81.

Trotter, M. & Gleser, G. C. (1952). Estimation of stature from long bones of American Whites and Negroes. *American Journal of Physical Anthropology* **10**, 463–514.

Truesdell, E. D. (1921). Inequality of the lower extremities following fractures of the shaft of the femur in children. *Annals of Surgery* **74**, 498–500.

Tsiklakis, K. & Nikopoulou-Karayianni, A. (1990). Multiple neurofibromatosis associated with mandibular growth and facial asymmetry. *Annals of Dentistry* **49**, 14–7.

Tupman, G. S. (1962) A study of bone growth in normal children and its relationship to skeletal maturation. *Journal of Bone and Joint Surgery* **44B**, 42–5.

Upadhyay, S. S., Burwell, R. G. & Moulton, A. (1986). Femoral anteversion in Perthes' Disease with observations on irritable hips. *Clinical Orthopaedics* **209**, 70–6.

Upadhyay, S. S., Burwell, R. G., Moulton, A., Small, P. G. & Wallace, W. A. (1990). Femoral anteversion in healthy children. Application of a new method using ultrasound. *Journal of Anatomy* **169**, 49–61.

Viljoen, D. L., Pearn, J. & Beighton, P. (1984). Manifestations and natural history of idopathic hemihypertrophy: a review of eleven cases. *Clinical Genetics* **26**, 81–6.

Viljoen, D. L., Nelson, M. M., de Jong, G. & Beighton, P. (1987). Proteus syndrome in Southern Africa: natural history and clinical manifestations in six individuals. *American Journal of Medical Genetics* **27**, 87–97.

Vogel, F. (1984). Short leg syndrome. *Clinical Podiatry* **1**, 581–99.

Wagner, H. (1990). Pelvic tilt and leg length correction. *Orthopaedics* **19**, 273–7.

Wakefield, E. C. & Hines, E. A. (1933). Congenital hemihypertrophy: A report of eight cases. *American Journal of Medical Science* **185**, 493–7.

Ward, J. & Lerner, H. H. (1947). A review of the subject of congenital hemihypertrophy and a complete case report. *Journal of Pediatrics* **31**, 403.

Westin, G. W., Sakai, D. N. & Wood, W. L. (1976). Congenital longitudinal deficiencies of the fibula; follow-up treatment by Syme amputation. *Journal of Bone and Joint Surgery* **58A**, 492–6.

Wojcik, A. S., Webb, J. K. & Burwell, R. G. (1990). An analysis of the effect of the Zielke operation on the rib-cage of S-shaped curves in idiopathic scoliosis. *Spine* **15**, 81–6.

Wiedemann, H. R., Burgio, G. R., Aldenhoff, P., Kunze, J., Kaufmann, H. J. & Schrig, E. (1983). The proteus syndrome. Partial gigantism of the hands and/ or feet, naevi, hemihypertrophy, subcutaneous tumours, macrocephaly or other skull anomalies and possible accelerated growth and visceral affectations. *European Journal of Pediatrics* **140**, 5–12.

Williams, T. & Heather, B. (1973). Laterality of fractures. *British Medical Journal* **4**, 52.

Willner, S. (1984). Prevalence study of trunk asymmetries and structural scoliosis in 10 year old school children. *Spine* **9**, 644–7.

Wythers, D. J., Burwell, R. G., Webb, J. K. & Wojcik, A. S. (1991). The segmental surface and rib deformity of progressive adolescent idiopathic scoliosis. In: *6th International Symposium on Surface Topography and Scoliosis*, ed. A. Alberti, B. Drerup & E. Hierholzer, pp. 119–35. Stuttgart: Gustav Fischer Verlag.

3 Intra- and inter-observer error in anthropometric measurement

STANLEY J. ULIJASZEK AND JOHN A. LOURIE

Introduction

Although the need for accurate anthropometric measurement has been repeatedly stressed by the great and the good (Krogman, 1950; Tanner, 1986), reports of growth and physique measurements in human populations rarely include estimates of measurement error. Cameron (1986) has suggested that this might be partly due to a lack of standardized terminology with which to describe the reliability of measurement in a clearly understandable manner. More recently, Mueller & Martorell (1988) and Frisancho (1990) have attempted to clarify this issue. Both suggest that the use of two error estimates, the technical error of measurement (TEM) and reliability (R) can give most of the information needed to determine whether a series of anthropometric measurements can be considered accurate.

The TEM is obtained by carrying out a number of repeat measurements on the same subject, either by the same observer, or by two or more observers, taking the differences and entering them into an appropriate equation. For intra-observer TEM, and for inter-observer TEM involving two measures, the equation is:

$$\text{TEM} = \sqrt{\frac{\Sigma D^2}{2N}}, \qquad (3.1)$$

where D is the difference between measurements, and N is the number of individuals measured. When more than two observers are involved, the equation is more complex:

$$\text{TEM} = \sqrt{\left(\sum_1^N \left[\sum_1^K M(n)^2 - \frac{\Sigma_1^K M(n)^2}{K}\right]\right)\Big/ N(K-1)} \qquad (3.2)$$

where N is the number of subjects, K is the number of determinations of

Table 3.1. *Reference values for technical error of measurement*

Measurement	Technical error of measurement	
	Intra-examiner	Inter-examiner
Cervical height (cm)	0.692	0.953
Sitting height (cm)	0.535	0.705
Biacromial breadth (cm)	0.544	0.915
Bitrochanteric breadth (cm)	0.523	0.836
Elbow breadth (cm)	0.117	0.154
Wrist breadth (cm)	0.115	0.139
Arm circumference (cm)	0.347	0.425
Triceps skinfold (mm)	0.800	1.890
Subscapular skinfold (mm)	1.830	1.530
Midaxillary skinfold (mm)	2.080	1.470

Source: Frisancho (1990).

the variable taken on each subject, and $M(n)$ is the nth replicate of the measurement, where n varies from 1 to K. According to Frisancho (1990), if intra- and inter- (where there is more than one measurer) observer TEM come close to a reference value in a series of repeated measurements, and if there are no biases in measurement, then the measurements can be considered accurate. The units of TEM are the same as the units of the anthropometric measurement in question. The TEMs which Frisancho (1990) recommends as reference are given in Table 3.1. These values were obtained by the measurement and re-measurement of 77 children aged 6 to 11 years and taking part in Cycle II of the US Health Examination Survey (Johnston, Hamill & Lemeshow, 1972; Malina, Hamill & Lemeshow, 1973).

Although this goes some way to resolving the problem, it is possible that these values may not apply to measured groups outside the age range of the population used to obtain them. Certainly, different values of TEM have been reported in different age groups for the following measures: biacromial breadth (Chumlea, Roche & Rogers, 1984), maxillary skinfold (Harrison *et al.*, 1988) and triceps skinfold (Harrison *et al.*, 1988). The coefficient of reliability, R, ranges from 0 to 1, and can be calculated using the following equation:

$$R = 1 - [(TEM)^2/(SD)^2], \qquad (3.3)$$

where SD is the total inter-subject variance, including measurement error. This coefficient reveals what proportion of the between-subject variance in a measured population is free from measurement error. In the case of a measurement with an R of 0.9, 90% of the variance is due to factors other than measurement error. It has been suggested that measures of R can be used to compare the relative reliability of different anthropometric measurements, and to estimate sample size requirements (Mueller & Martorell, 1988). Further, it can be used to determine the number of replicate measurements needed to obtain a reliable measure (Himes, 1989). There are few examples in the literature of R being used in these ways, however.

At present there are no recommended values for R in the literature. Himes (1989) has suggested that ideally, investigators should conduct their own reliability studies and decide what levels of R are needed for their purposes. Since TEM and R are related, this would then reveal acceptable values for TEM for that particular study. In most cases this is unlikely to happen, and in the absence of less vague guidelines, anthropometrists and auxologists are left with the TEM values recommended by Frisancho (1990).

The purpose of this paper is to examine the relationship of TEM to age for five commonly used anthropometric variables: height, sitting height, arm circumference, and triceps and subscapular skinfolds. Further, acceptable levels of R are explored using repeat measures collected by the authors, and values for TEM by sex and age groups are proposed on the basis of this exploration.

Technical error of measurement and acceptable levels of reliability

Measurement error consists of within-observer and between-observer error, as well as error due to other factors, such as equipment error, the physical state of the subject, the time of day at which the measurements are made, and error due to rounding up or rounding down the measured value to the nearest half or whole integer. Only the first two types of error will be considered here. A number of studies carried out by reputable authors have considered intra- and inter-observer TEM and R for length, height, arm circumference, triceps and subscapular skinfolds, and these are given in Tables 3.2 and 3.3.

Although it might be expected that intra-observer error should be smaller than inter-observer error, this is far from universally the case. Indeed, in the study reported by Pelletier, Low & Msukwa (1991) intra-observer error is greater than inter-observer error for length and arm circumference; the same is true for subscapular skinfold thickness in the US national sample reported by Johnston, Hamill & Lemeshow (1972). The intra-observer TEMs for length range from 0.4 to 0.8 cm; for height they vary between 0.3 and 0.7 cm. For sitting height, intra-observer TEMs vary between 0.1 and 0.7 cm. For arm circumference, the values range from 0.1 to 0.4 cm; for triceps and subscapular skinfold thicknesses the ranges are from 0.1 to 1.6 mm and from 0.1 to 3.4 mm, respectively. Inter-observer errors show similar ranges for most variables: 0.1 – 0.7 cm (height); 0.2 – 0.7 cm (sitting height); 0.05 – 0.3 cm (arm circumference); 0.2 – 1.9 mm (triceps skinfold); and 0.4 – 1.5 mm (subscapular skinfold).

Although the authors of these various studies have been careful not to apply value judgements to their TEM values, the implicit suggestion is that they are not excessively large. One way in which this can be evaluated is by examining the accompanying R values. A generous allowance for measurement error might be up to 10% of the observed inter-subject variance; this is equivalent to an R value of 0.9 or more. All R values for intra-observer error are above 0.9 (Table 3.2). For inter-observer error (Table 3.3), R values are above 0.9 for length, height and sitting height for most of the groups reported. For eight out of thirteen groups, however, the R value for triceps skinfold is below 0.9; the same is true for subscapular skinfolds in four out of eight groups. In the youngest age groups, triceps and subscapular skinfold measurements are characterized by both low TEMs and low values for R. This is because skinfolds have the highest level of measurement error of the measurements reported here, and because the variance of triceps and subscapular skinfolds is very low before about five years of age (Frisancho 1990).

The interpretation of TEM is complicated by its relationship with age. This is illustrated by four anomalies to be found in Table 3.3. If it is accepted that R must be 0.9 or greater for measurement error to be sufficiently small, than a TEM of 0.4 mm for triceps skinfold is good for 17–25-year-olds, but unacceptable for newborns. In addition, a TEM of 0.6 mm for subscapular skinfold is good for 17–25-year-olds, but too high for 1–2-year-olds. Finally, TEMs of 1.5 and 1.9 mm for triceps and subscapular skinfolds, respectively, are acceptable for 12–17-year-olds, but not for children aged 6–11 years. In order to examine the relationship between R and age, variances from the anthropometric standards developed from the combined National Health and Nutrition Examination Surveys (NHANES I and II) (Frisancho, 1990) have been used to calculate R for height, sitting height, arm circumference, triceps and subscapular skinfolds at different levels of TEM, and at different ages (Figs 3.1–3.5).

For height and sitting height, R values exceed 0.9 in all age groups at two reported values of TEM, 0.2 and 0.7 cm. With arm circumference, R is well above 0.9 at all ages when TEM is 0.1 cm, and only falls below this

Table 3.2. *Intra-observer technical error of measurement*

Age range (years)		Technical error of measurement	Reliability	Reference
Length				
1–2		0.4	0.99	1
1–2		0.8	0.98	2
Height				
6–11		0.5	0.99	3
6–12		0.5		4
6–14				5
	1978	0.1		
	1979	0.2		
8–18		0.5		6
9–14		0.5	0.99	7
12–17		0.3		8
5–30		0.3		9
20+		0.7	0.98	10
Sitting height				
6–11		0.5	0.98	3
6–12		0.6		4
6–14				5
	1978	0.1		
	1979	0.2		
9–14		0.7		7
12–17		0.3		8
20+		0.7		10
Arm circumference				
1–2		0.4	0.93	2
2–7		0.2	0.97	11
6–12		0.4		4
6–14				5
	1978	0.1		
	1979	0.1		
8–18		0.3		6
9–14		0.4	0.98	7
12–17		0.4		8
5–30		0.1		9
Triceps skinfold				
Newborns		0.1	0.95	12
1–2		0.6	0.94	2
2–7		0.5	0.92	11
6–11		0.8	0.97	13
6–12		0.8		4
6–14				5

(Continued)

Table 3.2 (*cont.*)

Age range (years)		Technical error of measurement	Reliability	Reference
	1978	0.2		
	1979	0.2		
8–18		0.7		6
9–14		0.5	0.97	7
12–17		1.6		8
5–30		0.4		9
Subscapular skinfold				
Newborns		0.1	0.96	12
1–2		0.4	0.92	2
2–7		0.3	0.94	11
6–11		1.8	0.99	13
6–12		0.7		4
6–14				5
	1978	0.3		
	1979	0.1		
8–18		0.4		6
9–14		0.6	0.96	7
12–17		3.4		8

Sources: 1, S. J.Ulijaszek, unpublished; 2, Pelletier *et al.*, 1991; 3, Malina *et al.*, 1973; 4, Malina, 1968; 5, Buschang, 1980; 6, Meleski, 1980; 7, Zavaleta & Malina, 1982; 8, Brown, 1984; 9, Malina & Buschang, 1984; 10, Spielman *et al.*, 1973; 11, Martorell *et al.*, 1975; 12, Branson *et al.*, 1982; 13, Johnston *et al.*, 1972.

cut-off in the 1 to 1.9 years age group at a TEM of 0.4 cm. For triceps skinfold, R is above 0.9 at all ages when TEM is either 0.4 or 0.8 mm. It should be noted that these measures only go down to 1 year of age, and that a TEM of 0.8 mm, or even 0.4 mm, may not be acceptable at earlier ages. When TEM is 1.9 mm, over 40% of the between-subject variance is due solely to measurement error, and it is not until about 11 years of age that such a high TEM is associated with an R value of 0.9 or more. For subscapular skinfold measurements, a TEM of 0.3 mm gives R values above 0.9 at all ages, whilst a TEM of 0.9 mm gives R values above 0.9 in age groups above 6 years. At a TEM of 1.8 mm, however, over 80% of between-subject variance is due to measurement error in age groups below 7 years; this value of TEM only becomes acceptable in age groups above 13 years, when the between-subject variance increases.

Size of measurement and measurement error

It is not clear to what extent the absolute size of a dimension affects measurement error; it is possible that some of the differences in reported

Table 3.3. *Inter-observer technical error of measurement*

Age range (years)		Technical error of measurement	Reliability	Reference
Length				
1–2		0.5	0.99	1
1.5–2.5		0.5	0.88	2
Height				
4–11	device:			3
	Harpenden stadiometer	0.4	0.99	3
	Raven magnimeter	0.2	0.99	
7–9		0.1	0.61	2
6–13		0.7	0.99	4
6–14		0.2		5
20–50		0.2		6
		0.4	0.99	7
20+	males	0.15	0.95	2
	females	0.3	0.65	2
54–85		0.2		6
Sitting height				
6–14		0.4		5
5–17		0.4		8
12–17		0.7	0.97	9
20–50		0.2		6
		0.5	0.99	7
54–85	males	0.2		6
	females	0.4		6
Arm circumference				
1–2		0.1	0.99	1
1.5–2.5		0.1	0.70	2
7–9		0.05	0.71	2
6–14		0.3		4
20+		0.3	0.99	10
	males	0.1	0.95	2
	females	0.25	0.90	2
20–50		0.1		6
54–85		0.1		6
Triceps				
Newborns		0.4	0.86	11
0–0.5		0.4	0.50	2
1–2		0.6	0.91	1
1–2		0.8	0.83	12
1.5–2.5		0.5	0.56	2
7–9		0.2	0.61	2

(Continued)

Table 3.3 (*cont.*)

Age range (years)		Technical error of measurement	Reliability	Reference
6–13		1.0	0.95	4
6–11		1.9	0.85	13
6–14		0.5		5
12–17		1.9	0.92	14
17–25	males			15
	Calipers:			
	Harpenden	0.4	0.98	
	Lange	1.0	0.90	
20+	males	0.4	0.69	2
	females	1.1	0.77	2
20–50		0.7		6
54–85		0.9		6
Subscapular skinfold				
Newborns		0.4	0.86	11
1–2		0.5	0.88	1
1–2		0.6	0.81	12
6–11		1.5	0.88	13
6–13		1.1	0.90	4
6–14		0.4		5
12–17		1.5	0.96	14
17–25	males			15
	Calipers:			
	Harpenden	0.6	0.98	
	Lange	1.2	0.95	
20–50		1.1		6
54–85	males	1.5		6
	females	1.2		6

Sources: 1, Pelletier *et al.*, 1991; 2, Harrison *et al.*, 1991; 3, Voss *et al.*, 1990; 4, Lohman *et al.*, 1975; 5, Buschang, 1980; 6, Chumlea *et al.*, 1984; 7, Gordon & Bradtmiller, 1992; 8, Johnston, Dechow & MacVean, 1975; 9, Malina *et al.*, 1974; 10, Callaway *et al.*, 1988; 11, Branson *et al.*, 1982; 12, Johnston & Mack, 1985; 13, Johnston *et al.*, 1972; 14, Johnston *et al.*, 1974; 15, Sloan & Shapiro, 1972.

TEMs between age groups could be attributed to this factor. Certainly, for a wide variety of body length, breadth and circumference measures, the relation between standard deviation and mean is curvilinear, the coefficient of variation declining with increasing mean value (Roebuck, Kroemer & Thomson, 1975). This is illustrated for length and circumference measures in Fig. 3.6.

The reasons behind this observation are obscure, but it has been suggested that they may be related to measurement error (Pheasant,

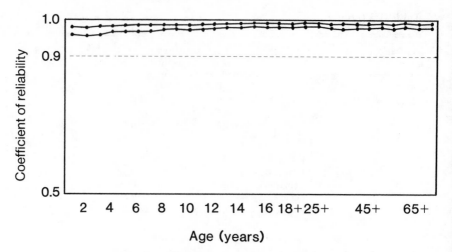

Fig. 3.1. Coefficient of reliability by age for height. Upper line, TEM = 0.2 cm; lower line, TEM = 0.7 cm.

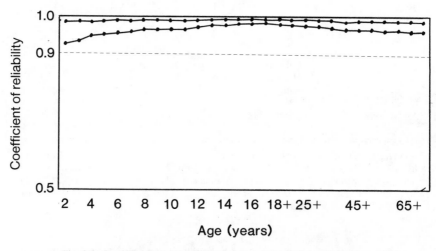

Fig. 3.2. Coefficient of reliability by age for sitting height. Upper line, TEM = 0.2 cm; lower line, TEM = 0.7 cm.

1988). That is, the larger the dimension being measured, the smaller the error of measurement is likely to be, as a proportion of the absolute measurement. This is not the case for skinfolds, after they have been logarithmically transformed to remove skewness (Fig. 3.7).

This lack of relation is probably due to the interaction of two effects

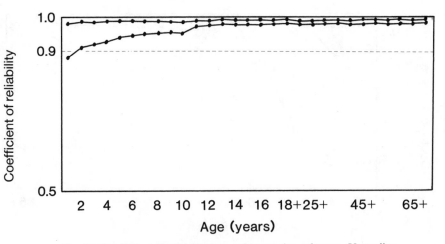

Fig. 3.3. Coefficient of reliability by age for arm circumference. Upper line, TEM = 0.1 cm; lower line, TEM = 0.4 cm.

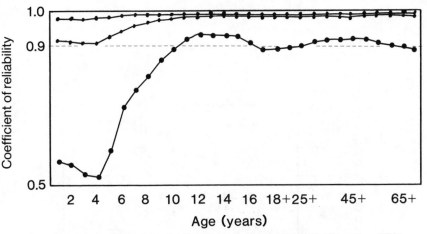

Fig. 3.4. Coefficient of reliability by age for triceps skinfold. Upper line, TEM = 0.4 mm; middle line, TEM = 0.8 mm; lower line, TEM = 1.9 mm.

which cancel each other out: the larger the measurement, the smaller the instrument error is likely to be. The error due to the observer's finding the site and measuring correctly is likely to be greater with the larger measurement, however. In order to examine the possibility of a relation between size of error and size of dimension, linear regressions of standard deviation scores (SDS) of within- and between-observer measurement

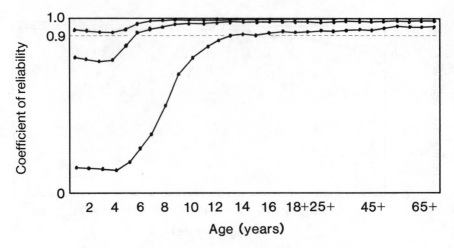

Fig. 3.5. Coefficient of reliability by age for subscapular skinfold. Upper line, TEM = 0.3 mm, middle line, TEM = 0.9 mm, lower line, TEM = 1.8 mm.

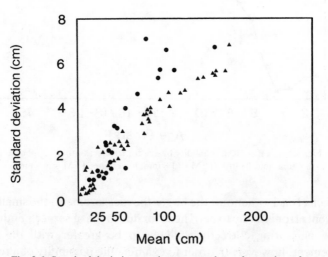

Fig. 3.6. Standard deviations against mean values of a number of anthropometric length and circumference measurements (from Roebuck *et al.*, 1975). Symbols: circles, length; triangles, circumference.

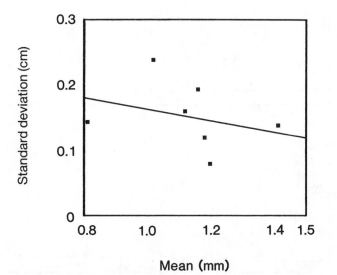

Fig. 3.7. Standard deviations against mean values of logarithmically transformed skinfold measurements (from Wong *et al.*, 1988).

Table 3.4. *Technical errors of measurement, adults, Papua New Guinea*

Two-way analysis of variance: between measurements $F = 0.1$; between intra- and inter-, $F = 10.1$; $p < 0.05$.

Measurement	Mean	CV	Intra		Inter	
			TEM	R	TEM	R
Height (cm)	150.9	3.8	0.25	0.99	0.22	0.99
Sitting height (cm)	77.9	4.2	0.42	0.99	0.55	0.97
Arm circumference (cm)	24.1	8.4	0.24	0.99	0.44	0.94
Triceps skinfold (mm)	5.3	15.0[a]	0.39	0.96	0.37	0.96
Subscapular skinfold (mm)	8.2	16.1[a]	0.58	0.96	0.63	0.95

[a]From log transformed data.

differences against size of dimension were carried out on data collected by the authors in Papua New Guinea. The use of SDS allowed the error–size relation for height, sitting height, arm circumference, and triceps and subscapular skinfolds to be compared directly. Table 3.4 gives means, coefficients of variation (CV) and intra- and inter-observer TEM and R values for the measured and re-measured sample.

The CVs of all the measurements are within the expected ranges (Roebuck *et al.*, 1975), with stature having the lowest CV and the two

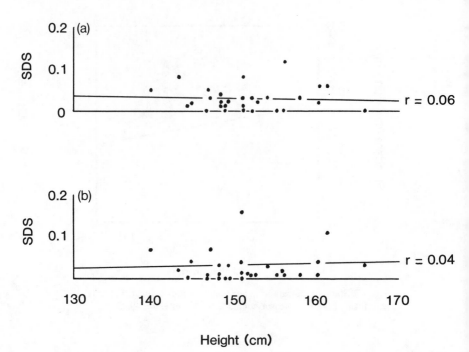

Fig. 3.8. Standard deviation score (SDS) of (a) within-observer and (b) between-observer difference in measurement by absolute size of measurement, for height.

skinfolds having the highest, even after logarithmic transformation. Two-way analysis of variance of TEM shows that there is no significant difference between any of the dimensions measured, while inter-observer TEMs are significantly greater than intra-observer TEMs ($F = 10.1$, df = $1.4, p < 0.05$).

Both intra- and inter-observer TEMs are within the ranges of reported values given in Tables 3.2 and 3.3. All R values are above 0.9, suggesting that the level of error associated with the measurement procedure is within the bounds thus far deemed to be acceptable in this paper. Figs 3.8–3.12 show SDS of within- and between-measurer differences plotted against size of dimension measured, for the five variables.

Of the anthropometric measurements shown here, triceps skinfold inter-measurer difference is significantly related to the size of the skinfold ($r = 0.41$, $F = 7.1$, df = 27, $p < 0.05$), while both intra- and inter-measurer differences in subscapular skinfold are related to size (intra-observer: $r = 0.82$, $F = 51.3$, df = $27, p < 0.001$; inter-observer: $r = 0.82$, $F = 52.5$, df = $27, p < 0.001$). However, the size of measurement error is

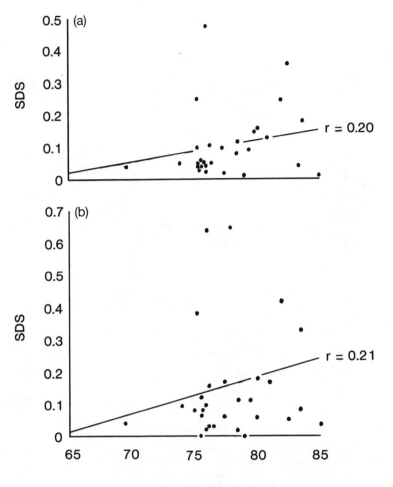

Fig. 3.9. Standard deviation score (SDS) of (a) within-observer and (b) between-observer differences in measurement by absolute size of measurement, for sitting height.

independent of the absolute value for height, sitting height and arm circumference, respectively. For adults, therefore, it is safe to assume that the size of the measurement has little or no influence on these three measurements, but not so for triceps and subscapular skinfolds. Indeed, the relation between error and absolute size is likely to be larger in Western populations, where there is a greater tendency to obesity than in populations from developing countries such as Papua New Guinea.

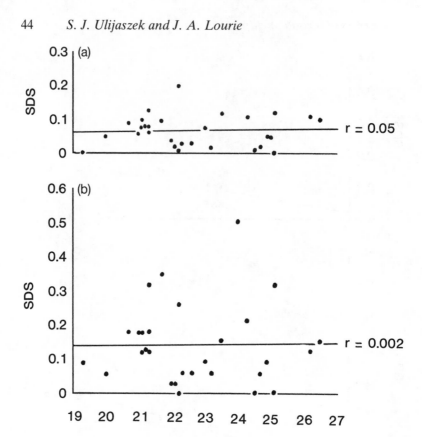

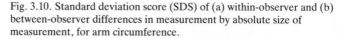

Arm circumference (cm)

Fig. 3.10. Standard deviation score (SDS) of (a) within-observer and (b) between-observer differences in measurement by absolute size of measurement, for arm circumference.

Although most of the TEMs given in Table 3.4 appear to be respectable by the standards of Frisancho (1990), Figs 3.8–3.12 show that there are considerable differences in the degree of scatter of SDS, and in homogeneity of error variance. For most of the variables, the scatter is greater for inter-observer differences than for intra-observer differences. For both sets of measurements, height shows the smallest amount of scatter, although the error variance is significantly heterogeneous for both intra- and inter-observer error (intra: $\chi^2 = 65.6$, df = 27, $p < 0.001$; inter: $\chi^2 = 77.4$, df=27, $p < 0.001$). This suggests that the errors are not systematic, and might be due to factors such as differences in posture and level of relaxation in the subjects measured, since the authors carried out the

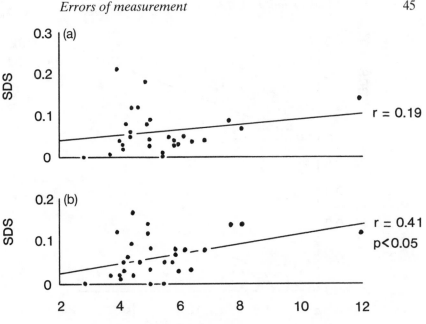

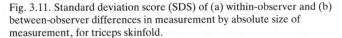

Fig. 3.11. Standard deviation score (SDS) of (a) within-observer and (b) between-observer differences in measurement by absolute size of measurement, for triceps skinfold.

repeat measurements at different times. Height measurement could therefore be made more accurate by standardizing the time of day at which measurements are made.

Sitting height shows the most scatter, with two outliers being in excess of 0.6 SDS. In addition, error variance is significantly heterogeneous for intra-($\chi^2 = 58.2$, df $= 27$, $p < 0.001$) and inter-($\chi^2 = 62.4$, df $= 27$, $p < 0.001$) observer error. This is a less accurate measure than height, and is subject to the same problems with the subjects' posture and state of relaxation as with height.

Subscapular skinfold SDS shows more scatter than triceps skinfold SDS, although most of this can be attributed to the error–size relation. For both measurements, error variance is homogeneous for within-observer differences (triceps: $\chi_3 = 35.8$, df$=27$; subscapular: $\chi^2 = 27.8$, df$=27$). This is also the case for between-observer differences in subscapular skinfold ($\chi^2 = 31.9$, df $= 27$). For triceps skinfold, between-observer error variance shows a low level of heterogeneity ($\chi^2 = 41.2$, df $= 27$, $p < 0.05$).

Inter-observer SDS for arm circumference is considerably greater than

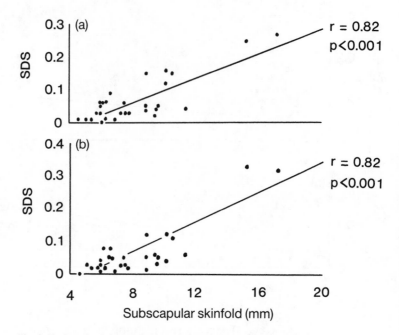

Fig. 3.12. Standard deviation score (SDS) of (a) within-observer and (b) between-observer differences in measurement by absolute size of measurement, for subscapular skinfold.

intra-observer SDS, with one outlier being 0.5 SDS. Between-observer error variance is significantly heterogeneous ($\chi^2 = 51.3$, df = 27, $p < 0.01$), whereas within-observer error variance is not ($\chi^2 = 33.0$, df = 27). This pattern is more difficult to interpret, but might be related to different levels of relaxation in the upper arm at the time of measurement. Regardless of the reason, the result suggests that the measurement of the upper arm is not the simple procedure that most people assume it to be.

In cross-sectional anthropometric surveys, variation due to error is likely to be cancelled out, if there is no systematic bias in the measurement and if the sample is large enough. In longitudinal studies and in situations where anthropometry is being used as a screening device, such outliers due to error give cause for concern, however. An SDS of 0.6 for the sitting height of an adult is about 2 cm; for a child aged between 5 and 10 years it is about 1.8 cm. This is a large amount of error which can be randomly thrown up once in 29 measures, if only one person is doing all the measuring, and twice in 29 measures, if there are two people involved. With respect to arm circumference, 0.5 SDS is equivalent to about 1.7 cm for an adult, and 1.1 cm for a child aged between 1 and 5 years. Assuming that the error is independent of arm circumference at circumferences below 19 cm, then a gross random measurement error could occur once in 29 measurements. In a rapid nutritional assessment in which large numbers of children are screened using arm circumference measurements, this could lead to large numbers of mis-classified children.

The repeat measurement data from which these conclusions are drawn were collected by the authors, two experienced and well-trained anthropometrists. It is therefore likely that the levels of error are higher in conditions where anthropometric training is poor, whether in Western countries or in the developing world.

Guidelines

The existing literature with respect to anthropometric measurement error either avoids making (Lohman, Roche & Martorell, 1988), is vague about (Mueller & Martorell, 1988), or is reluctant to make (Himes, 1989) recommendations about acceptable levels of error. It is our intention to propose guidelines for acceptable levels of measurement error, and for ways in which the reporting of anthropometric data could be improved by the incorporation of such data.

Reliability is a measure of the proportion of between-subject variance which is free from measurement error. A nominal value of 0.9 for R, which indicates that a measure is 90% free from measurement error, has been suggested. Although this might be an acceptable lower limit, examination of Table 3.4 and Figs 3.8–3.12 suggests that even at R values of around 0.95 there is occasional gross measurement error which is likely to have important consequences. Only when R is in the region of 0.99 is such error unlikely. Tables 3.5 and 3.6 give possible acceptable upper limits for total TEM by age group, at R values of 0.95 and 0.99.

In the case of a single observer, total TEM is equivalent to intra-observer TEM. When more than one observer is involved, total TEM can be obtained thus:

$$\text{Total TEM} = \sqrt{[\text{TEM(intra)}^2 + \text{TEM(inter)}^2]}. \qquad (3.4)$$

Tables 3.5 and 3.6 show that there are both age and sex differences in TEM. The 0.99 level of R gives values for TEM which in most cases are lower than the values recommended by Frisancho (1990) for sitting height, arm circumference, triceps and subscapular skinfolds. They are, however, attainable goals, as examination of Tables 3.2 and 3.3 reveals. Reliability of 0.95 might be more realistic in some circumstances, however. Further examination of Tables 3.2 and 3.3 shows some high values

Table 3.5. *Upper limits for total technical error of measurement at two levels of reliability (males)*

Age group (years)	Height (cm)	Sitting height (cm)	Arm circumference (cm)	Triceps skinfold (mm)	Subscapular skinfold (mm)
Reliability = 0.95					
1–4.9	1.03	0.40[a]	0.31	0.61	0.43
5–10.9	1.30	0.35	0.52	0.97	0.87
11–17.9	1.69	0.30	0.75	1.45	1.55
18–64.9	1.52	0.30	0.73	1.38	1.79
65+	1.52	0.30	0.74	1.29	1.74
Reliability = 0.99					
1–4.9	0.46	0.18[a]	0.14	0.28	0.19
5–10.9	0.58	0.16	0.23	0.43	0.39
11–17.9	0.76	0.13	0.33	0.65	0.69
18–64.9	0.68	0.13	0.33	0.62	0.80
65+	0.68	0.13	0.33	0.58	0.78

[a] 2 – 4.9 years.

Table 3.6. *Upper limits for total technical error of measurement at two levels of reliability (females)*

Age group (years)	Height (cm)	Sitting height (cm)	Arm circumference (cm)	Triceps skinfold (mm)	Subscapular skinfold (mm)
Reliability = 0.95					
1–4.9	1.04	0.34[a]	0.30	0.65	0.47
5–10.9	1.38	0.36	0.54	1.05	1.08
11–17.9	1.50	0.29	0.78	1.55	1.74
18–64.9	1.39	0.31	0.98	1.94	2.39
65+	1.35	0.32	0.98	1.86	2.27
Reliability = 0.99					
1–4.9	0.47	0.15[a]	0.13	0.29	0.21
5–10.9	0.62	0.16	0.24	0.47	0.48
11–17.9	0.67	0.13	0.35	0.69	0.78
18–64.9	0.62	0.14	0.44	0.87	1.07
65+	0.60	0.14	0.44	0.83	1.02

[a] 2–4.9 years.

for intra-observer TEM for arm circumference (Pelletier *et al.*, 1991) and subscapular skinfold (Johnston *et al.*, 1972), and for inter-observer TEM for triceps (Johnston & Mack, 1985; Johnston *et al.*, 1972; Johnston, Hamill & Lemeshow, 1974) and subscapular (Pelletier *et al.*, 1991; Johnston & Mack, 1985; Johnston *et al.*, 1972; Lohman, Boileau & Massey, 1975) skinfolds. Given that these reported values come from experienced anthropometrists, it is likely that the data of less experienced measurers may have greater TEMs than these. While one should strive to attain the levels of accuracy suggested in Table 3.5, this may not always be possible, particularly with skinfold measurements. Certainly, it is possible to calculate TEM off-cuts at lower levels of R, if it is felt by the practitioner or researcher that higher levels of error variance are acceptable. The reader is referred back to equation 3.2 to see how this can be done. It may not always be desirable to perform this procedure, however, and it is therefore important that ways should be sought in which measurement error can be taken account of in the interpretation of measurements.

Measurement error and interpretation of data

There are considerable problems associated with attempting to accommodate measurement error in the interpretation of longitudinal anthropometric information. If a measurer is able to attain a reliability of about 0.95, then it is possible that more than one measurement in about thirty may be substantially erroneous. For a five-year-old child, this level of error may be as high as 2.6 cm (height), 1.8 cm (sitting height), 0.9 cm (arm circumference), 6.6 mm (triceps skinfold) and 8.1 mm (subscapular skinfold), for a single reported measurement. We are sure that clinicians are aware of this phenomenon; the availability of R values for a measurer or group of measurers would help enormously in the interpretation of such a 'wild' measurement. If a measurer attains R values of 0.99, however, such a large difference between successive measurements is unlikely to be due to measurement error, and other explanations should be considered.

Sometimes serial differences in anthropometry are used for screening populations for health or nutritional interventions. Comparison of total TEM obtained by an observer or observers with values given in Tables 3.5 and 3.6 can allow a sensible value of measurement difference to be chosen, one which is unlikely to be attributed in large part to measurement error. For example, if an observer has a lower TEM for the triceps than for the subscapular skinfold, the former measurement should be used. Further, if their TEM is close to that which is associated with an R

value of 0.99, then the cut-off for the difference between serial measurements which should be used for screening should be the TEM for the appropriate age group, at $R = 0.99$. In the case of younger adults, this would be about 0.8 mm for triceps skinfold. Viegas *et al.* (1982) used a cut-off of 0.3 mm difference in triceps skinfold between the end of the first and second trimester of pregnancy to identify whether pregnant South Asian women in Birmingham, England, were at nutritional risk or not. In this case the cut-off was so small that a large number of women could have been mis-classified on the basis of measurement error alone, even if the anthropometrist was the best in the world. The TEM can therefore be used to determine what is measurable and what is not.

In cross-sectional studies, a proportion of the total variance observed in a population is due to measurement error. The partitioning of the variance can be summarised thus:

$$V(t) = V(b) + V(e,1) + V(e,2) + V(e,3), \qquad (3.5)$$

where

$\quad V(t) \quad$ = total variance observed;
$\quad V(b) \quad$ = biological, or true variance;
$\quad V(e,1)$ = variance due to intra-observer measurement error;
$\quad V(e,2)$ = variance due to inter-observer error;
$\quad V(e,3)$ = variance due to instrument error.

Usually, anthropometric data is reported as though $V(t)$ were $V(b)$. Although the two are usually so close that for all practical purposes the slight difference does not matter, this is not always the case. If the variances due to errors of one sort or another are large, they may mask true biological differences in anthropometric characteristics between groups, when statistical comparisons are being made.

As an example, one can consider the physical characteristics of men from the North Fly region of Papua New Guinea, the groups from which data presented in Table 3.4 and Figs 3.8–3.12 were obtained. Table 3.6. gives means and standard deviations (SD) for the three populations living in this region, together with standard deviations which have been corrected for both intra- and inter-observer error (CSD). One-way analysis of variance (ANOVA) and Scheffé tests were used to examine heterogeneity between the groups for the five variables, first with SD, and then with CSD. Statistical comparisons between groups for triceps and subscapular skinfolds were performed on logarithmically normalized data, the transformed means being given in Table 3.7 together with 5% and 95% confidence limits.

Table 3.7. *Means, standard deviations and corrected standard deviations of measurements of North Fly adult males*

Measurement	Scheffé (a)[a]	Wopkaimin N Mean (SD)[b] (CSD)[c]	Scheffé (b)	Ningerum N Mean (SD) (CSD)	Scheffé (c)	Awin N Mean (SD) (CSD)	ANOVA F	p
Height		152		66		56		
		156.8		157.6		158.4		
		(5.3)		(5.1)		(6.8)		
		(5.3)		(5.1)		(6.7)		
Sitting height		152		59		37		
		80.8		81.0		81.5		
		(5.7)		(2.6)		(3.1)		
		(5.6)		(2.5)		(3.0)		
Arm circumference		152		66		56		
		26.4		25.1		25.4		
	*	(2.2)	***	(2.2)		(2.0)	10.0	***
	*	(2.1)	***	(2.1)		(1.9)	10.6	***
Triceps skinfold		152		66		56		
		4.6		4.5		4.5		
		(2.9–7.2)		(2.9–6.8)		(3.3–6.4)		
		(3.6–5.9)		(3.5–5.7)		(4.1–4.9)		
Subscapular skinfold		38		55		56		
		8.4		7.5		7.9		
		(5.7–12.4)		(4.5–12.4)		(5.3–12.5)		
		(7.3–9.6)	**	(6.5–8.6)		(6.9–9.0)	5.6	**

[a]Scheffé tests (asterisks indicate levels of significance): (a) Wopkaimin vs. Awin; (b) Wopkaimin vs. Ningerum; (c) Ningerum vs. Awin.
[b](SD) Standard deviation, or 95% confidence limits.
[c](CSD) Corrected standard deviation, or 95% confidence limits.

For height, sitting height, arm circumference and triceps skinfold, intra- and inter-observer TEMs are too small to influence the statistical comparison between groups. That is, the between group differences revealed by the use of ANOVA and Scheffé test using SD as the distribution measure are the same as when CSD is used in the analysis. The error variance for subscapular skinfold is larger than for the other measurements, however, and is large enough to hide the true biological variance. Using SD, which is the square root of $V(t)$, there is no significant difference between the groups, as reported by Ulijaszek *et al.* (1989). When CSD, or the square root of $V(t) - (V(e,1) + (V(e,2))$, is used in the analysis, then a significant difference between the three populations is revealed (ANOVA: $F \simeq 5.59, p < 0.01$), with Wopkaimin men having significantly greater subscapular skinfold than Ningerum men ($p < 0.01$, Scheffé test).

In the reporting and analysis of cross-sectional anthropometric data, it is therefore recommended that CSDs be used. At the least, the possibility that measurement error might influence interpretation should be examined. Reorganizing equation 3.3 gives an easy way in which CSD can be calculated:

$$CSD = \sqrt{[SD^2 - (TEM(intra)^2 + TEM(inter)^2)]}. \qquad (3.6)$$

In this case CSD does not take into account measurement error due to other factors such as instrument error. This could be built into the equation quite easily, however, should it be needed.

Conclusions

This paper examines the use of technical error of measurement (TEM) and coefficient of reliability (R) as related anthropometric error-measurement variables. Values of TEM for sitting height, arm circumference, triceps and subscapular skinfolds suggested by Frisancho (1990) are deemed to be incorrect, because they do not take into account the age-dependence of TEM. Error variances for most of the anthropometric measures taken by the authors in Papua New Guinea are significantly heterogeneous, even with R values of 0.95 and greater. Although it is not always possible, it is recommended that for most purposes, intra-, and where applicable, inter-observer R should be at least greater than 0.95, and preferably greater than 0.99. Values for TEM at these two levels of R are presented by sex and age group, as possible acceptable upper limits for measurement error for height, sitting height, arm circumference, triceps and subscapular skinfolds.

Acknowledgements

We thank Dr J. Boldsen, Dr T. J. Cole, Professor G. Lasker and Dr C. G. N. Mascie-Taylor for their helpful comments and criticisms, and Professor R. M. Malina for making available technical errors of measurement from several studies carried out by University of Texas at Austin personnel.

References

Branson, R. S., Vaucher, Y. E., Harrison, G. G., Vargas, M. & Theis, C. (1982). Inter- and intra-observer reliability of skinfold thickness measurements in newborn infants. *Human Biology* **54**, 137–43.

Brown, K. R. (1984). Growth, physique and age at menarche of Mexican American females age 12 through 17 years residing in San Diego County, California. PhD thesis, University of Texas at Austin.

Buschang, P. H. (1980). Growth status and rate in school children 6 to 13 years of age in a rural Zapotec-speaking community in the Valley of Oaxaca, Mexico. PhD thesis, University of Texas at Austin.

Callaway, C. W., Chumlea, W. C., Bouchard, C., Himes, J. H., Lohman, T. G., Martin, A. D., Mitchell, C. D., Mueller, W. H., Roche, A. F. & Seefeldt, V. D. (1988). Circumferences. In: *Anthropometric Standardisation Reference Manual*, ed. T. G. Lohman, A. F. Roche & R. Martorell, pp. 39–54. Champaign, Illinois: Human Kinetics Books.

Cameron, N. (1986). The methods of auxological anthropometry. In: *Human Growth: a Comprehensive Treatise*, vol 3, ed. F. Falkner & J. M. Tanner, pp. 3–46. New York: Plenum Press.

Chumlea, W. C., Roche, A. F. & Rogers, E. (1984). Replicability for anthropometry in the elderly. *Human Biology* **56**, 329–37.

Frisancho, A. R. (1990) *Anthropometric Standards for the Assessment of Growth and Nutritional Status*. Ann Arbor: University of Michigan Press.

Gordon, C. C. & Bradtmiller, B. (1992). Interobserver error in a large scale anthropometric survey. *American Journal of Human Biology* **4**, 253–63.

Harrison, G. G., Buskirk, E. R., Carter, J. E. L., Johnston, F. E., Lohman, T. G., Pollock, M. L., Roche, A. F. & Wilmore, J. (1988). Skinfold thicknesses and measurement technique. In: *Anthropometric Standardisation Reference Manual*, ed. T. G. Lohman, A. F. Roche & R. Martorell, pp. 55–70. Champaign, Illinois: Human Kinetics Books.

Harrison, G. G., Galal, O. M., Ritenbaugh, C., Shaheen, F. M., Wahba, S.A.-A., Kirksey, A. & Jerome, N. W. (1991). Dependability and precision of anthropometric measures in a longitudinal field study in an Egyptian village. *American Journal of Human Biology* **3**, 479–87.

Himes, J. H. (1989). Reliability of anthropometric methods and replicate measurements. *American Journal of Physical Anthropology* **79**, 77–80.

Johnston, F. E., Dechow, P. C. & MacVean, R. B. (1975). Age changes in skinfold thickness among upper class school children of differing ethnic backgrounds residing in Guatemala. *Human Biology* **47**, 251–62.

Johnston, F. E., Hamill, P. V. V. & Lemeshow, S. (1972). Skinfold thickness of children 6–11 years, United States. National Health Survey Series II, #120, DHEW Publication #(HSM) 73-1602. Rockville, Maryland: National Center for Health Statistics.

Johnston, F. E., Hamill, P. V. V. & Lemeshow, S. (1974). Skinfold thicknesses in a national probability sample of U.S. males and females aged 6 through 17 years. *American Journal of Physical Anthropology* **40**, 321–4.

Johnston, F. E. & Mack, R. W. (1985). Interobserver reliability of skinfold measurements in infants and young children. *American Journal of Physical Anthropology* **67**, 285–9.

Krogman, G. M. (1950). A handbook of the measurement and interpretation of height and weight in the growing child. *Monographs of the Society for Research in Child Development* **13**, no. 3.

Lohman, T. G., Boileau, R. A. & Massey, B. H. (1975). Prediction of lean body mass in young boys from skinfold thickness and body weight. *Human Biology* **47**, 245–62.

Lohman, T. G., Roche, A. F. & Martorell, R. (eds) (1988). *Anthropometric Standardisation Reference Manual.* Champaign, Illinois: Human Kinetics Books.

Malina, R. M. (1968). Growth, maturation, and performance of Philadelphia negro and white elementary school children. PhD thesis, University of Pennsylvania, Philadephia.

Malina, R. M. & Buschang, P. H. (1984). Anthropometric asymmetry in normal and mentally retarded males. *Annals of Human Biology* **11**, 515–31.

Malina, R. M., Hamill, P. V. V. & Lemeshow, S. (1973). Selected body measurements of children 6–11 years, United States. Vital and Health Statistics, Series 11, No. 123. Washington, DC: US Government Printing Office.

Malina, R. M., Hamill, P. V. V. & Lemeshow, S. (1974). Body dimensions and proportions, White and Negro children 6–11 years, United States. Vital and Health Statistics, Series 11, No. 143. Washington, DC: US Government Printing Office.

Martorell, R., Habicht, J.-P., Yarbrough, C., Guzman, G. & Klein, R. E. (1975). The identification and evaluation of measurement variability in the anthropometry of preschool children. *American Journal of Physical Anthropology* **43**, 347–52.

Meleski, B. W. (1980). Growth, maturity, body composition and familial characteristics of competitive swimmers 8 to 18 years of age. PhD thesis, University of Texas at Austin.

Mueller, W. H. & Martorell, R. (1988). Reliability and accuracy of measurement. In: *Anthropometric Standardisation Reference Manual.* ed. T. G. Lohman, A. F. Roche and R. Martorell, pp. 83–6. Champaign, Illinois: Human Kinetics Books.

Pelletier, D. L., Low, J. W. & Msukwa, L. A. H. (1991). Sources of measurement variation in child anthropometry in the Malawi maternal and child nutrition survey. *American Journal of Human Biology* **3**, 227–37.

Pheasant, S. (1988). *Bodyspace. Anthropometry, Ergonomics and Design.* London: Taylor and Francis.

Roebuck, J. A., Kroemer, K. H. E. & Thomson, W. G. (1975). *Engineering Anthropometry Methods.* New York: Wiley.

Sloan, A. W. & Shapiro, M. (1972). A comparison of skinfold measurements with three standard calipers. *Human Biology* **44**, 29–36.

Spielman, R. S., da Rocha, F. J., Weitkamp, L. R., Ward, R. H., Neel, J. V. & Chagnon, N. A. (1973). The genetic structure of a tribal population, the Yanomama Indians. *American Journal of Physical Anthropology* **37**, 345–56.

Tanner, J. M. (1986). Physical development. *British Medical Bulletin* **42**, 131–8.

Ulijaszek, S. J., Lourie, J. A., Taufa, T. & Pumuye, A. (1989). The Ok Tedi health and nutrition project, Papua New Guinea: adult physique of three populations in the North Fly region. *Annals of Human Biology* **16**, 61–74.

Viegas, O. A. C., Scott, P. H., Cole, T. J., Eaton, P., Needham, P. G. & Wharton, B. A. (1982). Dietary protein energy supplementation of pregnant

Asian mothers at Sorrento, Birmingham. II: Selective during third trimester only. *British Medical Journal* **285**, 592–5.

Voss, L. D., Bailey, B. J. R., Cumming, K., Wilkin, T. J. & Betts, P. R. (1990). The reliability of height measurement (the Wessex growth study). *Archives of Disease in Childhood* **65**, 1340–4.

Wong, W. W., Cochran, W. J., Klish, W. J., Smith, E. O., Lee, L. S., Fiorotto, M. L. & Klein, P. D. (1988). Body fat in normal adults estimated by oxygen-18- and deuterium-dilution and by anthropometry: a comparison. *European Journal of Clinical Nutrition* **42**, 233–42.

Zavaleta, A. N. & Malina, R. M. (1982). Growth and body composition of Mexican-American boys 9 through 14 years of age. *American Journal of Physical Anthropology* **57**, 261–71.

4 *Statistical issues in anthropometry*

C. G. NICHOLAS MASCIE-TAYLOR

Introduction

Anthropometric measurements are used in a wide number of contexts in human biology. For instance, twin researchers compare monozygotic and dizygotic twins and find very high heritabilities for height and weight (Bouchard *et al.*, 1990). Others use height-for-age or weight-for-height of children to show the extent of undernutrition in a study area (Waterlow *et al.*, 1977). In adults low body mass index is thought by many to be a useful predictor of increased morbidity, reduced work capacity and increased risk of mortality (Ferro-Luzzi *et al.*, 1992).

The aim of this chapter is to discuss some of the main statistical issues and approaches when analysing cross-sectional anthropometric characters. The paper is divided into three sections. The first section deals with sample design and sample size determination; the second section concentrates on analyses of continuous characters and covers testing of normality, use of analysis of variance with main effects and covariates, testing for curvilinearity and the use of regression. The final section addresses the issue of the use of statistics for predictive purposes. It reviews the use of relative risk and odds ratio, sensitivity and specificity, logistic regression, discriminant analysis and modelling using multiple regression. Examples of many of the statistical tests and interpretation of results are provided.

Sample design and sample size determination
Study design

The term study design incorporates the type of research design, definition of the study sample, determination of sample size, method of treatment allocation (if applicable) and means by which the sample is obtained (random, cluster, quota, sequential, etc.). There are only two types of research design: either experimental or observational. In experimental studies the intervention is under the control of the researcher. The experimental design can be of many different types but the most powerful

56

design is the Randomized Control Trial (RCT) in which subjects are randomly allocated to one of two groups, usually called an intervention group and a control group. The aim of the study is to see how changes in the independent variable, the one under the researcher's control, affect some outcome (the dependent variable). An example of a RCT would be a study set up to examine the effects of de-worming on children's nutritional status. Children would be assigned randomly to treated and untreated groups and the treated children would receive regular chemotherapy while the untreated group would either receive nothing or, more commonly, a placebo. The dependent variable could be measurement of the change in height and weight over some fixed period.

By contrast the researcher does not control the intervention in observational studies, but rather observes the effects of an experiment in nature. For observational studies one of the main problems is selection of the subjects for study. Since it is usually impossible and impracticable to study everyone (the population) the survey is limited to a subset (sample) of the population. There are a number of sampling strategies. In random sampling (sometimes called strictly random sampling), each subject in the population has an equal chance of being chosen for the study. This approach maximizes the likelihood that the results of the study can be generalized to the entire population.

There are circumstances when it may be necessary to deviate from strictly random sampling. One problem with such sampling is that too few subjects may end up in one subgroup or another and it may not be possible to perform statistical tests with such small samples. One way to overcome this problem is to use stratified random sampling where the sample is divided into strata or levels, for instance by parity, educational level and/or other variables. Subjects are then sampled randomly from the stratum into which they fall.

In some designs it is impracticable to assign subjects to various groups. In nutritional surveys it is common to make use of multistage cluster sampling, where the cluster might be a family or household. However, the two, three or more people in the same household will share the same diet and environment, and are likely to have similar attitudes to health. Thus outcomes are likely to be correlated to some degree and studies that use cluster sampling usually need larger sample sizes than investigations which employ strictly random sampling.

Sample size determination
Whichever research design is used, it is essential to get some idea of how large a sample is required. There are many researchers who give little or

no thought to sample size, choosing the most convenient number (100, 250, etc.) or time period for their study. A study with too large a sample size may be deemed unethical if it involves clinical trials and may add considerably to the budget. On the other hand, a study with too small a sample will be scientifically useless, equally unethical in its use of subjects, and a waste of resources. Studies that are too small are extremely common, to judge by surveys of published results (Freiman *et al.*, 1978).

The calculation of sample size depends on the complexity of the study design. There are three components to the calculation of sample sizes: (i) the power of the test (β, the power is defined as the probability of correctly rejecting the null hypothesis H_0 given H_0 is false); (ii) the level of significance (α, the usual level of significance, is set at 0.95); and (iii) for means, the coefficients of variation of the changes and the percentage difference between group means or for proportions, the difference in proportions.

For example, a milk feeding trial on five-year-old children in which half the children are given extra milk is being set up. On average children at this age gain 6 cm in height over 1 year and the standard deviation is 2 cm. Suppose than an additional increase in height of 0.5 cm in the milk-fed group will signify an important difference. What sample sizes are needed to detect a true difference at least that large?

$$\text{The formula is } n = \frac{2\sigma^2[z_{1-\alpha} + z_{1-\beta}]^2}{(\mu_1 - \mu_2)^2}$$

$$n = \frac{2(2.0)^2[1.96 + 0.842]^2}{(0.5)^2}$$

$$n = 251.24.$$

Hence a sample of 252 subjects should be studied in each of the two groups. If the power of the test is increased to 85% and the significance to 0.99 then samples of 420 in each group are required.

If the researcher is interested in differences in proportions then a different formula is used. Suppose a study is planned to estimate the prevalence of undernutrition (using a cut-off of $-2Z$ weight-for-height, where Z is the normal deviate) for a predetermined confidence interval. The formula can also be modified to allow for cluster sampling (see Mascie-Taylor (1993) and Lemeshow *et al.* (1990) for further details).

The formula to calculate the confidence limit (CI) is:

$$\text{CI} = p \pm 2\{p(100 - p)/n\}^{1/2},$$

where CI gives the upper and lower limits of the confidence interval, p is the percentage of undernourished individuals, $100 - p$ is the percentage of well-nourished individuals, 2 is the approximate value for the 95% confidence interval, and n is the number of individuals included in the sample.

The width, W, of the confidence interval is expressed by the term $\pm 2\{p(100 - p)/n\}^{1/2}$. Consequently $W = 2 \times 2\{p(100 - p)/n\}^{1/2}$ and n can be derived by squaring both sides of the equation and multiplying by n:

$$W^2 n = 4 \times 4\{p(100 - p)/n\} \times n;$$

$$n = 16p(100 - p)/W^2.$$

To obtain n it is therefore necessary to choose a value of W and to know the value of p. Determining the value of p is, of course, the precise objective of the survey. However, it is not necessary to know the exact proportion and a rough 'guestimate' (based on previous experience) will give a satisfactory result. With a required precision for the estimate of change of ±5%, width of confidence interval of 10% and an estimated p value of 35% then,

$$n = 16 \times \frac{(35 \times 65)}{(10)^2} = 364.$$

So a sample size of 364 is required. If the p value was reduced to 30%, the sample size required would be 336.

Analyses of anthropometric characters
Testing for normality
Anthropometric variables tend to be continuous, quantitative characters. Most 'parametric' tests assume that the data conform to a normal distribution. A 'quick and dirty' way of getting some idea of whether the data are skewed is to compare the values of the mean and median. For normal distributions the mean and median are numerically identical. As the distribution becomes more skewed, the difference between mean and median increases.

There are a number of statistical tests available for testing 'normality' and the researcher may well get different results depending on which test is used. For example, the Kolmorogov–Smirnoff Test examines the cumulative distribution, while the Cox Test is used to determine the extent of skewness and kurtosis. Generally the Cox test is preferable but even so significant skewness and/or kurtosis may occur with large samples

Table 4.1. *Mean maternal weights and birth outcome*

F-test = 1.06, p = n.s.; t-test = 7.91, $p < 0.001$.

Birth outcome	Number	Mean	Standard deviation
Child died	345	45.33	6.72
Child survived	3805	48.40	6.92

even though the magnitude of the effect is very small. In general, skewness is more constraining than kurtosis.

If the distribution of an anthropometric character does show significant skewness then it is quite likely that a simple logarithmic (either $\log_{10}$ or $\log_e$) transformation will normalize the distribution. In such cases the geometric rather than arithmetic mean should be used. For instance, body mass index (BMI) has been shown to show skewness in some populations because of the extended tail at the upper end of the distribution.

For illustrative purposes only, data from a large maternal anthropometric Bangladeshi survey of 4150 mother–child pairs have been analysed. These data come from the work of Dr Halida Akhtar and her colleagues at the Bangladesh Institute of Research for Promotion of Essential & Reproductive Health and Technologies (BIRPERHT). Their study was conducted in ten medical centres in Bangladesh; all the women were full-term. Patients with antepartum haemorrhage, or undergoing miscarriage and abortion, with multiple pregnancy, eclampsia or gross foetal abnormalities were excluded.

A continuous dependent variable and an independent discrete variable with two categories (t-test)

One question of interest is whether there is any significant relation between maternal weight and birth outcome as expressed in perinatal mortality. Since there are only two categories (death or no child death) a t-test will suffice. The simple t-test assumes non-significant differences in sample variances and a test for homogeneity of variances (F-test) is usually performed before going on to the t-test. If the F-test shows significantly heterogeneity a separate variance t-test is used; most computer-based statistical packages (for example, SPSS/PC+, SAS or BMDP) provide both the pooled and separate variance t-tests.

The comparison of mean weights by birth outcome are presented in Table 4.1. The results show that the variances are very similar (non-

Table 4.2. *One-way analysis of variance and* a posteriori *test*

(a) Analysis of variance

Source	DF	Sum of squares	Mean squares	F ratio	F prob.
Between groups	3	22 517.8929	7505.9643	174.4589	<0.0001
Within groups	4146	178 378.5924	43.0243		
Total	4149	200 896.4853			

(b) Multiple range test (Student–Newman–Keuls)

Mean	Group	Group 0 1 2 3
45.3183	0	
46.8123	1	*
48.9616	2	**
51.6012	3	***

significant F-test) and so they can be pooled. The t-test indicates a highly significant difference in means; mothers whose child died are, on average, 3 kg lighter. In these analyses a two-tailed t-test was used because the null hypothesis (H_0) was that there was no difference between means. If, however, some previous study had shown a significantly reduced weight in mothers whose child had died the hypothesis would have been the alternative one (H_1) and a one-tailed t-test would have been used. The calculation of both one- and two-tailed t-tests are identical; the only difference is in the interpretation of the probability tables.

A continuous dependent variable and an independent variable with three or more categories (one-way analysis of variance)

It is frequently reported that weight varies between people with different educational levels, where educational level is taken as a proxy for a combination of knowledge of health matters and socioeconomic status. In Bangladesh it is usual to grade people's educational attainment into four levels: no education (coded as 0 here), primary (1), secondary (2) and tertiary (3). The mean weights for the four groups are shown in Table 4.2 together with the analysis of variance (ANOVA). Many computer packages also include tests of *a posteriori* differences. These are used, for example, if the F-test is significant and the researcher wants to know which means are significant. There are a number of *a posteriori* tests; the one illustrated here is the Student–Newman–Keuls test, but other frequently used tests are the Scheffé and *a posteriori* t-test.

The ANOVA shows that there are highly significant differences between the four means. The *a posteriori* test reveals that all group means are very different: the least educated mothers have the lowest mean weight and the more highly educated mothers, the highest mean weight.

A continuous dependent variable and two independent variables with two or more categories (analysis of variance)

A slightly more complex analysis occurs when the researcher wants to examine the simultaneous effect of two or more discrete characters in relation to a continuous variable. For instance, the researcher wants to examine the relationship of educational level and parity to maternal weight. The same categories for educational level are used as above. Parity has been coded from 0 to 5 (the last category referring to mothers who have 5 or more children). The results of the ANOVA are presented in Table 4.3.

The results show that there are significant additive effects of both educational level and parity on weight, but no significant interaction effect. The multiple classification analysis compares each group in relation to the overall (grand) mean. It is clear, for instance, that the initial pattern of means for parity change after educational level is taken into account; multiparous women have the lowest mean weight initially but after education is taken into account primiparous women have the lowest mean weights. The multiple R squared (R^2, the coefficient of determination) provides a measure of how much of the variation in maternal weight is explained by educational level and parity. In this example the two independent variables account for 12.4% of the total variation.

A continuous dependent variable and a continuous independent variable (regression analysis)

Regression analysis is used to examine the bivariate relationship between two continuous variables when there is dependency or when the researcher wants to plot the best fitting line. Alternatively, correlation analysis can be used if there is no dependent–independent relation. The results of regressing maternal weight on age are shown in Table 4.4. There is a clear positive relation with maternal weight. The regression line shows that maternal weight increases by approximately 0.198 kg per year.

It is always useful to examine the residual plot, which should show the residuals symmetrically arranged. Examination of the residuals for maternal weight and age show a curvilinear pattern, which suggests that a quadratic term should be included in the analysis.

Table 4.3. *Analysis of variance of maternal weight by educational level and parity*

(a) Total population statistics
Total
48.14
(4150)

Education

0	1	2	3
45.32	46.81	48.96	51.60
(1182)	(698)	(1355)	(915)

Parity

0	1	2	3	4	5
47.71	48.88	48.47	48.24	48.18	47.27
(1882)	(1013)	(604)	(349)	(122)	(180)

(b) Breakdown of population by education and parity

Education level	Parity					
	0	1	2	3	4	5
0	44.44	45.96	45.34	45.75	47.50	45.45
	(429)	(246)	(189)	(151)	(62)	(105)
1	46.11	46.46	47.12	48.71	47.32	48.96
	(286)	(163)	(116)	(67)	(29)	(37)
2	48.26	49.41	49.98	49.83	50.60	49.68
	(681)	(346)	(174)	(101)	(22	(31)
3	50.75	52.49	52.37	54.36	49.72	54.86
	(486)	(258)	(125)	(30)	(9)	(7)

(c) Analysis of variance

Source of variation	Sum of squares	df	Mean square	F	F prob
Main effects	24 851.369	8	3106.421	73.102	<0.001
Education	23 736.966	3	7912.322	186.198	<0.001
Parity	2 333.476	5	466.695	10.983	<0.001
2-way interactions	714.413	15	47.628	1.121	0.331
Education/Parity	714.413	15	47.628	1.121	0.331
explained	25 565.782	23	1111.556	26.158	<0.001
residual	175 330.703	4126	42.494		
total	200 896.485	4149	48.420		

(*Continued*)

Testing for curvilinearity: a continuous dependent variable and a continuous independent variable (regression analysis)

With the inclusion of a quadratic term, the regression equation changes from $Y = a \pm bX$ to $Y = a \pm bX \pm cX^2$. The output from an SPSS/PC $\pm$ regression of weight against age (linear and quadratic) is presented in

Table 4.3 (*cont.*)

(d) Multiple classification analysis (grand mean = 48.144)

Variable + category	N	Unadjusted		Adjusted for independents	
		Dev'n	Eta	Dev'n	Beta
Education level					
0 (no)	1182	−2.83		−3.01	
1 (prim)	698	−1.33		−1.41	
2 (sec)	1355	0.82		0.91	
3 (ter)	915	3.46		3.62	
			0.33		0.35
Parity					
0	1882	−0.44		−0.80	
1	1013	0.73		0.46	
2	604	0.33		0.53	
3	349	0.10		1.10	
4	122	0.04		1.47	
5	180	−0.88		0.87	
			0.07		0.11
Multiple R^2					0.124
Multiple R					0.352

Table 4.4. *Regression analysis of maternal weight on age*

(a) Step 1 Enter age

Multiple R	0.140 44
R^2	0.019 72
Adjusted R^2	0.019 49
Standard error	6.890 34

(b) Analysis of variance

	df	Sum of squares	Mean square
Regression	1	3 962.518 83	3962.518 83
Residual	4148	196 933.966 47	47.476 85

$F = 83.462\ 13$ Signif. $F = 0.0001$

Variable	B	se B	β	t	t prob.
Age	0.198 003	0.021 673	0.140 443	9.136	0.0001
(Constant)	43.291 905	0.541 817		79.901	0.0001

Table 4.5. *Test of curvilinearity of weight against mother's age*

At Step 1: enter age
Multiple R   0.14044
R Square   0.01972
Adjusted R Square   0.01949
Standard Error   6.89034

Analysis of variance

	df	Sum of squares	Mean square
Regression	1	3 962.518 83	3962.518 83
Residual	4148	196 933.966 47	47.476 85

$F = 83.462\ 13$ Signif. $F = 0.000\ 1$

Variable	B	se B	β	t	t prob.
Age	0.198003	0.021673	0.140443	9.136	0.0001
(Constant)	43.291905	0.541817		79.901	0.0001

At Step 2: enter age squared (age^2 entered)
Multiple R   0.16026
R Square   0.02568
Adjusted R Square   0.02521
Standard Error   6.87020

Analysis of variance

	df	Sum of squares	Mean square
Regression	2	5 159.64742	2579.82371
Residual	4147	195 736.83788	47.19962

$F = 54.65772$ Signif. $F = 0.0001$

Variable	B	se B	β	t	t prob.
Age	1.069 708	0.174 432	0.758 740	6.133	0.0001
Age^2	−0.016 522	0.003 281	−0.623 098	−5.036	0.0001
(constant)	32.254 216	2.257 279		14.289	0.0001

Table 4.5; a clear curvilinearity is demonstrated. The positive age effect and negative age^2 term indicates that with increasing age, maternal weight tends to plateau and to decline in the older age groups. The comparison of the linear and curvilinear lines are presented in Fig. 4.1.

A continuous dependent variable, a continuous independent variable and a number of discrete independent variables (analysis of variance or multiple regression analysis)

The previous analyses have shown that there are relationships between maternal weight and educational level, parity and maternal age. The simultaneous effects of these variables can be examined by using either

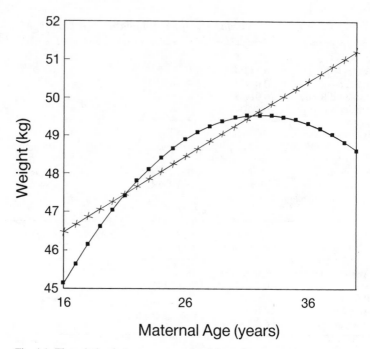

Fig. 4.1. The relation between maternal weight and age.

analysis of variance or multiple regression analysis. The analysis of variance with main effects and covariates is presented here, and the multiple regression analysis in the next main section.

There is considerable flexibility in analysis of variance in the order in which terms are entered. The analyses described in Table 4.6 remove the effects of the covariates (continuous characters) of age and age^2 initially before determining the effects of educational level and parity. The results show that after removing age and age^2 the educational effects remained very much as they were whereas the effects of parity were not significant. About 14% of the variance of maternal weight is explained by the three variables.

Multiple regression analysis would give similar results to analysis of variance; its use is discussed in the next section.

Use of statistics for predictive purposes
Introduction

One of the main aims of statistical analysis is to be able to identify factors for the purpose of prediction, although it should be noted at the outset that prediction does not necessarily imply causation. In the context of

Table 4.6. *Analysis of variance of weight with age and age^2, educational level and parity*

(a) Total population statistics

Total
48.14
(4150)

Education

0	1	2	3
45.32	46.81	48.96	51.60
(1182)	(698)	(1355)	(915)

Parity

0	1	2	3	4	5
47.71	48.88	48.47	48.24	48.18	47.27
(1882)	(1013)	(604)	(349)	(122)	(180)

(b) Breakdown by education and parity

Education	Parity					
	0	1	2	3	4	5
0	44.44	45.96	45.34	45.75	47.50	45.45
	(429)	(246)	(189)	(151)	(62)	(105)
1	46.11	46.46	47.12	48.71	47.32	48.96
	(286)	(163)	(116)	(67)	(29)	(37)
2	48.26	49.41	49.98	49.83	50.60	49.68
	(681)	(346)	(174)	(101)	(22)	(31)
3	50.75	52.49	52.37	54.36	49.72	54.86
	(486)	(258)	(125)	(30)	(9)	(7)

(c) Analysis of variance

Source of variation	Sum of squares	df	Mean square	F	F prob.
Covariates	5 159.647	2	2579.824	61.719	0.001
Age	1 775.068	1	1775.068	42.467	0.001
Age^2	1 197.129	1	1197.129	28.640	0.001
Main effects	22 559.388	8	2819.924	67.464	0.001
Education	20 350.069	3	6783.356	162.284	0.001
Parity	405.331	5	81.066	1.939	0.085
2-way Interactions	797.476	15	53.165	1.272	0.211
Education/parity	797.476	15	53.165	1.272	0.211
Explained	28 516.512	25	1140.660	27.289	0.001
Residual	172 379.974	4124	41.799		
Total	200 896.485	4149	48.420		

Covariate raw regression coefficient
Age   1.070
Age^2 −0.017

(*Continued*)

Table 4.6 (*cont.*)

(d) Multiple classification analysis (grand mean = 48.144)

Variable + category	N	Unadjusted		Adjusted for independents + covariates	
		Dev'n	Eta	Dev'n	Beta
Educ 1					
0 no	1182	−2.83		−2.96	
1 prim	698	−1.33		−1.24	
2 sec	1355	0.82		1.03	
3 high	915	3.46		3.26	
			0.33		0.34
Parity					
0	1882	−0.44		−0.16	
1	1013	0.73		0.47	
2	604	0.33		0.00	
3	349	0.10		−0.02	
4	122	0.04		0.14	
5	180	−0.88		−0.99	
			−0.07		0.05
Multiple R^2					0.138
Multiple R					0.371

adult anthropometry one of the current interests is whether or not maternal weight provides a useful prediction of morbidity and mortality.

Use of cut-off points

Frequently, researchers decide to use a particular cut-off point. This can either be based on a number of normal deviates (Z scores) above and below the mean (usually either ±2 standard deviations or ±1.96 standard deviations) or on the basis of some alternative criterion or criteria. In the context of maternal weight it is necessary to decide what constitutes 'low'. Some workers in Bangladesh have used a cut-off at 40 kg; this value will be used for illustrative purposes.

Use of χ^2 test

Table 4.7 shows the number of child deaths in relation to a cut-off of <40 kg. This is about 1 standard deviation below the mean. The chi-square test ($\chi^2 = 38.5$, $p \ll 0.001$) shows a very significant discrepancy between observed and expected results with an excess of deaths in the <40 kg category (observed 60, expected 29). Even so, mothers with weight of <40 kg only account for 60 out of 345 deaths.

Table 4.7. *Relative risk and odds ratio*

Maternal wt(kg)	Died	Survived	Total
<40	60 (*a*)	292 (*b*)	352 (*a* + *b*)
≤40	285 (*c*)	3513 (*d*)	3798 (*c* + *d*)
Total	345	3805	4150
	(*a* + *c*)	(*b* + *d*)	(*t*)

$$\text{Relative risk} = \frac{\text{Incidence rate of death in exposed group}}{\text{Incidence rate of death in unexposed group}}$$

$$= \frac{a/(a + b)}{c/(c + d)} = \frac{60/352}{285/3798} = \frac{0.170}{0.075} = 2.27.$$

$$\text{Odds ratio} = \frac{a/b}{c/d} = \frac{60/292}{285/3513} = \frac{0.205}{0.081} = 2.53.$$

Confidence limits for the odds ratio
1. Calculate $\log_e OR = \log_e 2.53 = 0.928$.
2. Calculate the estimated standard error.

$$SE(\log_e OR) = \left\{ \frac{1}{a} + \frac{1}{b} + \frac{1}{c} + \frac{1}{d} \right\}^{1/2}$$

$$= \left\{ \frac{1}{60} + \frac{1}{292} + \frac{1}{285} + \frac{1}{3513} \right\}^{1/2} = 0.154.$$

3. The 95% confidence limits of OR.

$$\log_e OR \pm 1.96 = \left\{ \frac{1}{a} + \frac{1}{b} + \frac{1}{c} + \frac{1}{d} \right\}^{1/2}$$

$\log_e OR \pm 1.96 = 0.928 \pm 0.154$.
95% confidence limit on $\log_e OR = 0.774$ and 1.082.
95% confidence limit on $OR = e^{0.774}$ and $e^{1.082} = 2.17$ and 2.95.

Relative risk and odds ratio

To measure the strength of the association between the risk factor
(<40 kg) and the condition (death) the relative risk (RR) and/or the odds
ratio (OR) can be calculated. Both ratios can take values between 0 and
infinity. A value greater than 1 signifies that the risk or odds of death are
greater when exposed to the risk factor (positive association); a value of 0
indicates no association, and a value of less than 1 indicates reduced risk
or odds of death with exposure to the risk factor (negative association).
Numerical differences in the RR and OR may occur but they always point
in the same direction.

The RR for the data shown in Table 4.7 shows that mothers with a
weight of <40 kg are 2.27 times as likely to have a child death as mothers
with a weight of ≥40 kg. The OR has advantages over the RR since it is

Table 4.8. *Sensitivity and specificity*

Maternal wt(kg)	Died	Survived	Total
<40	60 (*a*)	292 (*b*)	352 (*a+b*)
≤40	285 (*c*)	3513 (*d*)	3798 (*c + d*)
Total	345	3805	4150
	(*a + c*)	(*b + d*)	(*t*)

	True condition		
Maternal wt(kg)	Dead	Survived	Total
<40	True positive rate	False positive rate	Indicator positive
≥40	False negative rate	True negative rate	Indicator negative
Total	True positive	Total negative	Total

The true positive rate = $a/a + c$ = 60/345 = 17.4. This rate is also called the *sensitivity* of the test.
The true negative rate = $d/b + d$ = 3513/3805 = 92.3. This rate is also called the *specificity* of the test.
Positive predictive value = the percentage of the indicator positives who are true positives = $a/a + b$ = 60/352 = 17.00.

not dependent on how rare the condition is in the population and it provides consistent results whether a study is concerned with death or survival. The estimated OR for the Bangladeshi data is 2.53 (odds of a child death for a mother of <40 kg compared to one ≥40 kg). The 95% confidence interval for OR can also be calculated using Woolf's method and gives values between 2.17 and 2.95 (see Table 4.7).

Sensitivity and specificity
Another way of looking at the prediction is in terms of sensitivity and specificity. Screening tests use a procedure based on lot quality assurance sampling. As the name implies, the method originated in sampling and inspecting manufactured goods when the purchaser does not want to accept a batch of goods with more than a certain percentage defective and the manufacturer does not want to reject the batch unless a certain percentage are defective. Table 4.8 uses the same Bangladeshi data as shown in Table 4.7, classified according to the screening test (maternal weight) and true condition (died/survived). A number of terms are

calculated of which the sensitivity (Se), specificity (Sp) and positive predictive value are most commonly cited.

A good predictor is one which has a high sensitivity and high specificity. In addition a low false negative rate is important. Sensitivity and specificity are dependent on one another; high sensitivity is required with the identification of all the child deaths. Unfortunately this leads to lowered specificity and a high false positive rate, and results in incorrectly identifying women as high-risk. A high false positive rate is not as serious as a high false negative rate (i.e. failing to identify women as high-risk) but it will burden the screening system.

The obvious limitations to the use of sensitivity and specificity are that the measures depend on the prevalences of the condition (child death) and on the risk factor (maternal weight). If the prevalence rates differ between studies then it is illegitimate to compare sensitivities. In addition the sensitivity and specificity measures are constrained by what cut-off value(s) has (have) been chosen.

The example in Table 4.8 used <40 kg as the cut-off. This gave a fairly low sensitivity of 17.4, a high false negative rate and a high specificity. Clearly this cut-off value does not provide a particularly good prediction of child death.

An approach which gives equal weighting to the two forms of errors was developed by Youden (1950). He proposed an index $J = 1 - (\alpha + \beta)$ where α is the false negative rate and β is the false positive rate. If the test has no diagnostic value, $\alpha = 1 - \beta$ and $J = 0$. If the test is invariably correct, $\alpha = \beta$ and $J = 1$ (values of J between -1 and 0 could arise if the test result were negatively associated with the true diagnosis, but this situation is unlikely to arise in practice). Thus the closer J is to unity, the better the prediction. Although Youden's Index has been cited by some authors studying anthropometric measurements for predictive purposes, its use is limited since the two types of error are not treated equally: as noted above, it is more important to maintain a low false negative rate at the expense of a higher false positive rate. Another method which is occasionally cited is based on the summation of the sensitivity and specificity rates; this suffers from the same disadvantage as Youden's Index in that it gives equal weighting to both rates.

A better understanding of which cut-off to use can be obtained by plotting the sensitivity and specificity curves. Fig. 4.2 presents these curves for maternal weight and child death increasing at 5 kg intervals from <35 up to <85. Keeping in mind the aim (which is for an acceptable combination of higher sensitivity and low false negative rate) then a maternal weight of <50 kg provides a high specificity (75.4) and fairly low

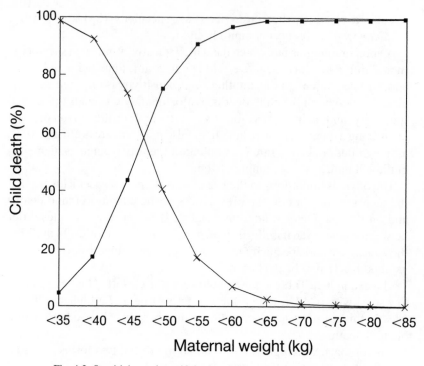

Fig. 4.2. Sensitivity and specificity for child mortality by maternal weight.

false negative rates. Of course the problem with such cut-offs in this range is that they result in a high false positive rate and the positive predictive value is only 10.3%.

Logistic regression analysis

In the examples so far, one predictor variable, maternal weight, has been used as a screening tool. In practice researchers may want to evaluate the impact of a number of potential predictors in relation to child death, for example taking into account the effects of weight, years of education and parity. The multivariate technique of logistic regression is designed to test for the relation between a binary dependent variable (such as death or no death, or low birth weight and normal) and a number of independent variables, which can be discrete (with many categories) and/or continuous. Thus the logistic regression analysis directly estimates the probability of an event occurring.

For more than one independent variable the model can be written as:

Table 4.9. *Use of logistic regression analysis*

Variable	B	Wald	P
Weight	−0.0457	24.01	<0.0001
Education	−0.1021	54.36	<0.0001
Parity	0.2188	55.59	<0.0001
Constant	−0.0736	0.03	0.8607

$\chi^2 = 211.7665$; df = 3; $p \ll 0.001$.

Probability (event) $= \dfrac{1}{1 + e^{-z}}$ where $z = B_0 + B_1X_1 + B_2X_2\ldots$

$z = -0.0736 + (-0.0457 \times \text{Weight}) + (-0.1021 \times \text{Education}) + (0.2188 \times \text{Parity})$

For Weight = 35, Education = 0 and Parity = 8, $z = 0.0773$; probability = 0.52.

For Weight = 50, Education = 5 and Parity = 3, $z = -2.2127$, probability = 0.10.

$$\text{Probability (event)} = \frac{1}{1 + e^{-z}}, \quad \text{where } z = B_0 + B_1X_1 + B_2X_2\ldots,$$

where e is the natural logarithm and $B_0 + B_1 + B_2$ refer to the coefficients for each independent variable. Table 4.9 presents the results of a logistic regression analysis for birth outcome by maternal weight, education and parity. It can be seen that mothers with low weight (35 kg) with little or no education and with a high parity have a high risk of having a child death whereas mothers with slightly above-average weight (50 kg), five years of education and three children have only a low risk of a child death.

These analyses show clearly the utility of logistic regression. Researchers should be encouraged to make use of this technique, since it does not have the limitations of Se and Sp measures. Furthermore, it allows the researcher to test for the simultaneous effects of a number of discrete or continuous variables.

Discriminant analysis

The extent to which it would be possible to predict whether a child will die or survive depends on the degree of overlap between the two sample distributions. As the difference between the two sample means increases so does the separation of the samples. Fig. 4.3 presents the generalized case of a variable, x, in which differences in means exist between two populations with the same variance; α is the false negative rate and β is the false positive rate. For any given α, the value of β depends solely on the standardized distance, θ, between the means. The equation is:

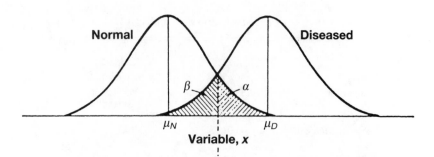

Fig. 4.3. Generalized model of standardized distance. (See text for details.)

Table 4.10. *Use of standardized distances* (θ)

Birth outcome	Number	Mean	Standard deviation
Weight			
Child died	345	45.33	6.71
Child survived	3805	48.40	6.92
Total	4105	48.14	6.96
Height			
Child died	345	149.10	5.25
Child survived	3805	150.83	5.11
Total	4105	150.68	5.14
Mid-upper arm circumference (MUAC)			
Child died	345	22.56	2.33
Child survived	3805	23.21	2.39
Total	4105	23.15	2.39

Standardized distances Variable	θ
Weight	0.45
Height	0.33
MUAC	0.28

$$\theta = \mu_1 - \mu_2/\sigma.$$

A critical value for the test is the mid-point between the means (e.g. $\frac{1}{2}(\mu_1 - \mu_2)$). The merits of different tests can be determined by comparing their values of θ. Tests with high values of θ will differentiate between the two populations better than low values. Table 4.10 presents an example

Table 4.11. *Discriminant analysis of pregnancy outcome by education, mother's age and weight*

Actual	No death	Death
No death	66.0%	34.0%
Death	34.8%	65.2%
Overall correctly predicted = 66.0%		

of the use of this standardized distance using mid-upper arm circumference (MUAC), weight and height for birth outcome (death/no death).

The standardized distances are based on the use of a single continuous variable as a predictor. When a number of continuous variables are to be used in combination then the discriminant function should be calculated. Most statistical packages have discriminant function routines and there is no need to calculate the function by hand. The principle of the method involves calculating the within-groups covariance matrix and its inverse together with the mean differences for each of the two variables. From these values the discriminant function can be calculated (a simple worked example is shown in Armitage & Berry (1987) for two continuous variables).

The results of a discriminant analysis of weight, years of education and age for birth outcome (death/no death) are presented in Table 4.11. The discriminant analysis shows that about 66% of birth outcome can be correctly classified on the basis of these three variables.

Modelling using multiple regression analysis

How well can we predict birth weight? Treating birth weight as a continuous variable and examining its relation to maternal weight reveals a highly significant positive relation in the Bangladeshi data set between birth weight and maternal weight. For each 1 kg increase in maternal weight, birth weight increases by, on average, about 15 g. However, even though the relation is significant there is considerable variation around the regression line as can be seen in Fig. 4.4 and from the coefficient of determination R^2 which was 0.052, i.e. maternal weight explains only 5.2% of the variance of birth weight. A test of curvilinearity indicates no significant quadratic or higher-order effect (see above for details of methodology).

The modelling can become more complex: multiple regression analysis can be used to examine how much variation can be explained using a large number of continuous and discrete variables. If discrete variables are

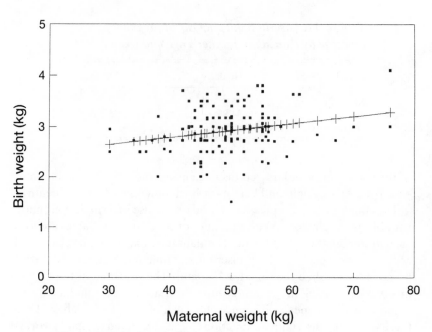

Fig. 4.4. Relation between birth weight and maternal weight.

Table 4.12. *Use of multiple regression analysis*

Step 1. Enter weight, height, MUAC, foot length (flength) and age

Analysis of variance

	df	Sum of squares	Mean square			
Regression	5	52 786 068.896 27	10 557 213.779 25			
Residual	4144	838 298 105.923 01	202 292.013 98			

$F = 52.18799$; significance of $F = 0.0001$.

Variable	B	SE B	β	t	t prob.
MUAC	9.087 816	3.842 520	0.046924	2.365	0.0181
Age	6.920 812	1.434 289	0.073 707	4.825	<0.0001
Height	1.900 458	1.773 822	0.021 083	1.071	0.2841
Flength	−6.666 161	7.909 326	−0.015 759	−0.843	0.3994
Weight	12.254 502	1.436 539	0.184 002	8.531	<0.0001
(Constant)	1728.730 161	224.559 996		7.698	<0.0001

used with two categories they must be coded at 0 and 1. If discrete variables with more than two categories are to be used, dummy variables must be created with binary coding of 0 and 1. The number of dummy variables corresponds to $n - 1$ categories.

To illustrate the use of multiple regression, an analysis of birth weight (the continuous dependent variable) was examined in relation to weight, mid-upper arm circumference (MUAC), height, maternal age and foot length. The analysis showed that weight, maternal age and MUAC were all significantly related to birth weight whereas height and foot length showed no significant association (Table 4.12). Even so R_2 only increased to 5.9% from the value of 5.2% when weight was the only independent variable.

References

Armitage, P. & Berry, G. (1987). *Statistical Methods in Medical Research.* Oxford: Blackwell Scientific Publications.

Bouchard, T. J., Lykken, D. T., McGue, M., Segal, N. L. & Tellegen, A. (1990). Sources of human psychological differences: the Minnesota study of twins reared apart. *Science* **250**, 223–8.

Ferro-Luzzi, A., Sette, S., Franklin, M. & James, W. P. T. (1992). A simplified approach of assessing adult chronic energy expenditure. *European Journal of Clinical Nutrition* **46**, 173–86.

Freiman, J. A., Chalmers, T. C., Smith, H. & Kuebler, R. R. (1978). The importance of beta, the type II error and sample size in the design and interpretation of the randomized control trial. *New England Journal of Medicine* **299**, 690–4.

Lemeshow, S., Hosmer, D. W., Klar, J. & Lwanga, S. K. (1990). *Adequacy of Sample Size in Health Studies.* Chichester: World Health Organization and Wiley and Sons.

Mascie-Taylor, C. G. N. (1993). Research designs and sampling strategies. In: *Research Strategies in Human Biology*, ed. G. W. Lasker & C. G. N. Mascie-Taylor, pp. 20–32. Cambridge University Press.

Waterlow, J. C. (1972). Classification and definition of protein-calorie malnutrition. *British Medical Journal* **3**, 566–9.

Waterlow, J. C., Buzina, R., Keller, W., Lane, J. M., Nichaman, M. Z. & Tanner, J. M. (1977). The presentation and use of height and weight data for comparing the nutritional status of groups of children under the age of 10. *Bulletin of the World Health Organization* **55**, 489–98.

Youden, W. J. (1950). Index for rating diagnostic tests. *Cancer* **3**, 32–5.

5 Statistical constructs of human growth: new growth charts for old

T. J. COLE

Introduction

Human growth has always fascinated statisticians, judging by the number of statistics books that use weight or height data for examples. The fascination may be due not only to the ready availability and statistically well-behaved nature of the data, but also to the fact that growth is universal: everybody has experienced it.

The most obvious statistical construct used in this study of human growth is the fiction that growth is a smooth process. Recent work on knemometry (Hermanussen *et al.*, 1988) has shown that on a sufficiently short time scale the process is anything but smooth, proceeding in fits and starts over periods of weeks. Equally, on a scale of months there are important seasonal influences on growth. This is particularly so in the Third World, where growth rates can vary enormously from one season to another, but even in the Western world there is clear evidence of seasonality (Marshall, 1971).

If height is measured annually, these oscillations ought to cancel out and give an impression of smooth progress. In practice, annual height velocities are far from smooth when plotted, so that even on this time scale growth is discontinuous. Despite this, it has been found useful over the years to retain the concept of smoothness in growth, on the grounds that when averaged over large samples, the oscillations do cancel out. This is particularly relevant for constructing growth charts.

Growth charts provide a simple and convenient means of displaying serial growth data in individual subjects. A growth chart consists of several smooth curves, usually seven, showing how centiles of the distribution of the chosen measurement change with age. The centile curves act as a backdrop to the subject's own data and allow for identification of unusual patterns of growth. The chart summarizes a growth standard based on some reference population of children, and the

78

relevance or irrelevance of this population to the individual plotted on the chart needs to be considered when interpreting the data. Thus it is unrealistic to expect children from a Third World country to follow the centiles of a chart based on European or American children.

A great many anthropometry measurements have been used to derive growth charts at different times, including weight and a variety of body lengths, widths, circumferences and thicknesses. Of these, the most studied measurement is standing height, or equivalently supine length in younger children. The reasons for this are not hard to find: it is (moderately) quick and easy to measure, requiring little in the way of specialized equipment, and in a social biological sense it is one of the most obvious human attributes.

To help diagnose height growth problems, several different types of growth chart have evolved. The purpose of this paper is to describe the various types of height chart, highlighting their strengths and weaknesses, and in turn to propose two new charts with useful properties.

Types of height growth chart

Tanner, Whitehouse & Takaishi (1966) published several different charts based on the heights and weights of British children around 1960. They distinguished between charts of *attained* height and weight, and charts showing the *growth* in height or weight over a period of a year or so; these two types of chart they termed *distance* and *velocity*, respectively, by analogy with a moving object.

Distance charts

The height distance chart is the simplest form of growth chart. It allows the height of individuals seen on a single occasion to be compared with the reference population. The construction of distance charts from reference data is an interesting statistical problem that has developed only recently (Healy, Rasbash & Yang, 1988; Cole, 1990; Pan, Goldstein & Yang, 1990; Thompson & Theron, 1990; Rossiter, 1991). The various proposals assume cross-sectional data, i.e. just one measurement per individual, but longitudinal data can also be used, albeit rather inefficiently. Longitudinal studies also tend to involve fewer subjects than cross-sectional surveys, so that their population estimates of mean and variance at each age are less precise or accurate.

A height distance chart is shown in Fig. 5.1, based on data for boys from the French longitudinal study of growth, one of seven such studies coordinated by the Centre International de l'Enfance (Falkner, 1961). Data, described earlier by Sempé, Pédron & Roy-Pernot (1979), were

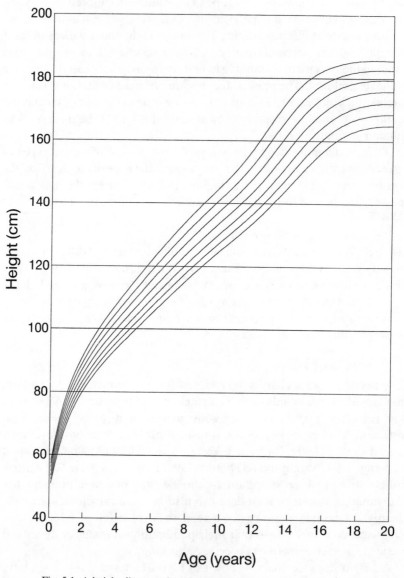

Fig. 5.1. A height distance chart for French boys. Seven centiles are shown, the 3rd, 10th, 25th, 50th, 75th, 90th and 97th from birth to age 20 years.

available on 239 boys and 257 girls, born between 1953 and 1960, at up to 35 ages from 1 month to 21 years, with 6 or 12 month intervals between measurements. The chart was obtained using the LMS method (Cole, 1990), which defines the centiles in terms of three curves called the L, M and S curves. The M curve is the 50th centile (median) curve, the S curve specifies the changing coefficient of variation of the distribution with age, and the L curve is a measure of the changing skewness of the distribution with age (actually its Box–Cox power transform).

The main purpose of a height distance chart like Fig. 5.1 is to decide, on the basis of a single measurement, whether or not an individual has been growing satisfactorily to date. The chart is relevant for assessing only height, not height velocity, as it is based on single reference measurements and contains no longitudinal information. However, even if it cannot *interpret* longitudinal data, the chart has the practical value that it can display them. Plotting two heights a year apart for the same individual gives a line whose slope is the height velocity. This emphasizes the value of charts for displaying growth data: they show both distance and velocity simultaneously.

Many other height distance standards have been published besides those of Tanner *et al.* (1966), most notably the NCHS standards of Hamill *et al.* (1979), which were subsequently adopted for use by the World Health Organization (Dibley *et al.*, 1987). The NCHS standard is made up of two distinct sets of centile curves, which do not coincide over the common age range between 2 and 3 years, and this has caused some problems of use and interpretation.

Velocity charts

A single height measurement is inefficient at identifying poor growth. Two measurements a year apart are much better as they define the height velocity. This then requires a height velocity chart to compare the observed velocity with reference velocity centiles. Fig. 5.2 shows the height velocity chart for the French boys, obtained by a simplified version of the LMS method. The full LMS method cannot be used because near adulthood, observed height velocity is close to zero and often negative, so it cannot be raised to a power (Healy, 1992). Thus the data are assumed to be normally distributed (so $L = 1$), and the centiles are estimated from just the M and S curves, i.e. based on the mean and coefficient of variation (CV) of height velocity at each age.

The resulting velocity chart is broadly similar to that of Tanner *et al.* (1966), although the adolescent growth spurt is somewhat different in shape, and some of the centiles are negative near adulthood. This latter

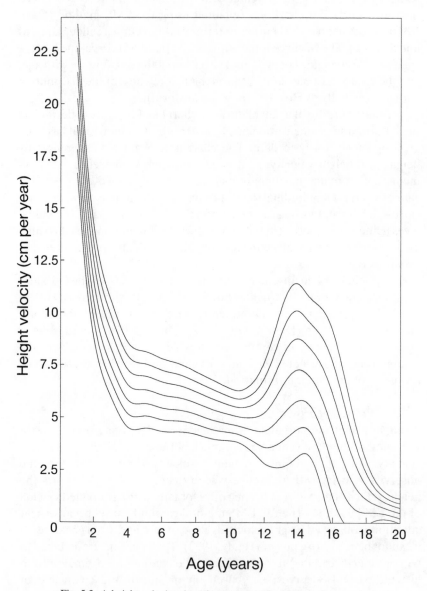

Fig. 5.2. A height velocity chart for French boys. Velocity is measured over a year, and is plotted at the age of the second measurement. The centiles are as in Fig. 5.1.

effect is the inevitable result of measurement error in the velocity. The chart confirms that for a small proportion of males, height gain continues beyond 20 years of age.

It is often assumed that velocity and distance are independent, i.e. that the growth velocity of tall and short individuals is on average the same. In practice this is not the case. At certain ages, particularly infancy and puberty, mean height velocity is different in tall and short individuals, and this can bias the assessment. During puberty, individuals who are tall are relatively more likely to have completed their growth spurt, whereas short individuals are more likely not to have spurted. Thus height gain over a year is likely to be greater in shorter individuals at this age. In infancy the same effect operates, as tall babies catch down and short babies catch up. So the velocity chart is biased, because it takes no account of the distance centile of individuals when displaying their velocity.

Combined velocity and distance charts

The space between centile curves on the distance chart represents the proportion of cross-sectional heights to be found there. It is also possible to provide sets of curves to assess velocity, such that the chance of an individual crossing from one curve to the next during a specified time period is known. This is how the Sheffield Weight Chart was constructed (Emery *et al.*, 1985). The Sheffield Weight Chart covers the first year of life with the conventional 3rd, 50th and 97th distance centiles, but it also includes another eight lines, rather closer together, which assess weight velocity. The channel widths between adjacent lines are chosen to ensure that a baby growing along the chart has a less than 5% chance of shifting one channel width up or down during any two week period. Over eight weeks the same chance applies for a two-channel-width shift.

Although the velocity centiles on the Sheffield Chart run parallel to the distance centiles, there is no reason *a priori* why they should (except for the 50th centile which is by definition the same for both). They could equally well cross. One difficulty with this type of chart is that the velocity centiles can easily be confused with the distance centiles, as the two are not obviously different.

Clinical longitudinal charts

Puberty causes problems with distance standards as well as velocity standards, in that distance centiles at puberty are widened owing to variation in the timing of the growth spurt. This in turn means that serial data for individuals plotted on the chart follow lines of steeper slope than

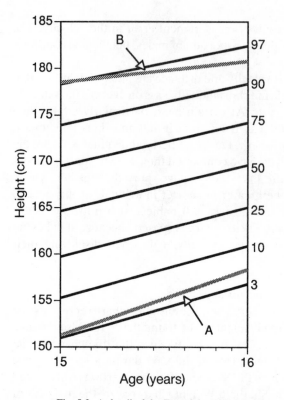

Fig. 5.3. A detail of the French boys' height distance chart, between 15 and 16 years. Subjects on the 3rd centile at age 15 grow more than average during the following year (A). Conversely, subjects on the 97th centile (B) grow less than average.

the centiles. This is potentially confusing, as it makes normal growth look abnormal. Tanner *et al.* (1966) addressed this problem by inventing the clinical longitudinal chart, which shrinks the distance chart centiles towards the median during puberty, so that their slope is similar to the observed height velocity. The chart is derived from a combination of cross-sectional and longitudinal data, with individual growth curves being fitted during puberty and the centiles derived from them. In practice the centiles are shown as both distance centiles and longitudinal centiles, in an attempt to make the chart dual-purpose. Another possibility is to provide extra median curves representing patterns of early and late maturation (Tanner & Davies, 1985).

To illustrate the need for a clinical standard, Fig. 5.3 shows seven centiles from the French boys' height distance chart between the ages of

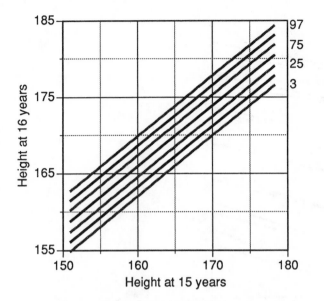

Fig. 5.4. A conditional standard for height of French boys at age 16, given their height at 15. The 50th centile is the regression of height at 16 on height at 15, and the other centiles are drawn parallel to it using the residual standard deviation.

15 and 16 years. Subject A in Fig. 5.3 is relatively short at age 15, on the 3rd centile. It happens that by age 16 he is likely to be relatively taller, midway between the 3rd and 10th centiles. Conversely subject B, who starts off on the 97th centile, is likely to be relatively *less* tall a year later by the same amount. Thus the distance centiles give a biased impression of the likely growth of individuals over a year, and the clinical chart attempts to compensate.

A deficiency of the clinical longitudinal standard is that although it improves the representation of growth during puberty, it provides no similar adjustment for growth during infancy, when the problem is just as acute. Also, the need to show both distance and longitudinal centiles is potentially confusing.

Conditional charts
The final category of chart is the conditional chart, a concept originally suggested by Healy (1974) and exploited by Cameron (1980). Like the velocity chart, it is derived from longitudinal data, typically with one year spacing, but unlike the velocity chart it is a regression standard, i.e. height one year hence is *predicted* from height now. Fig. 5.4 shows a

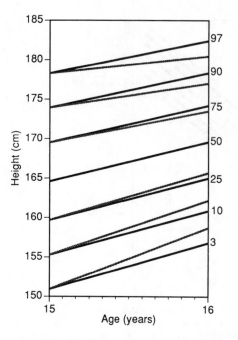

Fig. 5.5. The conditional chart of Fig. 5.4 redrawn to look like a distance chart. The solid lines represent the distance centiles, and the hatched lines, the conditional centiles.

conditional standard for height of French boys at age 16, given their height at 15. Reading from the median line in the figure, an average child of height 165 cm at age 15 grows 5 cm during the year. However, a small child, initially 155 cm tall, grows 7 cm, whereas a tall child of 175 cm gains only 3 cm. Thus at this age, height velocity depends inversely on the starting height. The conditional chart, unlike the velocity chart, takes this into account.

Cameron (1980) illustrates a chart like Fig. 5.4, and has similar charts for each age from 5 to 15 years, a total of 11 charts per sex. This is clearly impractical for clinical use, and the charts need to be combined in some way. Fig. 5.5 shows how Figure 4 can be redrawn like a distance chart, and it confirms the impression of Fig. 5.3 that conditional centiles, shown as dotted lines, are closer together than distance centiles, shown solid. The one centile which appears the same in both figures is the median. The fact that the conditional chart for age 16 (Fig. 5.4) can be shown as a section of a distance chart (Fig. 5.5) raises the important question: Can the charts for particular ages be combined into a single conditional chart covering the whole of childhood?

New types of height chart
Conditional velocity chart

Underlying the conditional height chart is the regression of height-next-year on height-now, or

$$\text{height}_{\text{next}} = \alpha + \beta \, \text{height}_{\text{now}} + \text{error}, \tag{5.1}$$

where α is the constant or intercept of the equation, β is the regression coefficient, usually close to 1 in value, and the error is given by the residual standard deviation (RSD) about the regression line. Thus $\text{height}_{\text{next}}$ is the mean predicted height for given $\text{height}_{\text{now}}$. The error term is assumed to be normally distributed, which allows centiles to be constructed using the formula

$$\text{centile}_z = \text{mean} + z\text{RSD}, \tag{5.2}$$

where z is a normal equivalent deviate defining the required centile. For example, on the 97th centile $z = 1.88$.

Table 5.1 gives the values by sex of α, β and RSD from the regressions of $\text{height}_{\text{next}}$ on $\text{height}_{\text{now}}$ over intervals of one year for 29 distinct ages between 1 and 19 years. (The earliest length was actually measured at 1 month rather than birth, so the first age interval is 11 rather than 12 months.) The value of β tends to be slightly greater than 1 for much of childhood, particularly at age 12, but during infancy and puberty it is very significantly less than 1. Cameron (1980) obtained similar results from his large sample of London schoolchildren, except that his β coefficients were smaller. This result is probably due to the large numbers of observers in his study, which would tend to increase the measurement error.

Equation 5.1 can be rearranged as follows:

$$\text{height}_{\text{next}} - \beta \text{height}_{\text{now}} = \alpha + \text{error}, \tag{5.3}$$

where the left side of the equation is here termed the *conditional height velocity* or CHV. The CHV has mean α and standard deviation RSD, and it is uncorrelated with $\text{height}_{\text{now}}$. Put another way, conditional height velocity is uncorrelated with height distance. This follows because the term $\beta \text{height}_{\text{now}}$ in the regression explains as much as it can of the variation in $\text{height}_{\text{next}}$, so that the remainder, i.e. CHV, is uncorrelated with $\text{height}_{\text{now}}$. This is an advantage over height velocity, particularly during infancy and puberty, which is negatively correlated with $\text{height}_{\text{now}}$ at these ages. When β is 1, conditional height velocity and height velocity are the same.

Table 5.1. *Conditional height regressions of height next year on height now, by age and sex*

In each case n is the sample size, RSD the residual standard deviation (cm), α the intercept (cm) and β the regression coefficient, with their standard errors SE.

Age now	Age next	Boys						Girls					
		n	RSD	α	SE(α)	β	SE(β)	n	RSD	α	β	SE(α)	SE(β)
0.08	1	210	1.85	34.4	3.4	0.748	0.063	197	1.99	32.6	0.763	4.0	0.075
0.5	1.5	195	1.64	12.7	3.6	1.019	0.054	178	1.98	16.1	0.970	4.4	0.067
1	2	184	1.37	4.0	3.1	1.099	0.042	170	1.61	6.3	1.074	3.7	0.051
2	3	169	1.23	1.8	2.7	1.079	0.031	148	1.09	2.1	1.076	2.6	0.031
3	4	145	1.06	2.1	2.4	1.045	0.025	132	1.06	3.5	1.030	2.6	0.028
4	5	138	0.92	-1.7	2.1	1.081	0.021	122	0.91	-2.1	1.087	2.3	0.023
5	6	130	0.88	-1.1	2.0	1.066	0.019	116	0.82	-1.8	1.073	2.1	0.020
6	7	116	0.84	0.0	1.9	1.053	0.017	113	0.92	-0.9	1.062	2.3	0.020
7	8	113	0.78	3.7	1.8	1.017	0.015	102	0.88	2.0	1.033	2.2	0.019
8	9	112	0.73	0.0	1.7	1.043	0.014	98	0.90	-1.8	1.058	2.4	0.020
9	10	107	0.67	0.6	1.7	1.035	0.013	96	1.02	-0.7	1.047	2.7	0.021
9.5	10.5	103	0.58	0.7	1.4	1.032	0.011	94	1.03	-3.0	1.065	2.8	0.021
10	11	101	0.77	-1.2	2.0	1.046	0.015	93	1.23	-3.8	1.073	3.2	0.024
10.5	11.5	99	0.87	-2.3	2.2	1.054	0.016	91	1.15	-5.3	1.086	3.0	0.022
11	12	95	1.31	-2.4	3.4	1.054	0.024	90	1.48	-2.6	1.067	3.7	0.027
11.5	12.5	89	1.48	-8.1	3.9	1.097	0.027	85	1.36	8.0	0.992	3.4	0.024
12	13	88	1.88	-13.6	4.8	1.138	0.033	84	1.61	18.5	0.918	4.0	0.027
12.5	13.5	84	2.07	-15.9	5.2	1.155	0.035	80	1.75	24.2	0.875	4.7	0.031
13	14	83	2.24	-6.2	5.2	1.090	0.035	78	1.85	24.5	0.868	5.2	0.034
13.5	14.5	76	1.81	8.6	4.0	0.990	0.026	71	1.89	11.2	0.950	6.1	0.039
14	15	73	1.84	24.3	4.1	0.889	0.026	64	1.72	7.2	0.969	6.0	0.038
14.5	15.5	65	1.83	34.0	4.4	0.826	0.027	58	1.24	5.1	0.978	4.7	0.029
15	16	63	2.09	38.3	5.4	0.795	0.033	54	0.83	0.4	1.004	3.2	0.020
15.5	16.5	51	1.95	34.3	6.8	0.816	0.040	48	0.55	1.0	0.998	2.3	0.014
16	17	48	1.79	22.3	7.2	0.882	0.042	43	0.45	0.6	0.999	2.0	0.012
16.5	17.5	42	1.46	10.4	6.5	0.949	0.038	31	0.28	-1.1	1.009	1.6	0.010
17	18	28	0.92	7.5	5.1	0.963	0.030	26	0.24	-0.5	1.005	1.5	0.009
17.5	18.5	14	0.45	12.8	4.0	0.931	0.023	18	0.22	0.8	0.996	1.5	0.009
18	19	13	0.44	7.1	4.4	0.963	0.025	14	0.29	-1.0	1.006	2.2	0.014
19	21	12	0.54	-2.7	5.6	1.017	0.032	13	0.48	4.1	0.974	3.6	0.022

Table 5.1 shows high values of α, the mean CHV in infancy and puberty, and relatively low and negative values just prior to puberty. These values are due to the corresponding β values moving in the opposite direction. Conversely, the values between infancy and puberty are close to zero, showing that here $height_{next}$ is very similar to $\beta height_{now}$. Where β is greater than 1, height velocity is relatively greater in tall individuals, so that the height centiles expand. The pattern of mean CHV with age is reminiscent of a height velocity curve, with a steep fall in the first year and a peak during puberty. However it should be thought of not as a velocity but as a *modified* velocity, where negative values are quite permissible.

It is now possible to construct a chart for conditional height velocity, as follows: the mean and RSD of CHV at each age are smoothed, and equation 5.2 is used to produce smooth centiles. Fig. 5.6 shows the resulting conditional height velocity centile chart. Also required is a smooth curve of β against age (not shown). To use the chart for a given child, β for the child's age is read from the curve and the CHV is calculated, then it can be plotted on Fig. 5.6.

The important property of CHV is that its expected value is unrelated to current height: both tall and short children can be plotted on the CHV chart without bias. The use of CHV rather than height velocity compensates for the phenomenon of 'regression to the mean', which causes initially short and initially tall children to grow respectively more and less than average. So to predict $height_{next}$ from $height_{now}$, $height_{now}$ is made less extreme by shrinking it towards the mean.

Conditional clinical chart

One problem with a conditional height velocity chart is that it gives no information about height distance. Ideally, both distance and conditional velocity should be displayed simultaneously, just as distance and velocity are on a conventional distance chart. However, if distance and conditional velocity are to be displayed together, the adjustment for regression to the mean has to be made graphically, and this is not possible on a conventional chart.

Fig. 5.5 shows a conditional chart superimposed on a distance chart. The solid lines represent the distance centiles and are all parallel, whereas the dotted conditional centiles become closer together during the year, so that the lower centiles are steeper than the higher ones. Now imagine Fig. 5.5 drawn on a rubber sheet, so that it can be stretched. The height axis at age 16 is lengthened by stretching it vertically, while the height axis at age 15 is kept the same length, and height at intermediate ages is stretched

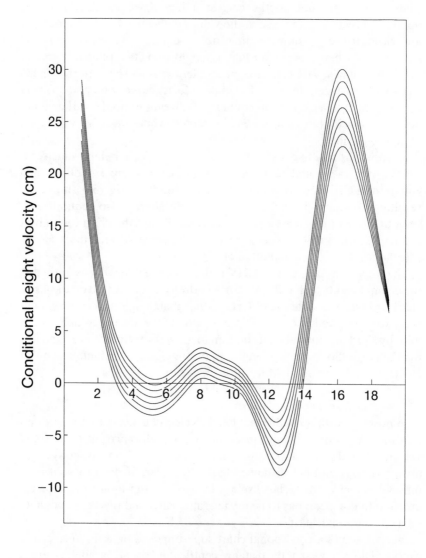

Fig. 5.6. A conditional height velocity chart for French boys. The 50th centile curve is based on the intercept α from the conditional height regression (Table 5.1), and the other centiles are drawn relative to it using the corresponding residual standard deviation (RSD). Both α and RSD are smoothed. (See text for details.)

intermediately. By this means, the conditional centiles can be made parallel. The stretching has the effect of keeping the distance centiles straight, but making them non-parallel. Conditional velocity is represented on the distance chart by the slope of the conditional centile, so if all the conditional centiles are parallel, then it follows that the conditional velocity is independent of the starting height.

Distorting the distance chart provides a way of displaying both distance and conditional velocity at the same time. From Table 5.1, the regression coefficient β of boys' height at age 16 on height at 15 is 0.795. Thus for the conditional centiles in Fig. 5.5 to be parallel, the height-at-15 axis has to be shrunk by a factor of 0.795, or equivalently height at 16 needs to be stretched by the inverse factor $1/0.795 = 1.26$.

Fig. 5.5 covers just the single year from 15 to 16, but the chart needs to extend from birth to adulthood. This requires the height axis at each age to be stretched by an amount $1/\beta$ relative to the same axis one year earlier. The process starts at age 0 and proceeds upwards; at age 0 the shrinkage factor β is 0.748, so height at age 1 is stretched by 1/0.748, or 1.34. At age 2, where β is 1.099, the factor is 1/1.099 or 0.91. However, the factor at 1 is 1.34 relative to age 0, so that for age 2 relative to age 0 the stretching factor is 1.34×0.91, or 1.22. The general rule is: set the factor to 1 at age 0 years (actually 0.08 years), and then for each successive year divide the factor by the value of β. Thus for years 0, 1 and 2 the factor is successively 1, 1/0.748 (=1.34) and 1/0.748/1.099 (=1.22).

Table 5.2 shows these calculations for each age, keeping separate those starting on the whole year and those on the half year. Between 10.5 and 18.5 years the same process operates, but the scaling factor at age 10.5 is obtained as the average of the factors at age 10 and 11. The value of β at age 0.5 years is not used, as there is no value a year later. The interval from 19 to 21 years is treated as being one year, since growth has essentially finished by this time. From Table 5.2 it can be seen that the scaling factor starts at 1, rises steeply in the first year, falls more or less linearly from 1 to 14 years, crossing the age axis at 5 years, and then ends up back near 1. Curiously, the final scaling factor for girls, at 0.87, is appreciably less than that for boys.

To preserve the appearance of the chart after scaling, the stretching of the height axis at each age is done relative to the 50th centile, so that the 50th centile curve itself is unchanged in shape. The other centiles at each age are shrunk towards or stretched away from the median according to whether the scaling factor is less than or greater than 1.

In order to produce a smooth centile chart incorporating the distorted height axis, the scaling factors in Table 5.2 need to be smoothed. The

Table 5.2. *Cumulative regression scaling factors by age and sex*

The factor b is that by which the height axis is scaled at each age to ensure that conditional height velocity is uncorrelated with height distance (see text for details).

Age now	Age next	Cumulative b	
		Boys	Girls
0.08	1	1.00	1.00
1	2	1.34	1.31
2	3	1.22	1.22
3	4	1.13	1.13
4	5	1.08	1.10
5	6	1.00	1.01
6	7	0.94	0.94
7	8	0.89	0.89
8	9	0.87	0.86
9	10	0.84	0.81
9.5	10.5	0.82	0.80
10	11	0.81	0.78
10.5	11.5	0.80	0.75
11	12	0.77	0.72
11.5	12.5	0.76	0.69
12	13	0.74	0.68
12.5	13.5	0.69	0.69
13	14	0.65	0.74
13.5	14.5	0.60	0.79
14	15	0.59	0.85
14.5	15.5	0.60	0.83
15	16	0.67	0.88
15.5	16.5	0.73	0.85
16	17	0.84	0.87
16.5	17.5	0.90	0.85
17	18	0.95	0.88
17.5	18.5	0.95	0.85
18	19	0.99	0.87
19	21	1.02	0.87

centile chart can then be drawn just as in Fig. 5.1, except that horizontal grid lines appear curved. Fig. 5.7 is the result. This is termed a *conditional clinical* chart. The effect of the scaling is best seen where the grid lines are a long way from the 50th centile. The grid lines to the top left of the figure are of the same form as Table 5.2, with a peak at age 1, but the peak gets larger the further away from the 50th centile the line is. Below the 50th

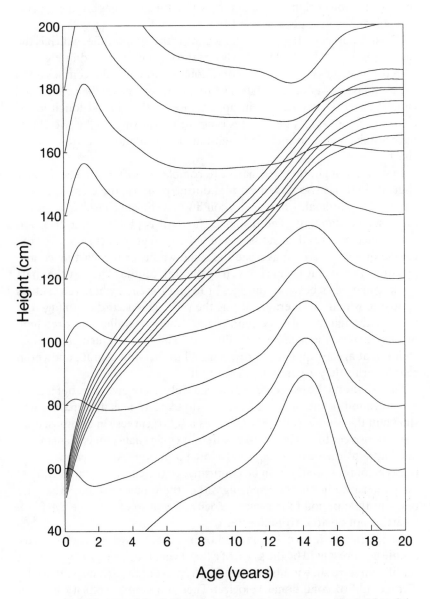

Fig. 5.7. A conditional clinical height chart for French boys. The height axis is scaled at each age to ensure that conditional height velocity is uncorrelated with height distance. (See text for details.)

centile the shape appears inverted. During puberty the same effect is seen towards the lower right of the figure, where the grid lines are the inverse of Table 5.2, with a peak at age 14.

The one curve unaffected by the scaling is the 50th centile, which is the same as in Fig. 5.1. The two charts are shown superimposed in Fig. 5.8, with the grid lines omitted. The conditional chart has wider centiles up to age 5 and narrower centiles later, so that during puberty the conditional clinical chart is very similar in appearance to the clinical longitudinal chart of Tanner *et al.* (1966). This is not too surprising, as the two charts have similar aims: to include longitudinal information on the distance chart.

In detail though, the two charts are completely different. The Tanner clinical chart has two sets of centiles during puberty, the cross-sectional and the longitudinal, whereas the conditional clinical chart has just one, the distance standard. The distance standard is plotted on a distorted scale which ensures that the slopes of individual growth curves, over the course of a year, are on average the same whatever the starting centile position. The average slope is given by the 50th centile. The way the chart works can be seen between the ages of 15 and 16 years, where the centiles appear to widen considerably during the year. This accords with Fig. 5.5, where although the distance centiles are actually parallel, the stretching process makes them appear to diverge. Thus on average, individual children at age 15 appear to grow parallel to the 50th centile, and yet in centile terms they are moving closer to it.

Fig. 5.7 shows the expected conditional velocity over a year, but it gives no indication of the *range* of velocities to expect. This information was shown in the Sheffield Weight Chart as a set of curves superimposed on the distance centiles, chosen to ensure a specific chance of crossing from one curve to the next during the follow-up period. Although effective, this type of presentation can be confusing, as the curves are not centiles: their relevance lies in their spacing rather than their position. Also, the relevant time period to measure velocity, 2 or 8 weeks for the Sheffield Chart, is not obvious from the chart.

An alternative form of display is shown in Fig. 5.9, where each velocity centile is represented by the slope of a line 1 year long. At each age, 7 such centile lines are shown, and their slopes represent the 3rd through to the 97th centile of conditional velocity. The 50th centile velocity line coincides with the 50th centile distance curve. To use this chart for a child with two height measurements one year apart, the *slope* of the line joining the child's height is compared with the *slopes* of the velocity centiles, and the child's velocity centile is obtained by interpolation.

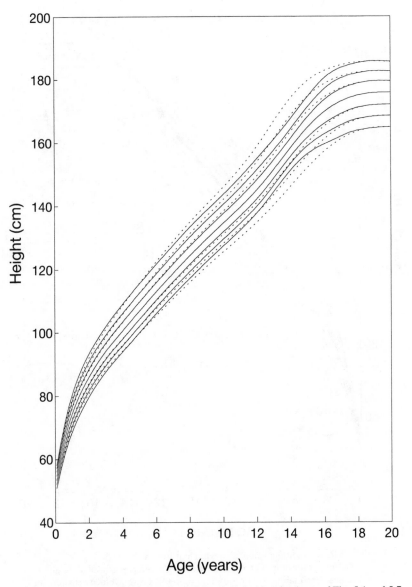

Fig. 5.8. The distance and conditional clinical height charts of Figs 5.1 and 5.7 are shown superimposed.

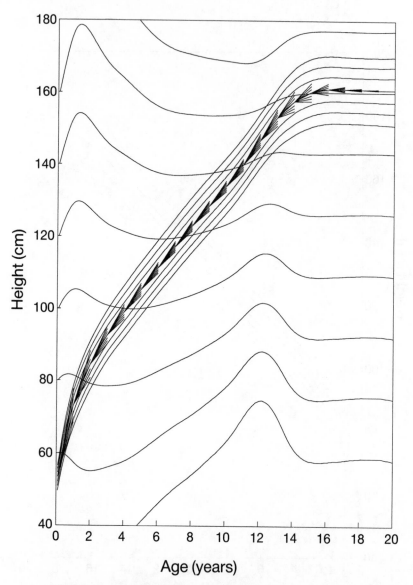

Fig. 5.9. A conditional clinical height chart for French boys (Fig. 5.7), including centiles for annual conditional height velocity as well as height distance. Each fan-like cluster of lines represents seven velocity clusters for that age, the slope of each line indicating the relevant centile velocity. (See text for details.)

Fig. 5.9 makes clear that the variability of height velocity changes with age. At 1 year, the velocity centiles extend from below the 10th to above the 90th distance centile, a span of more than four distance centile channels. The corresponding span at 15 years is less than two centile channels, while between 8 and 10 years it is only one, and at age 19 it approaches zero. A possible disadvantage of Fig. 5.9 is that subjects near the 50th centile may be obscured by the velocity centiles, but in practice such subjects are unlikely to be of concern as their heights are obviously unremarkable.

To conclude, Fig. 5.9 displays height data in such a way that both distance and velocity centiles are visible. The scaled axis used to draw the chart ensures that the distance and velocity centiles are uncorrelated with each other. Thus during infancy and puberty, tall and short children grow, on average, along lines of the same slope. Similar charts can be constructed for other measurements besides height, for example weight during infancy, and they should help to clarify the nature of growth and its variability during childhood.

Acknowledgements
I am grateful to Michel Sempé and Marie-Françoise Rolland-Cachera for making available the French height data.

References
Cameron, N. (1980). Conditional standards for growth in height of British children from 5.0 to 15.99 years of age. *Annals of Human Biology* 7, 331–7.

Cole, T. J. (1990). The LMS method for constructing normalized growth standards. *European Journal of Clinical Nutrition* 44, 45–60.

Dibley, M. J., Goldsby, J. B., Staehling, N. W. & Trowbridge, F. L. (1987). Development of normalized curves for the international growth reference: historical and technical considerations. *American Journal of Clinical Nutrition* 46, 736–48.

Emery, J. L., Waite, A. J., Carpenter, R. G., Limerick, S. R. & Blake, D. (1985). Apnoea monitors compared with weighing scales for siblings after cot death. *Archives of Disease in Childhood* 60, 1055–60.

Falkner, F. (1961). Croissance et développement de l'enfant normal, une méthode internationale d'étude. *Travaux et documents* XII. Paris: Masson CIE.

Hamill, P. V. V., Drizd, T. A., Johnson, C. L., Reed, R. B. & Roche, A. F. (1977). *NCHS growth curves for children birth–18 years*. National Center for Health Statistics, Vital and Health Statistics Series 11, No. 165. Washington, DC: NCHS.

Healy, M. J. R. (1974). Notes on the statistics of growth standards. *Annals of Human Biology* 1, 41–6.

Healy, M. J. R. (1992). Normalising transformations for growth standards. *Annals of Human Biology* 19, 521–6.

Healy, M. J. R., Rasbash, J. & Yang, M. (1988). Distribution-free estimation of age-related centiles. *Annals of Human Biology* **15**, 17–22.

Hermanussen, M., Geiger-Benoit, K., Burmeister, J & Sippell, W. G. (1988). Knemometry in childhood: accuracy and standardization of a new technique of lower leg length measurement. *Annals of Human Biology* **15**, 1–15.

Marshall, W. A. (1971). Evaluation of growth rate in height over periods of less than one year. *Archives of Disease in Childhood* **46**, 414–20.

Pan, H. Q., Goldstein, H. & Yang, Q. (1990). Nonparametric estimation of age related centiles over wide age ranges. *Annals of Human Biology* **17**, 475–81.

Rossiter, J. E. (1991). Calculating centile curves using kernel density estimation methods with application of infant kidney lengths. *Statistics in Medicine* **11**, 1693–701.

Sempé, M., Pédron, G. & Roy-Pernot, M.-P. (1979). *Auxologie: méthode et séquences*. Paris: Théraplix.

Tanner, J. M. & Davies, P. S. W. (1985). Clinical longitudinal standards for height and height velocity for North American children. *Journal of Pediatrics* **107**, 317–29.

Tanner, J. M., Whitehouse, R. H. & Takaishi, M. (1966). Standards from birth to maturity for height, weight, height velocity, and weight velocity: British children, 1965. *Archives of Disease in Childhood* **41**, 613–34.

Thompson, M. L. & Theron, G. B. (1990). Maximum likelihood estimation of reference centiles. *Statistics in Medicine* **9**, 539–48.

6 Growth monitoring and growth cyclicities in developed countries

STANLEY J. ULIJASZEK

Introduction

In Western nations, the causes of growth failure are usually genetic or constitutional rather than environmental, most children attending growth clinics having short stature as the main manifestation of growth failure. The causes of short stature include the following: (i) familial or congenital conditions; (ii) constitutional delay of growth and puberty; (iii) chronic systemic disorders; and (iv) endocrine abnormalities (Tanner, 1989). Regardless of aetiology, the initial aim of growth monitoring is to identify children with growth failure as early as possible for more detailed examination. It is therefore of some concern that a child, once identified as being small on the basis of one measurement of either length (in children below two years of age) or height (in children above two years of age), be designated as having acceptable or unacceptable growth velocity as soon as possible after this first measurement. This chapter examines why a potentially simple procedure is not always as straightforward as it might be.

Normal growth

The pattern of growth in any population can be represented by the centile distribution of stature by age; a number of developed countries have centile charts based on the measurement of their indigenous, healthy population, which is defined to be in some way normal. Countries with their own growth references include Britain (Tanner, Whitehouse & Takaishi, 1966), the United States (National Center for Health Statistics, 1977), the Netherlands (Roede & van Wieringen, 1985) and Belgium (Wachholder & Hauspie, 1986). All of these use the construct of anthropometric percentiles, as developed by Galton (1885).

Percentile (or centile) charts for any anthropometric variable seem to

99

imply that the growth of any single child should track a centile line from birth until the onset of adolescence. In particular, it is often assumed that between these ages growth in length, and subsequently height, is a smooth and continuous process. However, a number of studies have shown that the growth patterns of individual children are more likely to be cyclical, measured height oscillating about a centile line, rather than tracking it. Indeed, the normal growth curve, although representing population growth phenomena quite well, is not such a good representation of any individual growth pattern. Growth phenomena observed to contradict the tracking principle include: (i) catch-up and catch-down growth in the first two years of life (Tanner, 1989); (ii) mini growth spurts (Hermannussen *et al.*, 1988); (iii) seasonality of growth (Cole, 1993); and (iv) biennial cyclicity of growth, shown to take place in children between the ages of 3 and 11 years (Butler, McKie & Ratcliffe, 1989).

Catch-up and catch-down growth usually take place in the first two years of life. During this time, children may cross the centile lines either upwards or downwards, rather than tracking along them. Catch-up growth can occur after a period of restricted growth *in utero*. The mini growth spurt was first described for healthy German children, whose knee height was measured on a daily basis (Hermanussen *et al.*, 1988). These occur with a cyclicity of between 30 and 55 days. Hermanussen *et al.* (1988) give examples of individuals showing this phenomenon, and it appears that there is a 3–4-fold variation in the rate of skeletal growth between the fastest and slowest time of growth. For a girl aged 6.6 years, the maximum growth rate of the lower leg was 3.6 cm per year, the minimum, 1.1 cm per year. For a boy aged 8.9 years, the maximum and minimum rates were 4.2 and 1.1 cm per year, respectively. Another type of deviation from the tracking principle is the seasonality of growth reported for children in Japan (Togo & Togo, 1982), the Orkneys (Marshall, 1975) and Cambridge (Cole, 1993). The broad consensus is that height velocity is greatest in the spring, and weight velocity is greatest in the autumn (Cole, 1993).

Another phenomenon which is at odds with tracking principle suggested by the growth references is that of mid-childhood cyclicity of growth. A study in Edinburgh of mid-childhood growth of 80 boys and 55 girls between the ages of 3 and 11 years showed a cyclicity of statural growth with a periodicity of 2.2 years in males, 2.1 years in females (Butler *et al.*, 1989). Although cyclicity of growth was observed in all the children, periodicity and magnitude of peak growth rates varied.

Table 6.1. *Growth of lower leg over a 90 day period: variation according to the timing of the measurements*

Measurement (day)		Increase (mm/90 days)	
		girl, age	boy, age
1st	last	6.6 years	8.9 years
40	130	5.5	
50	140	5.4	6.3
60	150	6.7	4.9
70	160		4.8

Source: Data of Hermanussen *et al.* (1988).

Growth cyclicities and growth monitoring

The pattern of growth is important in assigning a child to a diagnostic category. Children with a congenital growth disorder will show a persistent deviation from the growth references from an early age, while children with an acquired growth abnormality will oscillate around a centile on the reference for a variable period of time, and then progressively deviate from that centile. Although a number of patterns of growth failure have been identified as being typical of various conditions associated with growth faltering, in practice, many cases of growth failure do not fit a diagnostic pattern in any straightforward manner. If, in any individual, there are several cyclicities of growth operating, then it is difficult to interpret growth patterns on the basis of a small number of measurements across time.

There is a need to identify deviation from the growth references as early as possible. However, under some circumstances growth cyclicity and measurement error may indicate such deviation in an individual for reasons other than growth faltering. The length of time between serial measurements is also important, for two reasons: (i) the expected growth in the period between measurements might be smaller than the size of the possible measurement error; and (ii) differences between two serial measurements might reflect reinforcement of various cyclicities at certain times. The importance of knowing the error of measurement for various anthropometric variables was considered in Chapter 3 of this volume. The possible effect of different time intervals between measurements in relation to growth cyclicity is illustrated for mini growth spurts in two German children, taken from data published by Hermannussen *et al.* (1988) (Table 6.1). This shows the estimated growth of lower leg over a 90 day period according to the timing of the measurements.

For the girl, measurements made on days 40 and 130, and on days 50 and 150 give very similar estimates of 90-day lower leg growth. If the measurements were made on days 70 and 160, then the 90 day growth estimate would be much greater. For the boy, measurements made on days 50 and 140 give an estimate of lower leg growth which is about 1.4 mm greater than that which would be obtained were the measurement days 60 and 150, and 70 and 160, respectively. At first glance this difference might seem trivial, but it is equivalent to a difference in estimate of stature of about 4 mm, due wholly to normal cyclicity of growth and the time of measurement. Although it is difficult to determine how other types of cyclicity might affect the interpretation of serial growth measurements, it suggests that caution is needed when attempting to diagnose growth failure in any individual.

Evaluation of growth measurements

Most measurement evaluations involve the plotting of the child's height on a length or height growth reference chart. If growth failure is suspected, knowledge of the heights of the parents is essential for further evaluation. These are incorporated on the child's chart, giving a parental height target range, which is the mid-parental percentile plus or minus 10 cm (after making corrections for the gender of the child). If the child is below this target range, this is suggestive of growth failure.

Alternatively, use of standard deviation (Z) scores can be used for the cross-sectional assessment of a group of children, or height velocity can be used to follow the longitudinal growth of the child. It is worth noting, however, that deviation from a centile is not an indicator of growth failure *per se*. This also applies to the low growth velocity as assessed by the difference between two serial measurements. A number of serial measurements are therefore needed to separate artifact from possible growth failure due to intrinsic reasons.

Modelling growth cyclicities in young children

The earlier in life growth failure is correctly identified in an individual the better, from the point of view of treatment. Across a short time frame, however, it is difficult to determine whether substantial deviations are due to error, natural cyclicity of growth, biological growth failure, or any combination of these factors. One way in which the maximum possible observed dampening of linear growth which could be attributed to normal cyclicity of growth can be examined is by modelling the effects of minimum growth rates due to a possible reinforcement of troughs in the growth rates due to mini growth spurts, seasonality, and two-year cyclicities. This is carried out in this section for hypothetical 50th centile British children aged 1, 2, 3, 4 and 5 years at the time of the first measurement.

In this model, it is assumed that troughs in all of these cyclicities occur at the same time. This is highly improbable in the real world, but by assuming the worst possible case, it is possible to determine rigorously the minimum length of time needed between measurements to be able to say with any certainty that the observed pattern of linear growth in an individual is not due simply to natural cyclicity of growth.

It is also assumed that the children are on the 50th centile for length or height at the time of the first measurement, and that there is no dampening or amplification of growth due to natural cyclicity at this time. At the time of the second measurement, three months later, it is assumed that the three types of cyclicity serve to dampen the growth rate, all to their maximum, as reported for a number of studies. At the time of the second measurement, the three types of cyclicity do not reinforce each other so much, while at the time of the third measurement they tend to cancel each other out. It is assumed that without the imposition of

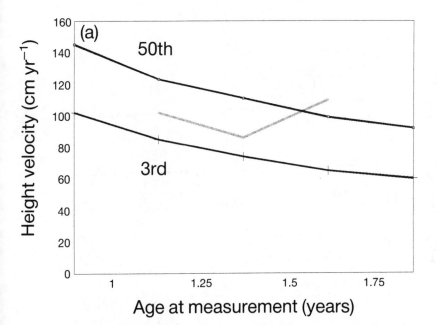

Fig. 6.1. Theoretical cyclical dampening of height velocities of hypothetical 50th centile children aged 1 (a), 2 (b), 3 (c), 4 (d) and 5 (e) years at the time of first measurement.

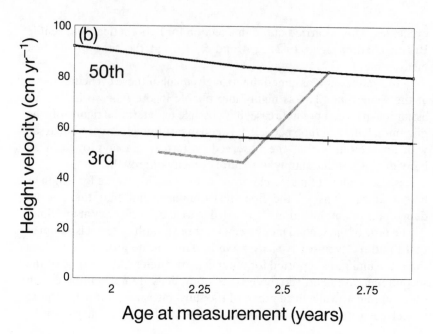

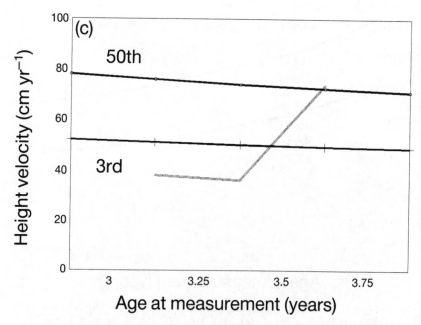

Fig. 6.1 (*cont.*)

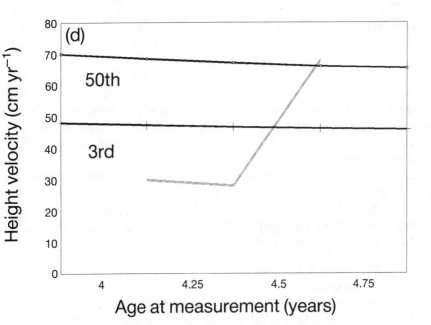

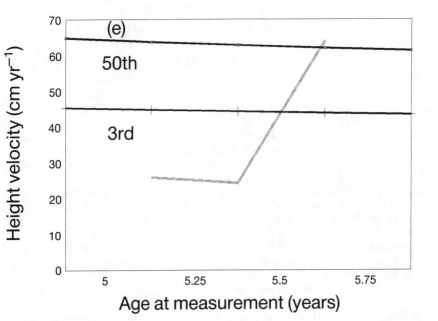

Fig. 6.1 (*cont.*)

cyclicities, growth would proceed smoothly along the 50th centile. Results from the modelling process are given as height velocities in Fig. 6.1.

The measured height velocity differs from annual quarter to quarter, according to the amplitude of the total natural growth cyclicity. At its maximum negative amplitude, cyclicity serves to make the growth velocity of a 50th centile child fall below the 3rd centile for the first two of the three velocity measures, at ages 2, 3, 4, and 5 years. At age 1, the effect is much less pronounced. This would suggest that low growth velocities in an individual based on only two serial measurements three months apart, could be accounted for simply by growth cyclicity. A minimum of three such serial measures is needed to determine whether slow growth rates are constant or cyclical. Growth monitoring should therefore take this into consideration.

Conclusion

In this chapter, growth phenomena which are known to contradict the tracking principle of following a centile line are described. These include catch-up and catch-down growth, mini growth spurts, seasonality, and biennial cyclicity of growth. It is argued that an understanding of growth cyclicities is important for accurate growth monitoring and diagnosis of growth failure, and a model is developed in which the effects of the reinforcement of various growth cyclicities on the growth patterns of hypothetical 50th centile children aged 1, 2, 3, 4 and 5 years are illustrated.

References

Butler, G. E., McKie, M. & Ratcliffe, S. G. (1989) An analysis of the phases of mid-childhood growth by synchronisation of growth spurts. In: *Auxology 88. Perspectives in the Science of Growth and Development*, ed. J. M. Tanner, pp. 77–84. London: Smith-Gordon.

Cole, T. J. (1993). Seasonal effects on physical growth and development. In: *Seasonality and Human Ecology*, ed. S. J. Ulijaszek and S. S. Strickland, pp. 89–106. Cambridge University Press.

Galton, F. (1885). Anthropometric per-centiles. *Nature* **31**, 223-5.

Hermanussen, M., Geiger-Benoit, K., Burmeister, J. & Sippell, W. G. (1988). Periodical changes of short term growth velocity ('mini growth spurts') in human growth. *Annals of Human Biology* **15**, 103–9.

Marshall, W. A. (1975). The relationship of variations in children's growth rates to seasonal climatic variations. *Annals of Human Biology* **2**, 243–50.

National Center for Health Statistics (1977). *NCHS Growth Curves for Children. Birth–18 Years*. US Department of Health, Education and Welfare Publication No. (PHS) 78-1650. Hyattsville, Maryland: National Center for Health Statistics.

Roede, M. J. & van Wieringen, J. C. (1985). Growth diagrams, 1980. *Tijdschrift voor Sociale Gezondheidszorg* **63** (suppl. 1985), 1–34.

Tanner, J. M. (1989). *Foetus into Man*. Ware: Castlemead Publications.

Tanner, J. M., Whitehouse, R. H. & Takaishi, M. (1966). Standards from birth to maturity for height, weight, height velocity, and weight velocity: British children, 1965. *Archives of Disease in Childhood* **41**, 454–71.

Togo, M. & Togo, T. (1982). Time series analysis of stature and body weight in five siblings. *Annals of Human Biology* **9**, 425–40.

Wachholder, A. & Hauspie, R. C. (1986). Clinical standards for growth in height of Belgian boys and girls, aged 2 to 18 years. *International Journal of Anthropology* **1**, 327–38.

7 Growth monitoring, screening and surveillance in developing countries

ANDREW TOMKINS

Hundreds of thousands of children have their weight measured daily. Somewhat fewer have their length or height measured and others receive measurement of their mid-upper arm circumference (MUAC). Such measurements are often considered to be core skills of nutritionists or nutritionally orientated health workers. Why? What is the use of collecting such data in so many individuals and so frequently? Does it really assist in the assessment of an individual, or guide those who are trying to improve that individual's nutrition? Does anthropometry lead to action, or, at the very least, to the development of policies aimed at improving the nutrition of entire communities or particularly vulnerable groups within those communities? This paper examines current practices and assesses the different purposes of anthropometric measurements in a range of situations.

There is now a wide range of equipment for measuring weight, to varying degrees of accuracy. In less developed countries (LDC) the most commonly used scale reads up to 25 kg in intervals of 100 g; such a scale, consisting of an accurate torsion spring with a dial display, costs around £30–40. More sensitive measurements, to 10 g of accuracy, may be obtained using machines with battery-powered digital displays, costing around £160. Even more accurate balances, involving integration with multiple readings taken every second over a 10 s time period cost over £1000. There are variants on these scales. The recent development of a torsion coil spring enables the observer to mark a chart which is placed alongside the scale in such a way that the weight is recorded at the appropriate age band on a Road to Health chart (TALC, UK). A simple spring has been developed for detection of low birth weight infants (less than 2.5 kg). This is cheap, around £2, but its accuracy is limited. It is to be hoped that more scales will be produced for different situations. There is an urgent need for the development of scales which are sensitive, accurate and robust during transport in field surveys for measurement of adult weight.

Length measurement is much less satisfactory. Accurate position of infants or children is critical and errors are easily made. Height measurements are somewhat more easily made because children over 36 months are often more cooperative. Several lightweight, portable, robust height measuring devices are now available (CMS Weighing Equipment, UK). A range of devices has been developed for specific lengths. Measurement of knee–heel length using a calliper-type apparatus with constant pressure to minimize errors appears to be promising. Measurements of mid-upper arm circumference are open to considerable bias because of the variations in pressure that different observers may exert. Nevertheless, with careful standardization of procedures, measurements of MUAC to the nearest millimetre can be accurately performed by workers with only basic education. None of these measures, however, has value unless there is some reference population or standard against which individual values may be compared.

Debates over the last few decades about the advisability or need to have 'local' standards as opposed to 'international' standards which are based on populations in the USA or UK have become less vehement of late. Many studies now show that children of the majority of ethnic groups in the world can grow as well as international standards if they belong to elite socioeconomic groups, the implication being that in such groups adequate diets are available and exposure to infection is minimal. Recent data from India show that diet and disease rather than ethnicity are responsible for the short stature of many Indian children (Gopalan, 1989). However, there is still a need for careful consideration; there are secular changes in growth rates in children in various populations including Britain, where growth standards, developed several decades ago, are not now suitable for contemporary 'normal' UK infants. For most of this paper, however, reference will be made to the National Center for Health Statistics (NCHS) standards because they are, for the present at least, recommended for international use by the World Health Organization (WHO, 1983).

Growth monitoring

Most child survival, health and development programmes involve regular growth monitoring. Enthusiasm for this activity has been fanned by UNICEF in its promotion of GOBI (Growth monitoring, Oral rehydration, promotion of Breastfeeding and Immunization). There are considerable differences in the way that growth charts are displayed within child survival and development programmes. In some, as in the situation with the Government of Indonesia, there is a gradation of intensity of a single group of colours (yellow/green) between centiles of weight/age. In others, such as in Tanzania, Road to Health charts use clearly demarcated bands (red, grey and green) between the centiles. Other countries, such as Kenya and Mozambique, add measurements of 'growth faltering' measured over several months.

There is no doubt that satisfactory weight gain is a reasonable sign that the infant is being fed adequately and is relatively free from serious infection. In this regard the visual display of growth on a card may give comfort to the parent and nutrition health worker alike. It is less certain how such people should respond to growth faltering or persistent growth along a rather low centile. For growth faltering to be detectable using conventional scales measuring to 100 g there needs to be at least 8 weeks between the measurements. Does the information that growth faltering has occurred during the past two months tell the mother or health/ nutrition worker something that she/he does not already know? Undoubtedly in some cases it does and appropriate intervention such as dietetic advice or more intensive treatment of infection can be given. In situations where the infant started on a low centile for age at birth and is growing along but not crossing centile lines, appropriate intervention may be more difficult to formulate.

In long-standing illness such as measles which is complicated by pneumonia, dysentery or TB, there is considerable value in terms of clinical case management in using the growth chart (Tomkins & Watson, 1989). In situations where food intake is persistently less than ideal, perhaps because of long-standing poverty or problems with maintaining adequate child care, it may be more difficult to respond. In this situation an approach towards the family and community is indicated.

Future research will need to examine how information on growth is explained by professionals and perceived by parents using different methods. Growth monitoring is a time-consuming exercise, often demanded by maternal and child health units as part of routine clinic protocol. Whereas the data displayed as points on a trajectory is understood by many parents, to others it is little more than a dot on a card. Graphs are conceptually more complex and less easily understood by those with elementary education than is generally recognized. It will be necessary to explore optimal ways of generating and sharing community-based anthropometric information such that there is maximum involvement and stimulation of action.

Screening

The concept of 'at risk' is well recognized by health professionals. Complications in pregnancy, for instance, are known to occur more frequently in those with twins, those who are multiparous or those of short stature. The risks associated with these problems are remarkably constant across a wide range of culturally different populations. Similar approaches to identification of 'at risk' children have been developed in relation to anthropometry. The health professional/nutritionist therefore often asks 'What is *the* appropriate anthropometric indicator to use as a cut-off in child development programmes? Which anthropometric indicators can best detect children with a high risk of developing a particularly severe response to infection or death?'

The last decade has seen the publication of studies using similar screening instruments (weight for age, height for age, weight for height and MUAC) as predictors of morbidity or mortality in communities of young children. A study in Nigeria, West Africa, showed that children who were somewhat arbitrarily classified as undernourished or better nourished in terms of weight, length or thinness at the beginning of the rainy season had significantly longer episodes of diarrhoea during the four months of the rainy season if they were malnourished at the start (Tomkins, 1981). Subsequently a more substantive study in The Gambia examined the interaction between anthropometry at the beginning of the rains and prevalence of diarrhoea, respiratory symptoms and febrile episodes during the next four months. It was possible to show the levels of malnutrition at which the risk for infection increased (Tomkins, Dunn & Hayes, 1989). Several other studies have examined anthropometry as a risk factor for mortality, especially from infection. Recent data from south-west Uganda show the proportion of children who died during the twelve months after nutritional assessment according to various anthropometric indices at the beginning of the study (Figs. 7.1–7.3) (Vella *et al.*, 1992).

There are sources of confounding in such studies. Those who are underweight, short and thin are often from disadvantaged households with lower-quality housing, cramped accommodation and inadequate sanitation or water supplies, often living near mosquito breeding sites and unable to afford mosquito nets. Thus increased prevalence of infection and mortality are not necessarily attributable to the malnutrition, this being a proxy indicator of a household which is disadvantaged in many respects.

Because of these obvious caveats a wide range of socioeconomic, environmental and behavioural indicators were included in the Gambian

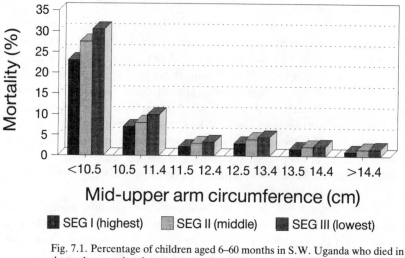

Fig. 7.1. Percentage of children aged 6–60 months in S.W. Uganda who died in the twelve months after assessment by mid-upper-arm circumference (MUAC). Rates are predictions of the logistic model. (SEG: socio-economic group.)

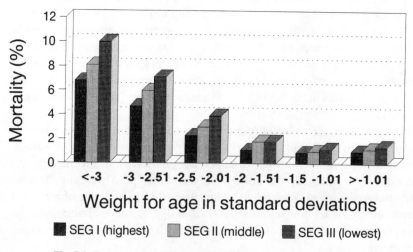

Fig. 7.2. Percentage of children aged 6–60 months in S.W. Uganda who died in the twelve months after assessment by weight for age. Rates are predictions of the logistic model. (SEG: socio-economic group.)

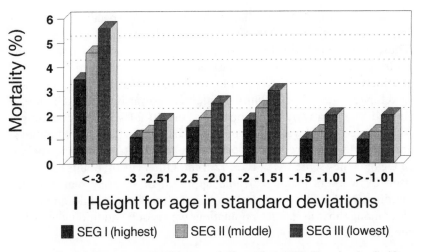

I Height for age in standard deviations

■ SEG I (highest)　　▨ SEG II (middle)　　▨ SEG III (lowest)

Fig. 7.3. Percentage of children age 6–60 months in S.W. Uganda who died in the twelve months after assessment by height for age. Rates are predictions of the logistic model. (SEG: socio-economic group.)

(Tomkins *et al.*, 1989) and Ugandan studies (Vella *et al.*, 1992). They made rather little difference to the overall relation between malnutrition and risk of infection or death. Thus, anthropometric indices can be used to predict high-risk individuals, and the findings link nutrition with severity of infection and mortality in a biologically plausible relation. The question of what anthropometric cut-off to screen at is often asked. Health professionals and nutritionists would value advice.

There seem to be two possible responses at least. Reviews of the literature on nutrition as related to risk of mortality–morbidity show that a single anthropometric cut-off is not associated with the same level of risk of infection or death in all communities (Tomkins, 1986). There are marked differences in the nutrition–mortality interactions between Bangladesh, Papua New Guinea and Zaïre, and cut-off levels need to be considered in their local context. The reasons for these differences have been reviewed, and it is evident there are many intermediate variables between malnutrition and outcome. These include epidemiology of certain diseases, access to health care facilities for prevention and treatment, and behavioural differences in relation to household management of infection. In addition there may be important confounding factors due to differences in micronutrient status. The rather striking influence of vitamin A deficiency on morbidity and mortality, which acts independently of anthropometric status, may well explain some of the differences (Ghana VAST Study Team, 1993).

The second question is that of sensitivity and specificity. This has important implications for resources, mostly in terms of manpower. Thus, if the sensitivity for prediction of death is set too low and the anthropometric indicator is not particularly specific, a large proportion of routinely screened subjects will be identified as 'at risk'. In many less developed countries the ability to intervene towards 'at risk' children is limited to a relatively low proportion, say 10–20% of the population. Thus the 'correct' level for screening will be dictated by local conditions. In Bangladesh, village health workers screen MUAC at 11.5 cm, whereas in Uganda they screen MUAC at 12.5 cm. Other cut-off points have been used by workers making a rapid appraisal of severely malnourished children (MUAC less than 11.0 cm) for identifying the children most at risk among those in refugee populations who require additional intensive feeding.

Monitoring and evaluation

It is now widely recognized that sustained improvement in health or nutrition is dependent on a series of improvements in socioeconomic status, physical environment, community participation, household food security, access to health services, education, care and improved dietary intake. Non-governmental organizations (NGOs), and fortunately an increasing number of governments, are active in promoting multisectoral approaches. As in many areas of human endeavour, there is a need to be seen to achieve results. Thus the number of village health committee meetings held, the number of women's groups formed, the number of credit and income-generating schemes started, are all valid indicators of activity. And yet many governments and NGOs require answers to the question 'Does all this have any impact?'

Many agencies seize on anthropometric indices for this purpose. Indeed there are well documented examples of the changes in the prevalence of children with severe protein energy malnutrition (less than 60% weight for age) or moderate malnutrition (less than 80% weight for age) as a result of concerted multisectoral approaches. One of the most recently described programmes (in Iringa, Tanzania) has documented a reduction of the prevalence of severely malnourished children from 6.8% to 2.3% during five years of an integrated primary health care/nutrition programme (UNICEF/WHO, 1988). There was a reduction of the proportion of young children less than 80% weight for age from 35% to 19% during three years of an agricultural development programme in Malumfashi, Nigeria (Tomkins *et al.*, 1991).

It is tempting to use anthropometry as an indicator of stress as a result of economic adjustment programmes in which welfare, health, food subsidies and educational activities are reduced. Deterioration in nutritional indices is sometimes used as an 'objective' indicator of the human cost of economic adjustment. It should be noted, however, that there are many intermediate variables which influence the relation between adversity and nutritional status. In the Gambia, for instance, an apparently successful diarrhoeal disease control programme was associated with a decrease in anthropometric indices. There did not appear to be much wrong with the programme: dehydrating episodes of diarrhoea were treated for the most part rather successfully using locally produced oral rehydration solution. However, the severe drought in the Sahel had reduced food supplies.

Conversely, it may well be that economic adjustment is associated with increasing costs of food and a deterioration in the standard of living, but if primary health care (PHC) activities increase at the same time, nutritional status as assessed by anthropometry in children, may not change much. There is a need for work on the value of anthropometry of children, siblings and parents as family profiles during economic and other stress.

Community involvement in anthropometry

The value of involvement of community groups in PHC and nutrition activities, not only in the establishment of programmes but also in their planning and re-forming, has been underestimated. In this respect it is particularly interesting to see how community-based growth monitoring, often run separately from health-related activities such as epidemiological reporting (EPI) and maternal and child health (MCH) clinics, has provided a focal point for communities interested in improving the health and nutrition of their children. Well documented examples of such anthropometric activities have occurred in Tanzania, Indonesia and Thailand. Mothers agree to meet for measurements of weight of their children, sometimes monthly, up to 60 months of age. Evidently the aggregate results of a group of village children expressed on wall charts for all to see, sometimes in a comparative, competitive way, contrasting with neighbouring communities, have been central to the development of other innovative approaches for the improvement of nutrition.

To be fair, not all communities share such enthusiasm. Many in fact regard weighing as a necessary obstacle to be overcome before the child is seen by a nurse or physician at a health centre or hospital. Future research would do well to examine the reasons for success and enthusiasm in certain programmes which involve regular community-based growth monitoring compared with low level of commitment in other communities.

Conclusions

Measurements of anthropometric indices are justified in LDC for a variety of reasons. There is strong evidence that they provide a clinically useful indicator of growth and health for many children in disadvantaged circumstances. However, the benefits of regular anthropometric measurements and growth monitoring do not seem to have been realized. There is a need to examine how the indices are understood by health professionals and communicated to parents. There is an even greater need to see how simpler, more regular measurements, such as weight, can stimulate a range of activities within communities that together will improve nutritional status among children.

References

Ghana VAST Study Team (1993). Vitamin A supplementation in northern Ghana: effects on clinical attendances, hospital admissions and childhood mortality. *Lancet* **342**, 7–12.

Gopalan, C. (1989). Growth standards for Indian children. *Bulletin of the Nutritional Foundation of India* **10**, 1–4.

Tomkins, A. M. (1981). Nutritional status and severity of diarrhoea among preschool children in rural Nigeria. *Lancet* **ii**, 860–2.

Tomkins, A. M. (1986). Protein-energy malnutrition and risk of infection. *Proceedings of the Nutritional Society* **45**, 289–304.

Tomkins, A. M., Bradley, A., Bradley-Moore, A., Greenwood, B. M., MacFarlane, S. & Gilles, H. (1991). Morbidity and mortality at Malumfashi, Nigeria, 1974–1979. Studies of child health in Hausaland. In: *Disease and Mortality in Sub-Saharan Africa*, ed. R. G. Feachem & D. T. Jamison, pp. 325–41. Published for the World Bank by Oxford University Press.

Tomkins, A. M., Dunn, D. T. & Hayes, R. J. (1989). Nutritional status and risk of morbidity among young Gambian children allowing for social and environmental factors. *Transactions of the Royal Society of Tropical Medicine and Hygiene* **83**, 282–7.

Tomkins, A. M. & Watson, F. (1989). *Malnutrition and Infection.* Administrative Committee on Coordination/Subcommittee on Nutrition. Geneva: World Health Organization.

UNICEF/World Health Organization (1988). *Joint Nutrition Support Programme (Iringa) 1983–1988. Report.* Geneva: Unicef.

Vella, V., Tomkins, A. M., Ndiku, J. & Marshall, T. (1992). Determinants of child mortality in South West Uganda. *Journal of Biosocial Sciences* **24**, 103–12.

World Health Organization (1983). *Measuring Change in Nutritional Status.* Geneva: World Health Organization.

8 *Variability in adult body size: uses in defining the limits of human survival*

C. J. K. HENRY

Introduction

Human body size may be surveyed from three standpoints: (i) measurement of height or stature (which is one-dimensional); (ii) measurement of surface area (which is two-dimensional); and (iii) measurement of ponderal growth or weight (which is three-dimensional). Of the three, weight and height measurements are widely used to quantify the dynamic state of human growth. Although the assessment of body size has been extensively used to quantitatively describe nutritional status in children (Waterlow, 1972) there is little information for its use in defining the lower limits of human survival in adults. James, Ferro-Luzzi & Waterlow (1988) attempted to define chronic energy deficiency (CED) in adults in terms of their body mass index (BMI) and basal metabolic rate (BMR). This novel approach based its definition of CED on specific physiological criteria rather than the socioeconomic status of the individual. The authors proposed three cut-off points based on BMI: 18.5, 17 and 16. Subjects with BMI above 18.5 were classified as normal and below 16 as grade III CED. Although BMI alone was used to classify CED at the two extremes, it was combined with BMR values to define various degrees of grades I and II CED. The paper also proposed that a BMI of 12 may be the absolute lower limit compatible with life. A considerable body of information exists on the relationship between BMI and health in affluent societies (James, 1984; Garrow, 1981; Keys, 1980; Waaler, 1984). Much of the discussion has centred around the range and upper limits of BMI compatible with health. In contrast, less attention has been focused on the relation between being underweight (low BMI) and health. The aim of this chapter is to determine, to borrow a term from engineers, the inbuilt factor of safety in the human machine, using weight and height as indicators of body size.

117

Use of the Body Mass Index (BMI)

In 1870 Quetelet, a Belgian astronomer, showed that body weight (in kilograms), divided by the square of height (in metres) (W/H^2) was least biased by height. Today the Quetelet index is often referred to as the 'Body mass index' (BMI). Several researchers have used BMI (Special Report, 1985; Vague, Vague & Barré, 1988), to classify obesity or show a relationship between BMI and health in affluent societies (Garrow, 1981, Waaler, 1984). Garrow (1981) has proposed the following classification of obesity according to BMI. It should be acknowledged that the scheme is based more on the need for simplicity than scientifically determined cut-off points.

Grade 0, W/H^2 = 20–24.9;
Grade I, W/H^2 = 25–29.9;
Grade II, W/H^2 = 30–40;
Grade III, $>W/H_2 > 40$.

Significantly, the range 20–25 is the value associated with minimum mortality. The mortality risk rises steeply with BMI greater than 30. Although the range and upper limits of BMI compatible with health have been extensively examined, less attention has been focused on using BMI in undernourished or underweight subjects and on its ability to predict mortality risks in people suffering from food restriction. In the first part of this chapter the lower range of BMI is examined, and it is demonstrated that BMI (as a proxy for body size) may be successfully used to define the lower limits of human survival.

Starvation as a model for determining the lower limits of BMI

At times in history and prehistory, human populations have experienced starvation and famine; the metabolic and physiological adaptations of individuals undergoing starvation has fascinated scientists for over a century. However, knowledge of the biology of starvation in humans is still imperfect owing to the great difficulty of obtaining reliable data from subjects undergoing severe food deprivation. In the past 50 years alone millions have died in famines, or as a result of policies of genocide. These situations do not generally lend themselves to scientific investigation. Ideas about the metabolic changes in starvation, particularly total starvation, are derived largely from a few experimental studies of fasting, dating from the early twentieth century (see Table 8.1), and from a large and recent corpus of work on therapeutic fasting in grossly obese subjects and its effects on metabolism (see Table 8.3). Much of the work presented here comes from an analysis of the literature, and it must be remembered that death by starvation limits the amount of information available. It is stressed that the investigation is concerned specifically with total food restriction or deprivation, not semi-starvation (although data on individuals having *ad libitum* intake of water are included).

Human survival during total starvation

The antiquity of the habit of voluntary fasting by humans is well documented, although the reasons have been many and varied. A major reason is religious belief; another is therapy, hoping to gain relief from a variety of ailments ranging from gout to lunacy (Benedict, 1915). Some have fasted for fame and pecuniary gain, the most notable among them being Succi, an Italian professional faster who in the late nineteenth century made repeated fasts.

Fasting attracted the attention of the nineteenth century physiologists, and Table 8.1 gives a summary of the studies performed in the nineteenth and early twentieth centuries. The early studies were not elaborate, being confined to measurements of the loss of body weight, urinary nitrogen and chlorides. In all of these, nitrogen loss in the urine and weight loss received by far the greatest attention. In 1915, Benedict published his monumental work *A study of prolonged fasting*, which investigated for the first time not only the gross physiological changes during fasting, but also the metabolic and psychological changes. The book is a classic, and to date no other study on complete fasting can match its meticulous detail. But although Benedict's study was a detailed one, it described only one subject and thus was of limited use in making any comparative observations in humans. In contrast to this study, the little known work by the Japanese investigator Takahira (1925) provides an in-depth study of fasting in a group of five Japanese subjects of varying body weight. This document, along with other studies collated from the literature, provides useful information on the variability and limits of survival during starvation. Starvation studies therefore may be a useful model to use in the quest to understand the lower limits of BMI compatible with life.

Table 8.2 shows a compilation of values from the literature of subjects undergoing total starvation in 'normal' weight subjects. The maximum recorded value for total starvation is 43 days for a subject with BMI 22.5. In contrast, in grossly obese subjects (Table 8.3) the maximum recorded length of total starvation is 382 days.

Having established some guidelines on the duration of starvation in normal weight and obese subjects, the BMI below which death ensues can now be examined. Normal weight subjects in the following categories have been taken from the literature and considered:

Table 8.1. *Summary of studies on fasting in humans*

Investigator[1]	Year	Subject	Duration of fast(days)	Measurements made
Seegen	1871	Male	25	Nitrogen excretion
Luciani	1886	Male (Succi, Milan)	30	Body weight, nitrogen loss
Lehman	1887	Male	6	Body weight, nitrogen loss
Zuntz	1887/88	Male (Cetti)	10	Body weight, nitrogen loss
Paton and Stockman	1888	Male (Jacques)	30	Body weight, nitrogen loss
Luciani	1888	Male (Succi, Florence)	30	Urinary nitrogen loss, urinary chlorides
Luciani	1890	Male (Succi, London)	40	Body weight, nitrogen loss
Tigerstedt	1897	Male	5	Nitrogen loss, energy expenditure
Van Hoogen	1905	Female	14	Urinary nitrogen loss
Brugschid	1906	Female	15	Body weight, nitrogen loss
Cathcart	1907	Male (Beauté)	14	Nitrogen loss

[1]All references may be found in Keys *et al.* (1950), vol. 2, pp. 1256–333.

Table 8.2. *Duration of total fasting in 'normal' weight subjects*

Subject no.	Initial body weight (kg)	Height (m)	Initial BMI	Duration of fast (days)	Investigator
1	50	1.69	17.5	12	Takahira (1925)
2	43	1.55	17.9	16	Takahira (1925)
3	54	1.58	21.6	17	Takahira (1925)
4	78	1.56	32.05	26	Takahira (1925)
5	58	1.69	20.3	30	Takahira (1925)
6	65	?	?	14	Cathcart (1907)[1]
7	55	1.63	20.7	15	Kunde (1926)[1]
8	62	?	?	30	Paton (1888)[1]
9	65	1.7	22.5	42	Kleitman (1926)
10	56	?	?	40	Luciani (1898)[1]
11	60	?	?	30	Luciani (1888)[1]
12	60	1.70	20.8	31	Benedict (1915)
13	63	?	?	45	Sunderman (1947)[1]
14	65	1.7	22.5	43	Labbe (1922)

[1]These references may be found in Keys *et al.* (1950), vol. 2, pp. 1256–68.

Table 8.3. *Duration of total fasting in obese subjects*

Subject no.	Initial body weight (kg)	Duration of fast (days)	Investigator
1	156	117	Drenick (1964)
2	130	139	Tompson (1966)
3	128	236	Tompson (1966)
4	120	249	Tompson (1966)
5	131	315	Barnard (1969)
6	207	382	Stewart (1973)

(a) Subjects who died from starvation;
(b) Subjects who died from famines;
(c) Subjects who died from anorexia nervosa.

Tables 8.4 and 8.5 show the BMI in males and females who died from starvation, and Figs 8.1 and 8.2 illustrate this graphically.

Despite the diversity of sources, the data of Table 8.4 show a remarkable consistency. In males, a BMI of around 13 appears to be fatal. The coefficient of variation (CV) of the BMI is 8.7%. In contrast, in females a lower BMI of around 11 was found to be fatal. The CV of BMI in females

Table 8.4. *Body mass index in males who died from starvation*

Subject no.	Last body weight recorded (kg)	Height (m)	BMI (W/H^2)	Investigator	
1	36.6	1.72	12.4	Meyer	(1917)
2	38.0	1.68	13.4	Burger *et al.*	(1950)
3	40.4	1.75	13.2	Burger *et al.*	(1950)
4	40.5	1.72	13.7	Burger *et al.*	(1950)
5	36.8	1.80	11.3	Burger *et al.*	(1950)
6	45.8	1.77	14.6	Burger *et al.*	(1950)
7	36.5	1.65	13.4	Porter	(1889)
8	36.0	1.66	13.0	Krieger	(1921)
9	36.0	1.60	14.0	Krieger	(1921)
10	40.0	1.67	14.3	Krieger	(1921)
Mean ± sd	38.6 ± 3.0	1.70 ± 0.06	13.3 ± 0.95	—	

Table 8.5. *Body mass index in females who died from starvation*

Subject no.	Last body weight recorded (kg)	Height (m)	BMI (W/H^2)	Investigator	
1	28.0	1.65	10.3	Burger *et al.*	(1950)
2	33.6	1.65	12.3	Wilkinson *et al.*	(1877)
3	37.0	1.68	13.1	Fernet	(1901)
4	22.3	1.62	8.5	Stephen	(1895)[1]
5	27.0	1.52	11.6	Oppenheimer	(1944)[1]
6	29.0	1.56	11.9	Krieger	(1921)
Mean ± sd	29.4 ± 5.17	1.61 ± 0.06	11.28 ± 1.64	—	

[1] These references may be found in Henry (1990).

showed a greater variability (14%). From these two figures, a mean BMI of 12 as the lower limit for survival emerges, a value first proposed by James *et al.* (1988). Although the figures presented here lend general support to the initial proposal to set a BMI of 12 as the lower limit, the clear sex difference in the lower limit of BMI may need to be further considered. This sex difference is further exemplified by examining Tables 8.4 and 8.6. A mean BMI of 13 (Table 8.4) is fatal in males, whereas a mean BMI of 13 in females with anorexia nervosa (Table 8.6) appears to be non-fatal. Indeed, several female subjects had BMIs as low as 9, 10 and 11. Admittedly patients with anorexia are perhaps not comparable with individuals with chronic energy deficiency. Neverthe-

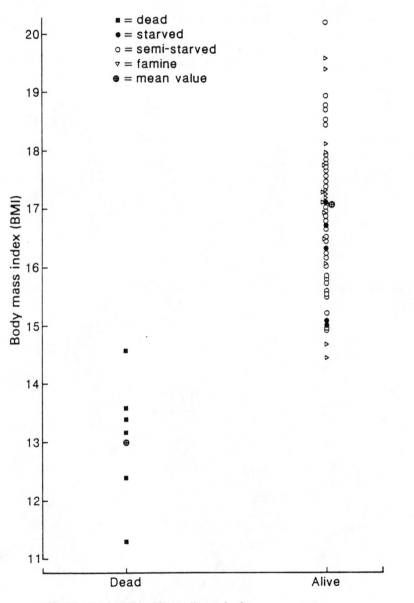

Fig. 8.1. BMI in male subjects, alive or dead.

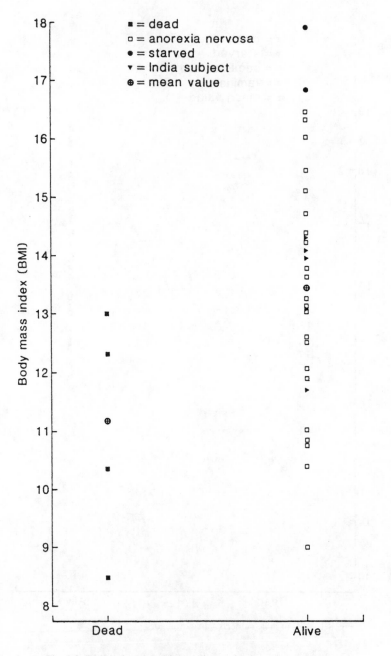

Fig. 8.2. BMI in female subjects, alive or dead.

Table 8.6. *Body mass index in female subjects with anorexia nervosa*

Subject no.	Lowest recorded body weight (kg)	Height (m)	BMI (W/H^2)	Reference
1	32.0	1.60	12.5	
2	44.8	1.72	15.1	
3	40.4	1.62	15.4	
4	30.6	1.52	13.2	
5	34.2	1.62	13.0	Farquharson (1941)
6	24.8	1.52	10.7	
7	39.1	1.65	14.3	
8	39.5	1.57	16.0	
9	28.8	1.45	13.7	
10	53.8	1.80	16.6	
11	29.3	1.68	10.4	
12	26.2	1.57	10.6	Berkman *et al.* (1947)
13	22.2	1.57	9.0	
14	27.2	1.57	11.0	
15	36.3	1.67	13.0	
16	36.3	1.60	14.2	
17	31.3	1.62	11.9	Berkman *et al.* (1947),
18	35.9	1.62	13.7	p. 385
19	37.7	1.52	16.3	
20	36.3	1.57	14.7	
21	33.1	1.65	12.1	
22	41.2	1.73	13.8	
23	45.5	1.65	16.7	
24	44.5	1.64	16.5	
25	42.4	1.59	16.8	Ljunggren *et al.* (1961)
26	38.9	1.73	13.0	
27	39.8	1.62	15.2	
28	27.8	1.60	10.8	
29	22.0	1.41	11.0	Bruckner *et al.* (1938)
30	26.3	1.52	11.4	
Mean ± sd	34.9 ± 9.4	1.60 ± 0.80	13.5 ± 2.2	

less this highlights the problem of using a single lower limit of BMI for both sexes. More importantly, it serves to illustrate a sex difference in the limits of survival.

Decrease in body weight is the most obvious observation during chronic energy deficiency. The loss of body weight represents the utilization of body tissues as an energy source. However, the relationship between energy deficit and weight loss is not a simple one. Several factors such as degree of adiposity, level of hydration, sex of the individual, and P ratio (Henry, Rivers & Payne, 1986) influence weight loss. Dugdale &

Payne (1977) suggested that the fraction of energy stored as, or mobilized from, protein is constant for a given subject. They have defined this by the P ratio, which is calculated on the assumption that body protein is 16% nitrogen and has a metabolizable energy value of 16.7 kJ g^{-1}. Thus P ratio can be calculated as:

$$\frac{\text{urinary nitrogen excretion} \times 6.25 \times 16.7}{\text{total energy expenditure}},$$

or as:

$$\frac{\text{energy stored on protein}}{\text{total energy stored}}.$$

It has been shown that during starvation females lose less protein than males (Widdowson, 1976; Henry, 1984) and are better able to withstand food shortages (Widdowson, 1976). It was Chossat (1843) who first proposed that death would ensue when animals lost 40–50% of their body weight. Although this generalization appears to be valid in human males it appears not to be so for females. For example, the patients of Berkman (1947) (Table 8.6) with anorexia nervosa lost up to 58% of their body weight and were all alive at the time of treatment. From an inspection of Fig. 8.1, the general 'cut-off' in the BMI of around 13 divides survivors from non-survivors in males. This distinct cut-off point is not apparent in females (Fig. 8.2). Females show a much larger variability in BMI, in both the survivors and the non-survivors. Moreover, the sex difference in the cut-off point is vividly illustrated.

Sex differences in human survival

Under normal conditions, requirements for nutrition are met by intermittent feeding. During starvation, however, nutrient needs are met by the breakdown of body stores. The results presented thus far clearly indicate that females are capable of withstanding greater weight loss during food deprivation than males. There may be several biological and physiological reasons for this difference. At any given body weight, females have greater fat stores than males. Differences between males and females in fatness levels during growth represent one of the clearest examples of human sexual dimorphism (Tanner, 1978). Fat, being an energy dense material, is a rich source of metabolic fuel during starvation. It is available in greater amounts in the female. In addition, females appear to break down less protein or lean tissues (important for cellular integrity)

Table 8.7. *Contribution of protein and fat (%) to total energy expenditure of rats during complete starvation*

	Males	Females
Protein	33	8
Fat	67	92

Source: Widdowson (1976).

during starvation than males (Henry, 1984; Widdowson, 1976); Table 8.7 illustrates this point. Thus the pattern and site of tissue mobilization in males and females may influence their limits of survival. Finally, females may be capable of withstanding greater weight loss during starvation (hence greater use of body stores) because they are able to mobilize fat tissues efficiently from all sites in their body. Males, on the other hand, may be incapable of mobilizing all their fat stores in the face of food deprivation. To coin a metaphor, females are able to raid their entire larder, whereas males appear to be unable to get to their half-filled larders. Although evidence in support for a sex difference in the ability to mobilize fat stores is only circumstantial, cadaver analysis in subjects who have died from starvation provides indirect support for this. For example, Wilkinson *et al.* (1877) commented on their post-mortem examination of Harriet Stanton as follows: 'There was a total absence of fat.' Conversely, Meyers (1917), who examined a male who died of starvation, commented: 'In the remaining remnants of the sub-pericardial fat, the cells are better preserved.' Although these statements should be interpreted with caution, they may illustrate a difference in the amount of residual fat that remained in males and females who died from starvation.

Conclusion

This paper has shown that body size (using BMI as a proxy) may be used to define the limits of human survival. A BMI below 13 in the males and 11 in females may be the lowest limit compatible with life. The variability in BMI seen between the sexes, and the ability of females to withstand a greater degree of food deprivation, may be due to the following reasons: (i) females have greater body stores of fat than males, and this can be used as a source of energy for a much longer period; (ii) the contribution of fat energy to total energy expenditure is greater in the female, there being a greater conservation of protein; and (iii) females appear to be better able to mobilize adipose tissue from most sites in the body than are males. These three factors appear to give females a biological advantage. It is clear that men and women respond differently to food deficits. It is hoped that this paper will stimulate further research in the biology of inanition.

The results presented here endorse the initial proposition of James *et al.* (1988) that a BMI of around 12 may be the lower limit for survival. Further refinements may need to be considered in view of the distinct sex difference in the lower limit of BMI. Nevertheless it is clear that BMI may be a useful proxy indicator in defining CED. Much remains to be learned concerning the critical levels of BMI and body weight and its implications for health and function. Although the desire to know more precisely the lower limit of survival in males and females may be more academic than practical, it nevertheless provides further support for the view that men and women respond differently to energy deficits.

References

Barnard, D. L. & Ford, J. (1969). Changes in body composition produced by total starvation. *Metabolism* **18**, 564–9.

Benedict, F. G. (1915). A study of prolonged fasting. Carnegie Institute, Washington, Publication no. 203.

Berkman, J. M., Weir, J. F. & Kepler, E. J. (1947). Clinical observations on oedema, serum protein and the effects of forced feeding in anorexia nervosa. *Gastroenterology* **9**, 357–90.

Bruckner, W. J., Wies, C. H. & Lavietes, P. H. (1938). Anorexia nervosa and pituitary cachexia. *American Journal of Medicine* **196**, 663–73.

Burger, G. C. E., Drummond, J. C. & Sandstead, H. R. (eds) (1950). *Malnutrition and Starvation in Western Netherland*, vol. 2. The Hague: General State Printing Office.

Chossat, C. (1843). Recherches experimentales sur l'initiation. *Memoires de l'Academie des Sciences, Paris*, no. 8.

Drenick, E. J. (1964). Prolonged starvation as a treatment of obesity. *Journal of the American Medical Association* **187**, 100–5.

Dugdale, A. E. & Payne, P. R. (1977). Pattern of lean and fat deposition. *Nature* **366**, 349–51.

Farquharson, R. F. (1941). Anorexia nervosa. III. *Medical Journal* **80**, 193–7.

Fernet, M. (1901). Amaigrissement extreme, et mort par inanition. *Bull. Mem. Soc. Hop., Paris* **1**, 1361–3.

Garrow, J. S. (1981). *Treat Obesity Seriously*. London: Churchill Livingstone.

Henry, C. J. K. (1984). Protein energy interrelationships and the regulation of body composition. PhD thesis, University of London.

Henry, C. J. K. (1990). Body mass index and the limits of human survival. *Human Nutrition; Clinical Nutrition* **44**, 329–35.

Henry, C. J. K., Rivers, J. P. W. & Payne, P. R. (1986). Does the pattern of tissue mobilisation dictate protein requirements? *Human Nutrition; Clinical Nutrition* **40**, 87–92.

James, W. P. T. (1984). Treatment of obesity, the constraints on success. *Clinical Endocrinology and Metabolism* **13**, 635–53.

James, W. P. T., Ferro-Luzzi, A. & Waterlow, J. C. (1988). Definition of chronic energy deficiency in adults. *European Journal of Clinical Nutrition* **42**, 969–81.

Keys, A. (1980). Overweight obesity, coronary heart disease and mortality. *Nutrition Reviews* **38**, 116–27.

Keys, A., Brozek, J., Henschels, A., Mickelsen, O. & Taylor, H. (1950). *The Biology of Human Starvation*, vol. 2, p. 1133. Minneapolis: University of Minnesota Press.

Kleitmann, N. (1926). Basal metabolism in prolonged fasting. *American Journal of Physiology* **77**, 223–44.

Krieger, M. (1921). Ueber die Atrophie der menschlichen Organe bei Inanition. *Zeitschrift für Angewandte Anatomie Konstitutionsl.* **7**, 87–134.

Labbe, M. (1922) Echanges respiratoires et metabolisme basal au cours d'un jeune de 43 jours. *Comptes Rendus Soc. Biol.* **87**, 607–10.

Ljunggren, H., Ikos, D. & Luft, R. (1961). Basal metabolism in obese and anorexic women. *British Journal of Nutrition* **15**, 21–34.

Meyer, A. W. (1917). Some morphological effects of prolonged inanition. *Journal of Medicine* **36**, 51–77.

Porter, A. (1889). *The Diseases of the Madras Famine of 1877-1878.* Madras, India: Government Press.

Special Report (1985). Body weight, health and longevity: conclusions and recommendations of the workshop. *Nutrition Reviews* **43**, 61–3.

Stewart, W. K. (1973). Features of a successful therapeutic fast of 382 days. *Postgraduate Medical Journal* **49**, 203–9.

Tanner, J. M. (1978). *Fetus Into Man. Physical Growth from Conception to Maturity.* Cambridge, Massachusetts: Harvard University Press.

Takahira, H. (1925). Metabolism during fasting and subsequent refeeding. *Report of Metabolism, Tokyo* **1**, 63–82.

Tompson, T. J. (1966). Treatment of obesity by total fasting up to 249 days. *Lancet* **ii**, 992–6.

Vague, J., Vague, P. & Barre, A. (1988). Fat distribution, obesities and health: evolution of concepts. In: *Fat Distribution during Growth and Later Health Outcomes*, ed. C. Bouchard & F. E. Johnston, pp. 9–41. New York: Alan R. Liss.

Waaler, H. (1984). Height, weight and mortality. The Norwegian experience. *Acta Medica Scandinavica* (suppl.) **679**, 1–59.

Waterlow, J. C. (1972). Classification and definition of protein-calorie malnutrition. *British Medical Journal* **3**, 566–9.

Widdowson, E. M. (1976). The response of the sexes to nutritional stress. *Proceedings of the Nutrition Society* **35**, 175–80.

Wilkinson, J. E., Bright, J. M., Langriss, D., Piggot, A. & Lister, C. H. (1877). Report of postmortem examination and on the cause of death of Harriet Stanton. *Lancet* **i**, 604.

9 Anthropometry and body composition

PETER S. W. DAVIES

Introduction

Humans have been concerned with the composition of the human body for many centuries. Since *ca.* 440 BC, when Hippocrates postulated his ideas of the four constituents of man, we have come a long way in our understanding of the composition of the body. Most current techniques might be regarded, however, as a retrograde step as usually the body is split into two components, fat-free mass (FFM) and fat mass (FM). Describing the body as two compartments began in earnest when a number of workers produced equations relating the specific gravity or density of the body to the percentage of fat within it (Rathbun & Pace, 1945; Siri, 1956). The principle on which these equations are based was derived hundreds of years ago by Archimedes, namely, that if a body has two components of different densities, the proportion of the components can be calculated from the density of the body. Using these and other equations a great deal of work has been done to assess the percentage of the body which is fat, and hence calculate body FM. Much of the early work involved US Navy personnel (Behnke, Feen & Welham, 1942; Morales *et al.*, 1945). Another measure, subcutaneous 'fatness', has been assessed by using skinfold callipers, the skinfold measurements often being related to total body fat measurements. More complex techniques are laboratory-based, while anthropometric techniques are used to assess body composition under field conditions.

Measurement of body composition in children offers a number of problems not necessarily encountered in studies of adults. This chapter concentrates on the difficulty of using anthropometry to assess body composition in children, and presents a possible new anthropometric tool.

Considerable attention has been focused on fatness in childhood, yet there is little information on total body fat at this time. Data obtained from direct cadaver analyses are rare, and detailed indirect body compo-

130

sition analysis, including underwater weighing, *in vivo* neutron activation and potassium-40 counting, is restricted because of practical and sometimes ethical problems (Davies & Preece, 1988).

There are a number of areas in the study of child growth and development and in paediatric medicine where accurate and reliable knowledge of body composition would be advantageous. In the study of the physical growth and development of children and adolescents, anthropometric measures such as stature and sitting height have long been used to obtain information on linear growth. Detailed knowledge regarding the growth of the tissue compartments of the body, including body fat, water and lean body mass, has been less easily forthcoming using anthropometry. Changes in body weight tell us little about the growth of individual tissues, although the additional use of skinfold callipers for the measurement of skinfold thickness allows some estimate of change in FM and FFM to be made. However, there is increasing recognition that skinfold measurements and their extrapolation to measures of total body fatness are fraught with problems and assumptions that are not easily overcome or validated (Martin *et al.*, 1985; Davies, Jones & Norgan, 1986).

To understand and describe the changes that occur in body composition throughout growth would certainly give a new insight into the growth process. There is still much to be learnt of the effect of different hormones on specific body tissues and of the influence of body composition abnormalities in early life on subsequent growth and development. Furthermore, the possible role of body composition in pubertal and reproductive events is still far from clear (Frisch & McArthur, 1974; Cameron, 1976; Frisch, 1984; Malina, 1983).

Moreover, there are situations where disturbances in body composition are of clinical importance to the paediatrician. For example, the characteristic changes in body composition experienced by many individuals when receiving corticosteroids as treatment for a variety of inflammatory conditions, including rapid weight gain and changes in fat distribution (Horber *et al.*, 1986), can often be more disturbing to children and adolescents than the disease process itself.

There are also marked body composition changes in some endocrine disorders, such as Cushing's disease and growth hormone deficiency. While the effects of the initiation of growth hormone treatment on body fat and muscle have been investigated (Tanner *et al.*, 1971; Collip *et al.*, 1973; Parra *et al.*, 1979) the potentially more important changes that occur in the quantity and histology of body muscle and fat after the cessation of treatment have only recently been addressed (Preece, Round & Jones, 1987).

The study of human body composition is confounded by the obvious necessity of using indirect techniques. Also, there are very few body composition techniques that allow individual tissues or body constituents to be assessed. The vast majority of available indirect techniques consider the human body as a two-compartment model consisting of FM and FFM. The FFM consists of many different tissues, including bone, muscle and the viscera. The number of techniques of body composition assessment appropriate to paediatrics are fewer than those available when studying adults because of special problems encountered in this field. Ethical considerations reduce the number of techniques that can be used; for example, the use of radioactive tritium oxide for the assessment of total body water is usually precluded.

In addition, the detailed analysis of body composition using *in vivo* neutron activation (Allen, Gaskin & Stewart, 1986) has important ethical considerations because of exposure to radiation, although the incurred radiation dose is relatively small, being about 30 cGy (Forbes, 1978). The recent development of photon activation analysis (Ulin *et al.*, 1986) for the measurement of total body carbon, oxygen and nitrogen has yet to be applied to paediatric body composition analysis, but again the radiation dose incurred may be restrictive.

No less an important consideration when studying paediatric body composition is that the technique used should be acceptable to the child. Thus, the procedure of measuring body density by underwater weighing or volumetric displacement, while being non-invasive, can prove difficult to use in children, especially sick ones. The measurement of the naturally occurring isotope potassium-40 (used as an index of the lean body mass) can prove disturbing to many children because of the claustrophobic nature of the counting chamber. So the use of simple, non-invasive methods such as anthropometry has been explored on many occasions.

However, there are few data that can be used as a standard against which to validate less invasive and more acceptable techniques such as anthropometric measurements of height, weight or skinfold thicknesses. Indeed, there are few validated equations for predicting total body fatness in children from any simple anthropometric measurements.

Prediction of body composition from skinfold measurements

Although a number of equations for the prediction of total body fatness from skinfolds in children have been proposed (e.g. Parizkova, 1961; Brook, 1971; Dauncey, Gandy & Gardner, 1977; Frerichs, Horsha & Berenson, 1979; Deurenberg, Pieters & Hautvast, 1990) they are either cumbersome, based on limited data, or not applicable throughout the childhood years.

For example, Dauncey *et al.* (1977) produced an equation to predict total body fat using triceps and subscapular skinfold measurements and nine body dimensions such as circumferences of the arm and leg and segmental lengths. These authors claim that the equation can be applied 'tentatively' in infants up to 40 weeks of age, and in pre-term infants. Nevertheless, the large number of measurements required in order to use the prediction equation has meant that it has not enjoyed widespread use. On the other hand, the equations derived by Brook (1971) have been used quite frequently.

Brook's (1971) equations purport to predict body density, and hence FM, in boys and girls aged from 1 to 11 years. However, the equations are based on the detailed analysis of body composition in 23 children of which 10 were of short stature and 13 were obese. Thus, it is questionable whether equations based on such a small sample size, ranging in age from 1 to 11 years, is applicable to the more generally non-obese child of normal stature.

Frerichs *et al.* (1979) used a much larger sample size (214 children aged from 10 to 14 years) in order to develop regression equations that related height, weight and triceps skinfold thicknesses to percentage body fat. These equations, however, are age-dependent and therefore their extrapolation to younger children and infants cannot be recommended.

Parizkova (1961) also produced age-dependent equations based on the triceps and subscapular skinfold measurements from a large sample size. Separate equations exist for boys and girls in the age ranges 9–12 years and 13–16 years. However, one of the largest sample sizes reported in the literature involving the estimation of total body fatness from skinfold measurements is that reported by Deurenberg *et al.* (1990). Body density, calculated from underwater weighing, was related to skinfold measurements in a group of 378 boys and girls. Unfortunately, for those interested in young children, the youngest children involved in this study were 7 years old. Once again the extrapolation of these equations to younger children or infants cannot be recommended.

Thus there are few equations that exist for the assessment of body fatness from anthropometric measurements. Also, the problems that can be encountered in obtaining reliable skinfold measurements in the very young has led to the consideration of other anthropometric methods for assessing body fatness in childhood.

Prediction equations involving skinfolds are known to be highly population-specific and are rarely of general validity (Jackson & Pollock,

1978; Norgan & Ferro-Luzzi, 1985). That is, equations based upon highly homogeneous populations are usually the most accurate and reliable, with R^2 values in the order of 0.8 to 0.9. In more diverse populations the equations are less robust. The possibility emerges that children may be inherently heterogeneous populations with regard to their body fat stores. Notably, the percentage of body fat changes rapidly in early life.

Any predictive equation that relates subcutaneous measures of body fat from skinfolds to total body fatness assumes that the ratio between internal and subcutaneous stores are constant at any given level of fatness. Variation in the proportion of fat situated subcutaneously has been postulated as a reason why predictive equations derived for adults are rarely of general validity (Davies, Jones & Norgan, 1986). It is possible that between-subject variation in the distribution of internal and external fat stores may be a major factor accounting for the poor predictive value of skinfold thickness often found.

Prediction of body composition using height and weight

Simple indices relating weight to height have been used in the assessment of obesity and nutritional status since the time that Quetelet (1869) observed the proportional relation between weight and height squared in normal adults. Cole, Donnet & Stanfield (1981) have shown that Quetelet's Index (weight/height^2) is a good index of obesity in childhood, while more recently Garrow & Webster (1985) have shown that Quetelet's Index can be used to derive reliable and accurate measurements of FM in lean and obese adults. The derivation of FM and hence percentage body fat from an index requiring only accurate measurement of weight and length would be extremely valuable in paediatric body composition studies.

Such an approach would be of particular interest in infancy when rapid and dramatic changes occur in the percentage of body weight that is fat and the absolute amount. However, the ability of a weight–height relation (in the form of Quetelet's Index) and triceps and subscapular skinfold measurements to predict total body fat in early infancy has been investigated and shown to be poor (Davies & Lucas, 1989, 1990).

As observed previously (Garrow & Webster, 1985) some of the variation in the relationship between fat mass/height^2 and weight/height^2 will be due to error induced by the use of total body water to derive FFM and hence FM. There is no evidence, however, that levels of hydration in the FFM vary more in children than in adults and therefore there is no reason to place more emphasis on this particular error in childhood.

The basic premise which allows Quetelet's Index to be used as a measure of fatness is that variation between individuals is due to difference in FM. If the change in Quetelet's Index is due to a combination of FM and FFM changes, or to change in FFM alone, then the ability of Quetelet's Index to predict FM will be poor. Infants undergo rapid growth in both length and weight. If the nature of this rapid growth varies between individuals in terms of FM and FFM or if the relative rates of growth in weight and length vary significantly, then Quetelet's Index will not be closely related to FM. This may also apply to children.

Although the simplicity of prediction equations to relate weight and height to parameters such as FFM is appealing, such equations have yet to be established. The equation devised by Mellits & Cheek (1970) for the prediction of total body water using weight and height has been criticized as having poor reliability, while Quetelet's Index has been shown to be unable to predict fat mass with the degree of accuracy one would require in young infants (Scott, 1984). It is possible that natural biological variation in the components of weight gain in children will never allow the generation of a simple and accurate weight–height predictive equation.

Criteria for an adequate anthropometric measure of body composition

A number of criteria need to be satisfied before a body composition technique can be used in paediatric studies. The repeatability and reliability of any potential body composition technique should be carefully evaluated; this is no less important in paediatric studies than in adult body composition analysis.

Techniques for the assessment of body composition should ideally be applicable in both health and disease. A disturbance in body fat distribution, or an unusual distribution in some diseases (such as Cushing's disease) may, for example, affect the ability of skinfold calliper measurements to predict total body fatness. Techniques should also be non-invasive, rapid, inexpensive and applicable in the field.

In the last few years a number of new body composition techniques have been developed that may have a role to play specifically in paediatric body composition analysis. These include the measurement of total body electrical conductivity (Cochran *et al.*, 1986; Van Loan & Mayclin, 1987) and the measurement of total body water using total body electrical impedance (Lukaski *et al.*, 1985; Kushner & Schoeller, 1986). The latter technique, although the subject of a certain amount of criticism in the literature (Cohn, 1985) is gaining popularity worldwide.

The technique of measuring total body electrical impedance is remarkable if only for its simplicity. More importantly, the technique is non-invasive and rapid, and the equipment required is relatively cheap. These factors make the measurement of total body impedance as an index of total body water an ideal technique for paediatric body composition analysis. If the definition of anthropometry is taken as the measurement of man, impedance technology is simply another measure and is often quicker to achieve satisfactorily than more classical anthropometric measures such as sitting height. Thus, bioelectrical impedance is an anthropometric technique.

The term 'total body impedance' refers to the electrical resistance offered by the human body when an alternating electrical current is passed through the body. The term 'impedance' usually refers to a 'resistance' due to the combination of simple electrical resistors and capacitors, which offer their own resistance in the form of capacitative reactance. Therefore, although there are differences between the exact definitions of the terms resistance and impedance, empirical testing (Lukaski *et al.*, 1985) has shown that within the human, the resistance component is the most important. There are a number of factors that influence the resistance of any conduction body, including the human, to an alternating electrical current. These are: (i) conductor length; (ii) conductor configuration; (iii) frequency of the current; and (iv) conductor cross-sectional area. Using a constant signal frequency and assuming a relatively constant conductor configuration, the mathematical equation relating these parameters to resistance is:

$$\text{Resistance} \propto \frac{\text{length}}{\text{cross-sectional area}} \qquad (9.1)$$

If one multiplies by length/length the relationship becomes:

$$\text{Resistance} \propto \frac{\text{length}^2}{\text{volume}} \qquad (9.2)$$

and simple rearrangement gives:

$$\text{Volume} \propto \frac{\text{length}^2}{\text{resistance}}. \qquad (9.3)$$

Conductor length is taken to be the height of the individual, and thus the volume of the conducting medium, being total body water, is proportional to a simple relation involving only height and resistance.

Knowledge of total body water is a useful body composition parameter *per se*. However, its usefulness to body composition analysis in the broader sense lies in its application in predicting lean body mass and

Table 9.1. *Some equations that relate measure-ments of height²/resistance to indices of body composition*

TBW, total body water; FFM, fat free mass.

Reference	n	Equation
Davies *et al.* (1988)	26	$TBW = -0.5 + 0.60 \, H^2/R$
Cordain *et al.* (1988)	30	$FFM = 6.86 + 0.81 \, H^2/R$
Gregory *et al.* (1991)	34	$TBW = 0.79 + 0.55 \, H^2/R$
Davies & Gregory (1991)	60	$TBW = 0.13 + 0.58 \, H^2/R$

hence fat mass. It is accepted that fat is anhydrous and that the water content of the lean tissue is remarkably constant (Forbes, 1962; Behnke & Wilmore, 1974). Indeed, the concept of a consistent composition of the lean body mass is essential to most indirect body composition techniques. Thus if body water can be measured using the electrical resistance of the body it is possible to derive values for the FFM and FM.

Bioelectrical impedance technology has now been validated in a number of studies involving children, and Table 9.1 shows equations relating total body water (TBW) or FFM to resistance and height. The final equation of Davies & Gregory (1991) was produced by a combination of the data they individually published in 1988 and 1990. It is noteworthy that regression equations relating TBW to resistance reported in the literature have a high degree of similarity; intercepts are close to zero while the regression coefficients are usually between 0.6 and 0.7. This would indicate that the relation between height²/resistance and total body water is constant in children, adolescents and adults, for both males and females.

The phenomenon is in marked contrast to other methods of predicting body composition parameters such as the use of skinfold thicknesses. The technique of measuring body resistance is non-invasive and rapid, although cross-validation studies are required in order to assess the general validity of the bioelectrical impedance technique.

The conversion of total body water measurements to estimates of lean body mass and fat mass requires that the water content of lean tissue be known and constant. There is evidence that the proportion of water in lean tissue changes considerably during growth (Boileau *et al.*, 1984). The concept of a constant lean body mass composition is one that pervades many indirect body composition techniques, such as densitometry. However, the technique of measuring total body resistance, in conjunction with other body composition techniques, may allow the changes that occur in the water content of the lean body mass, and in body composition in general, to be studied more easily in the growing child.

Anthropometry is usually thought of as the classical techniques used by anthropologists to describe human form. Bioelectrical impedance is a simple measurement and could be included in this category. Its use may provide measurements of body composition that can be used in the field, simply, non-invasively and at a reasonable cost.

References

Allen, B., Gaskin, K. & Stewart, P. (1986). Measurement of body composition by *in vivo* neutron activation. *Medical Journal of Australia* **145**, 307–8.

Behnke, A. R., Feen, B. G. & Welham, W. C. (1942). The specific gravity of healthy men. *Journal of the American Medical Association* **118**, 495–8.

Behnke, A. R. & Wilmore, J. H. (1974). Evaluation and regulation of body build and body composition. *International Research Monograph series in Physical Education*, ed. H. Harrison Clarke. New Jersey: Prentice-Hall.

Boileau, R. A., Lohman, T. G., Slaughter, M. H., Ball, T. E., Going, S. B. & Hendrix, M. K. (1984). Hydration of the fat-free body in children during maturation. *Human Biology* **56**, 651–66.

Brook, C. G. D. (1971). Determination of body composition of children from skinfold measurements. *Archives of Disease in Childhood* **46**, 182–4.

Cameron, N. (1976). Weight and skinfold variation at menarche and the critical body weight hypothesis. *Annals of Human Biology* **3**, 279–82.

Cochran, W. J., Klish, W. J., Wong, W. W. & Klein, P. D. (1986). Total body electrical conductivity used to determine body composition in infants. *Pediatric Research* **20**, 561–5.

Cohn, S. H. (1985). How valid are bioelectrical impedance measurements in body composition studies? *American Journal of Clinical Nutrition* **42**, 889–90.

Cole, T. C., Donnet, M. L. & Stanfield, J. P. (1981). Weight-for-height indices to assess nutritional status – a new index on a slide rule. *American Journal of Clinical Nutrition* **34**, 1935–43.

Collip, P. J., Curti, V., Thomas, J., Sharma, R. K., Maddaiah, V. T. & Cohn, S. H. (1973). Body composition changes in children receiving human growth hormone. *Metabolism* **22**, 589–98.

Cordain, L., Whicker, R. E. & Johnson, J. F. (1988). Body composition determinants in children using bioelectrical impedance. *Growth, Development and Aging,* **52**, 37–40.

Dauncey, M. J., Gandy, G. & Gardner, D. (1977). Assessment of total body fat in infancy from skinfold thickness measurements. *Archives of Disease in Childhood* **52**, 223–7.

Davies, P. S. W. & Gregory, J. W. (1991). Body water measurements in growth disorders. *Archives of Disease in Childhood* **66**, 1417.

Davies, P. S. W., Jones, P. R. M. & Norgan, N. G. (1986). The distribution of subcutaneous and internal fat in man. *Annals of Human Biology* **13**, 189–92.

Davies, P. S. W. & Lucas, A. (1989). Quetelet's Index as a measure of fatness in young infants. *Early Human Development* **20**, 135–41.

Davies, P. S. W. & Lucas, A. (1990). The prediction of body fatness in infancy. *Early Human Development* 21, 193–8.

Davies, P. S. W. & Preece, M. A. (1988). Body composition in children: methods of assessment. In: *The Physiology of Growth*, ed. J. M. Tanner & M. A. Preece, pp. 95–107. Cambridge University Press.

Davies, P. S. W., Preece, M. A., Hicks, C. J. & Holliday, D. (1988). The prediction of total body water using bioelectrical impedance in children adolescence. *Annals of Human Biology* 15, 237–40.

Deurenberg, P., Pieters, J. J. L. & Hautvast, G. A. J. (1990). The assessment of body fat percentage by skinfold thickness measurement in childhood and adolescence. *British Journal of Nutrition* 63, 293–303.

Forbes, G. B. (1962). Methods for determining composition of the human body. *Pediatrics* 29, 477–94.

Forbes, G. B. (1978). Body composition in adolescence. In: *Human Growth*, 2nd edition, ed. F. Falkner & J. M. Tanner, Vol. 2, pp. 239–72. New York: Plenum Press.

Frerichs, R. R., Horsha, D. W. & Berenson, G. S. (1979). Equations for estimating percentage body fat in children 10–14 years old. *Pediatric Research* 13, 170–4.

Frisch, R. E. (1984). Body fat, puberty and fertility. *Biological Reviews* 59, 161–88.

Frisch, R. E. & McArthur, J. (1974). Menstrual cycles: fatness as a determinant of minimum weight for height necessary for their maintenance or onset. *Science* 185, 949–51.

Garrow, J. S. & Webster, J. (1985). Quetelet's Index (W/H^2) as a measure of fatness. *International Journal of Obesity* 9, 147–53.

Gregory, J. W., Greene, S. A., Scrimgeor, C. M. & Rennie, M. J. (1991). Body water measurements in growth disorders: a comparison of bioelectrical impedance and skinfold thickness techniques with isotope dilution. *Archives of Disease in Childhood* 66, 220–2.

Horber, F. F., Zurcher, R. M., Herren, H., Crivelli, M. A., Ribolti, G. & Frey, F. J. (1986). Altered body fat distribution in patients with glucocorticoid treatment and in patients on long term dialysis. *American Journal of Clinical Nutrition* 43, 758–70.

Jackson, A. S. & Pollock, M. L. (1978). Generalized equations for predicting body density of man. *British Journal of Nutrition* 40, 497–504.

Kushner, R. F. & Schoeller, D. A. (1986). Estimation of total body water by electrical impedance analysis. *American Journal of Clinical Nutrition* 44, 417–24.

Lukaski, H. C., Johnson, P. E., Bolonuchuk, W. W. & Lykken, G. I. (1985). Assessment of fat-free mass using bioelectric impedance measurements of the human body. *American Journal of Clinical Nutrition* 41, 810–7.

Malina, R. M. (1983). Menarche in athletes: a synthesis and hypothesis. *Annals of Human Biology* 10, 1–24.

Martin, A. D., Ross, W. D., Drinkwater, D. T. & Clarys, J. P. (1985) Prediction of body density by skinfold calliper: assumptions and cadaver evidence. *International Journal of Obesity* 9, 31–9.

Mellits, E. D. & Cheek, D. B. (1970). The assessment of body water and fatness from infancy and childhood. Monograph, *Society for Research on Child Development* **35**, 12–26.

Morales, M. F., Rathbun, E. N., Smith, R. E. & Pace, N. (1945). Studies on body composition. *Journal of Biological Chemistry* **158**, 677–84.

Norgan, N. G. & Ferro-Luzzi, A. (1985). The estimation of body density in men: are general equations general? *Annals of Human Biology* **12**, 1–5.

Parizkova, J. (1961). Total body fat and skinfold thickness in children. *Metabolism* **10**, 794–807.

Parra, A., Argote, R., Garcia, G., Cervantes, C., Alatorre, S. & Perez-Pasten, E. (1979). Body composition in Hypopituitary dwarfs before and during human growth hormone therapy. *Metabolism* **28**, 851–7.

Preece, M. A., Round, J. M. & Jones, D. A. (1987). Growth hormone deficiency in adults – an indication for therapy. *Acta Paediatrica Scandinavica* (suppl.), **331**, 76–9.

Quetelet, A. (1870). *Anthropometrie, on Mésure des Différentes Facultés de l'Homme-Brussels: Muquardt.*

Quetelet, L. A. J. (1869). *Physique Sociale* 2. Brussels: Muquardt.

Rathbun, E. N. & Pace, N. (1945). Studies on body composition. *Journal of Biological Chemistry* **158**, 667–76.

Scott, E. C. (1984). Estimation of total body water and fatness from weight and height: Inaccurate for lean women. *American Journal of Physical Anthropology* **64**, 83–7.

Siri, W. E. (1956). Gross composition of the body. In: *Advances in Biological and Medical Physics*, vol. 4, ed. J. H. Lawrence & C. A. Tobias, pp. 239–80. New York: Academic Press.

Tanner, J. M., Whitehouse, R. H., Hughes, P. C. R. & Vince, F. P. (1971). Effect of human growth hormone treatment for 1 to 7 years on growth of 100 children, with growth hormone deficiency, low birth weight, inherited smallness, Turner's syndrome and other complaints. *Archives of Disease in Childhood* **46**, 745–82.

Ulin, K., Meydani, M., Zammenhof, R. G. & Blumberg, J. B. (1986). Photon activation analysis as a new technique for body composition. *American Journal of Clinical Nutrition* **44**, 963–73.

Van Loan, M. & Mayclin, P. (1987). A new TOBEC instrument and procedure for the assessment of body composition: use of Fourier coefficients to predict lean body mass and total body water. *American Journal of Clinical Nutrition* **45**, 131–7.

10 *Anthropometry and physical performance*

N. G. NORGAN

Introduction

This chapter examines the extent to which body size, shape and composition determine or correlate with indices of physical performance. Although a relationship between size and performance is obvious and well documented, performance is influenced by a multitude of other factors which may confound or obscure the simple relationship such that the correlation is, at best, weak. It begins with a statement of what is understood by the term anthropometry and a description of the different types of physical performance and the factors affecting them. The theoretical relationships are summarized and then the empirical evidence relating performance to anthropometric indices is reviewed.

Anthropometry

Anthropometry means, literally, the measurement of people; taken literally, it could include any human characteristic including, for example, intelligence. Indeed, Stephen Jay Gould's provocative and highly readable book *The Mismeasure of Man* (Gould, 1984) is mainly concerned with psychological characteristics. But anthropometry has come to be used in a more restrictive sense to mean the comparative study of sizes and proportions of the human body. Here, anthropometry is considered to include size and shape (the proportionality of sizes) and the composition of the body (the masses and proportions of its constituents). These are commonly described, in the first instance, in anatomical terms as lean body mass (LBM) and adipose tissue (AT) or the similar but not identical chemical model of the body as fat-free mass (FFM) and fat mass (FM). It is both legitimate and more informative to include these, or, say, skeletal muscle mass than to consider height, weight and shape indices alone. To be consistent, cardiac muscle mass or heart weight ought

141

Table 10.1. *Types of energy systems and physical performance*

Each type of physical performance requires skill, flexibility and motivation. See text for further details.

Energy systems	Time frame	Activities	Attributes
Anaerobic, alactic	0–10 s	lift, jump, sprint	strength, speed
Anaerobic, lactic	10–120 s	chasing the dog	speed
Aerobic–anaerobic, mixed	1–2 min	heavy work	stamina, endurance
Aerobic, maximal	4 min	fitness test	cardio-respiratory fitness
Aerobic endurance (75% of maximum)	100 min	team games	high muscle glycogen
Aerobic, submaximal	400 min	daily occupation, productivity	see Fig. 10.1
Aerobic, submaximal	40 years	lifetime	see Fig. 10.1

to be included but as it is difficult to measure *in vivo* it is not necessary to debate whether to include it or not. Total haemogloblin can be measured accurately and is well correlated with aerobic performance, but can it be regarded as an anthropometric measurement? Twenty years ago, the term 'physiological anthropometry' appeared in the literature but without any common clear understanding or definition of what it encompassed; the term has fallen out of use, perhaps because of that. Many of its measures might have been better considered as 'anatomical anthropometry'. A much more widespread term to describe the quantitative relationships between structure and function is 'kinanthropometry', but this is used only by kinesiologists and biomechanicists concerned with movement.

Anthropometry is a method and as such is a means to an end. It matters less what size a person is, but rather how that person performs. What is important is whether anthropometric measurements have functional correlates and significance. Therefore, measurements should not be made for measurement's sake but from a pre-measurement rationale as to what questions are being posed and why.

Types and indices of physical performance

Table 10.1 shows a description of the different types of physical performance on the basis of the energy transduction systems involved. It includes an indication of time frames for maximal effort and what these mean in terms of everyday activities. Strength, the ability to exert force against an external resistance, requires anaerobic alactic energy transduction at least in the short term. Speed, too, involves this system in addition to anaerobic metabolism producing lactic acid. Maximal effort at a level that can be sustained for 5 min or more depends largely on the ability to transport and utilize oxygen. Most everyday tasks are below this level of intensity (submaximal) but are aerobic in nature. The importance of the energy transduction system and its dimensions should not, however, be over-emphasized. Physical fitness, the ability to perform, requires not only appropriate aerobic capacity and endurance, muscular strength and endurance, flexibility and body composition but also skill and motivation. Neuromuscular and psychological factors are particularly important in maximal performance. Components of motor skill, of particular importance in the developing child, include agility, balance, coordination, power and speed. However, the ability to transduce energy by the various systems can be expected to be matched to the mechanical design and size of the system and its metabolic machinery. This can be examined theoretically, by observation, and empirically.

Determinants of physical performance
Proportionality theory

Static differences
Two geometrically and compositionally similar individuals of stature 1.2 and 1.8 m have statures in the ratio 1.5 : 1. It follows that all linear dimensions, e.g. length of limbs, muscles, conductors, etc., and all levers and ranges of movements will be proportional at 1.5 : 1. All cross-sectional areas, e.g. muscles, bone, blood vessels, lung surfaces, and so on, scale as $(1.5)^2 : 1$ or 2.25 : 1. All volumes and (assuming density is independent of size), masses, e.g. body, heart, skeletal muscle, or bone mass, scale as $(1.5)^3 : 1$ or 3.375 : 1.

Dynamic effects
The maximal force a muscle can develop is proportional to its cross-sectional area. An individual 1.5 times as tall as another should be able to lift a 2.25 times larger weight but as the levers are 1.5 times as long too, torque or work will scale to stature or length cubed, L^3, but pulling and pushing to L^2. Time scale is proportional to length scale so power indices, i.e. rates, such as maximum oxygen uptake, are divided by L and proportional to L^2.

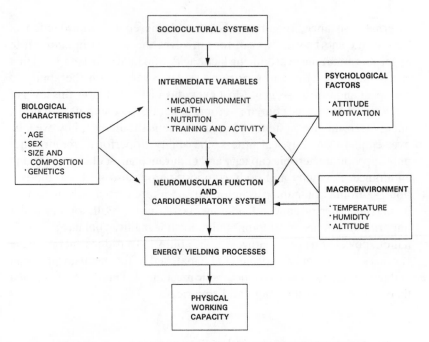

Fig. 10.1. A model of the factors influencing the capacity for physical work, illustrating how size, shape and composition do not impinge directly on work capacity but act through sets of other variables.

Empirical findings

Fig. 10.1 shows a general model of factors influencing physical working capacity. It illustrates the following points:

1. There are a large number of factors, biological, environmental and sociocultural, influencing work capacity and physical performance.
2. The influences are not always simple and linear. They may be additive or multiplicative and in cases such as altitude the effects may be antagonistic.
3. These factors operate at different levels. Sociocultural factors are further removed from the outcome, working capacity, than for example cardiorespiratory factors. This enables views on the relative roles of anthropometric and other factors to be refined.
4. The importance of size and composition should not be over-emphasized. Indeed, this model is based on that of Beall & Goldstein (1988), who did not include size and composition.

However, it is usually agreed that size and composition explain a significant proportion of the variance in some types of performance.

The role of size, shape and composition
Muscle strength and endurance

Muscle strength and endurance are required for everyday activities, not only for the maximum effort of emergencies and occasional hard work. In the elderly, a minimum strength or muscle endurance may determine whether an individual is regarded as capable of continuing an independent existence or requires home or institutional care.

Strength, the ability to exert force against some external resistance, is directly related to the number and size of the muscle fibres recruited, that is the cross-sectional area (CSA) of the muscles. The isometric force that can be developed depends on the number of actin–myosin cross-bridges that are activated in the muscle, which depends in part on the CSA and partly on the coordination of the contractile units. It also depends on the available leverage. On average, 50% of the variance in arm strength is explained by CSA. The degree of recruitment of the muscle fibres may explain much of the rest but within the CSA are non-contractile components which will reduce the fit of the relation. Formerly, measurements of strength were usually measures of static strength at one selected angle using simple strain gauges and dynamometers. Nowadays, dynamic measures of isokinetic or isotonic strength using the newer dynamometers over a range of movement are the norm. With dynamic effort, the external force developed is also affected by the coordination of the sequencing of contraction and relaxation of antagonist muscle and the viscosity of the tissue.

An early classical study of strength and composition is that of Ikai & Fukunaga (1968) who measured elbow flexion strength and the CSA of the biceps brachii with the then new *in vivo* technique of ultrasound. They found a good correlation between the two but no significant difference between sexes or between trained judomen and controls. There was a wide range of ages and a wide range of values of strength or CSA, which seems a characteristic of this attribute (Maughan, Watson & Weir, 1983a). The intercorrelation of strength measurements in the same individual depends on which muscles are being compared and can be low, moderate or high.

Pheasant (1986) has published a detailed analysis of male–female differences in strength from 112 data sets in the literature. The average female : male ratio was 61%, close to the commonly quoted value of 2/3.

The range was from 37 to 90%. Sex can account for a major (85%) or minor (3%) amount of the total variance in the different studies. Not all muscle groups seem to behave in the same way. Upper limbs show greater differences than lower limbs and upper arm and shoulders more than hand and forearm. The smallest differences were found in pull, push or lift categories. When expressed per unit of lean body weight, hip flexor and extensor strength have been found to be the same in men and women, some 20% lower for forearm and trunk flexors and extensors and 50% lower in chest, arm and shoulders in women (Wilmore, 1974).

Maughan *et al.* (1983a) examined the strength of the knee extensor muscles and its relation with mid-thigh CSA from computed tomography. There were no significant correlations between strength and weight in either sex or between strength and LBM in women. In both groups, there was a significant correlation between strength and CSA. The strength : CSA ratio was higher in men but not significantly so. The wide variation was suggested to be due partly to differences in the proportions of fast-twitch anaerobic and slow-twitch aerobic muscle fibres or to anatomical differences in leverage. Maughan, Watson & Weir (1983b) went on to look at runners and non-runners. Again, a feature was the wide variation in strength : CSA, nearly two-fold in the controls. Neither sprinters nor endurance runners differed significantly from controls. Sprinters were stronger than endurance runners; this result may be related to a higher proportion of fast-twitch muscle fibres. Indeed, variation in strength in the untrained population may be due in part to variation in fibre type. Although Schantz *et al.* (1983) confirmed the absence of a difference in strength : CSA in physical education students of both sexes and of body builders, they did, however, find no significant correlation with fibre type.

Maximal strength is reached at between 20 and 30 years of age and falls gradually to some 80% at 65 years of age, the rate of decline being greater in the leg and trunk muscles than in the arm muscles. Loss of force is associated with a loss of muscle mass, which occurs mainly through a decrease of fibre diameter, but a lower level of training consequent on reduced physical activity may also have an effect.

Muscle strength and motor performance in childhood and youth

Muscle CSA increases two- to three-fold during growth, not by increasing the number of fibres (as these are set in the first year), but by the attachment of new contractile filaments. Muscles grow in length in step with bone growth by adding new contractile units at the junction of muscles and tendons. The curves of strength increase during childhood and youth are similar to those of height and weight but with important differences.

Pre-adolescent boys are stronger than girls per unit of body weight or CSA, in contrast to there being no difference in adults. This may reflect motivational differences rather than biological factors. Sex differences in lower limb strength in children reflect stature and size differences (Asmussen, 1973). Upper limb and trunk strength are higher in boys aged 7–17 years than in girls after adjusting for stature. Both boys and girls increase more in strength than expected from their height gain, especially during and after adolescence. Between 6 and 20 years of age one third of total stature is gained but four fifths of strength is developed.

During adolescence, acceleration in strength gain is more marked in boys than in girls. The peak of the strength spurt in boys occurs after peak height and weight velocities. In the longitudinal Amsterdam Growth and Health study, the greatest increases took place about one year after peak height velocity (Kemper & Verschuur, 1985). Such observations have led to the proposal that boys may outgrow their strength. Rather, they do not have the same strength as an adult of the same size (Tanner, 1962). Strength gain may continue until the third decade of life. The peak is more variable in girls but, on a group basis, strength appears to increase linearly with age. In individuals, however, it usually peaks between peak height velocity and menarche. These data can be related to growth of the muscle mass. In boys, peak growth of muscle mass occurs during or after peak weight gain (Malina, 1986). Muscle appears to increase in mass first and then in strength, suggesting that neuromuscular factors may be as important as increases in size.

Parker *et al.* (1990) examined elbow and quadriceps isometric strength in over 550 5–17-year-old London private school children. Strength rose steadily from 8 to 12 years, followed by a rapid increase in boys that continued even when height and weight growth had virtually ceased. In the pre-adolescent phase, elbow flexor strength increased as a function of height squared, L^2, and quadriceps as height cubed, L^3. They suggested that stretch, as a result of elongation of the long bones, and, for the quadriceps, loading, may be the primary stimuli. Post-pubertally, the variation in the data increased and it was suggested that some other stimulus, such as direct action of hormones on the muscle, must be responsible for the continued strength gain in boys. Parker *et al.* (1990) reported that 40–50% of the variance in strength is associated with height and weight.

Motor performance in children is dependent on age, size, sex, physique, body composition and biological maturity status (Malina,

1975). With the exception of age, the correlations are generally low to moderate and less than for strength, particularly when age is partialled out. The relation of specific body segments, for example leg length, and motor performance are similarly low. Physique does not markedly influence motor performance except at the extremes of the ranges.

In summary, correlations of body weight, muscularity and FFM with strength are generally low to moderate in children. Correlations between body size and strength in boys in year groups from 11 to 18 years range from 0.33 to 0.64 for weight and from 0.25 to 0.60 for height (Malina, 1975).

Effects of training

Both strength and muscle size can show large and parallel increases in response to training. This means that the ratio of isometric strength to CSA is the same in trained and untrained subjects (Maughan, 1986). However, this is not always the case; gains in force development of 30–40% invariably exceed the increase in CSA of the muscle (Faulkner & White, 1990). The extra increase is due in part to improved recruitment patterns. Some types of training, for example body building, attempt to affect mainly CSA, while in others, for example weight lifting, where competitions are in weight classes, performance must be increased by skill rather than by an increase in muscle mass. Those parts of the body that receive less use, for example the arms, are more trainable than the legs.

Faulkner & White (1990) consider that the extent of sex differences in adaptation to training has not been determined, but it is rare to see in female athletes the muscle bulking seen in men. However, progressive resistance weight training can induce large strength gains. Wilmore (1974) has shown that men and women may both have significant absolute and relative gains in strength, have similar gains in LBM and losses in FM but that the muscular hypertrophy is substantially greater in men than women. How do female body builders develop large muscles? Do they have a genetic endowment of more fast-twitch fibres that hypertrophy? Do they use anabolic steroids? Most are not as excessively developed as they look. The effect is achieved through 'pumping up' by blood engorgement, muscle control or 'rippling' and by training for 'definition' rather than size. Fibre type differences do not seem to affect the strength–CSA relation in maximal voluntary strength.

Children have larger increases in strength than adults with training, suggesting that they have a lower degree of strength utilization in everyday life (Asmussen, 1973). However, Malina (1986) suggests that children and adolescents may be more sensitive to a training stimulus than adults. Debate continues over whether skeletal muscle becomes less trainable with age. Differences in the size of the training response exist between young and old but these could be a result of differences in the training stimulus (Faulkner & White, 1990).

Anaerobic power
Alactic power

Power output varies inversely with the duration of maximum effort. During a standing jump, values of 3.9 and 2.3 kW have been recorded in men and women, respectively (Davies, 1971). In a staircase climb of a few seconds, values may be only 25% of these. In both forms of activity, maximal power output depends on age and sex, size, stature and to a lesser extent, body composition. In young men and women, power outputs are highly correlated to estimates of LBM and thigh muscle ($r =$ 0.86 and 0.74, respectively) but this is not so in older subjects (Davies, 1971).

The effects of body size are further illustrated by the observations of Kitagawa, Suzuki & Miyashita (1980) that young obese men had higher anaerobic power outputs than normal in a standard stair climb, both in absolute terms and per kilogram of LBM. Adding inert weights to normal-weight individuals increased power output, suggesting that it is the degree of loading that causes this paradox (Kitagawa *et al.*, 1980; Caiozzo & Kyle, 1980). Increases of 20% in power output can be obtained when carrying loads of 45% of the body weight.

Lactic power

Work at a lower intensity for a longer period depends on anaerobic glycolysis with the production of lactic acid. A typical protocol is a 30 s all-out effort on a cycle ergometer. The test is extremely strenuous, requires high motivation and has a prolonged recovery. The appearance of lactic acid in the blood (the anaerobic threshold) occurs in both sexes at the same relative work intensity. In children, maximal post-exercise levels are lower than in adults, indicating a lower glycolytic capacity and tolerance of acidosis in pre-adolescents.

Maximum oxygen uptake (V_{O_2max})

V_{O_2max} (litres per minute) is regarded as the best single index of the ability to perform most types of daily work. V_{O_2max} increases with weight and size in children and adults; it has been common to express V_{O_2max} in individuals and groups of differing sizes as millilitres O_2 per minute per kilogram body weight (ml min^{-1} kg^{-1}). The increases are less in women than in men, reflecting the differences in composition of the sexes. However, expressing V_{O_2max} as ml O_2 kg^{-1} LBM or FFM does not equate the sexes: men have values some 5–15% higher. Is this a true sex difference? There is no reason why the sexes should have the same V_{O_2max} per unit mass or composition. Men may be more active and fitter. They have higher total haemoglobin content for the same blood volume. Lean body mass is a heterogeneous entity, mostly water and including bone, neither of which are direct determinants of oxygen transport or uptake. Sparling (1980) performed a meta-analysis of the results of 15 studies reporting V_{O_2max} and body composition data of men and women; V_{O_2max} values in absolute terms of litres per minute were some 50% higher in men. Expressed as millilitres per kilogram body weight, this reduced to 25%; and as millilitres per kilogram FFM, 5–15%. He concluded that 66% of the variance in V_{O_2max} (l min^{-1}) was explained by knowing the sex of the individual.

Regional measures of body composition seem to perform better in that differences between the sexes tend to disappear. Leg volume or lean leg volume is more highly correlated with V_{O_2max} than is body weight or FFM. Davies *et al.* (1973) found that a single equation fitted the data of European adults and children and African adults of both sexes.

$$V_{O_2max} (l \ min^{-1}) = 0.36 + 0.22 \times leg \ volume \ (l);$$

$$r^2 = 0.81.$$

The high correlation reflects, to some extent, the range of the data in these wide age groups. The relations are not good enough for estimation purposes; the measurement of leg volume is complex and largely unvalidated. However, Davies & Van Haaren (1973) found that the lower V_{O_2max} of Africans compared with Europeans was a function of their smaller estimated muscle mass. Differences in the V_{O_2max} of Europeans, Nigerians, Kurds and Yemenite Jews standardized for size and composition were small and of doubtful biological significance (Davies *et al.*, 1972a).

A similar range effect may explain in part the high correlation of 0.97 between V_{O_2max} (l min^{-1}) and total haemoglobin (g,) in ninety-four 7–30-year-old males and females (Astrand & Rodahl, 1977). Cureton *et al.* (1986) determined the effect of experimentally equating haemoglobin concentrations in the sexes by withdrawal of blood in 10 men. The sex difference in V_{O_2max} was reduced from 47% to 36% but this was only 60% of the change expected by reducing the O_2 carrying capacity. Sex differences or changes in the distribution of fast- and slow-twitch muscle fibres do not, however, seem to be important here (Wells, 1985). Matching subjects for training status has shown smaller sex differences in V_{O_2max} (18% as ml kg^{-1} body weight, 3–5% as ml kg^{-1} FFM) than those mentioned earlier (Sparling & Cureton, 1983).

V_{O_2max} is less pliant than other common performance attributes such as strength and aerobic endurance. Increases with training depend on the initial level of V_{O_2max}, and on the frequency, intensity and duration of training, but they are usually less than 20%. Even so, these gains exceed the changes in size or composition of 1–2 kg FFM or FM (American College of Sports Medicine, 1990) and occur before them. All these observations suggest that other dimensions of the oxygen transport system and musculature are involved, such as cardiac output and arterio-venous O_2 differences.

V_{O_2max} in growth and ageing

Childhood is a time when considerable changes in size, physique and composition occur and when considerable inter-individual variation exists. Aerobic power and muscle strength are related to body size and they show growth patterns similar to those of weight, stature and composition. Young adult values of FFM are reached at 15–16 years in girls and at 19–20 years in boys (Malina & Bouchard, 1991). The FFM is 1.5 times higher in the young adult male than in the female. A few longitudinal and many cross-sectional studies have examined the development of V_{O_2max} from 6 years to adulthood. The data have been reviewed by Krahenbuhl, Skinner & Kohrt (1985). Boys have consistently higher V_{O_2max} values than girls, a difference that becomes magnified at around age 12–13 years. There is a steady increase in boys, best described by a quadratic function, but in girls there are falls after the age of 15 years such that the data are best described by a cubic function. When V_{O_2max} is expressed as millilitres per kilogram body weight, there is no change with age throughout childhood and adolescence in boys but a fall in girls.

Results from the longitudinal Saskatchewan Growth and Development study (Cameron, Mirwald & Bailey, 1980) have been presented as chronological age-based distance and velocity standards. These show a similar pattern to those of structural dimensions: a fairly gradual rise, with an acceleration at 13–14 years of age in boys. Peak velocity occurred at about 14.25 years following a take-off at 12.5 years, presumably corresponding to that of height. There was also a mid-growth spurt between 10 and 11 years, which was more noticeable in the lower percentiles of velocity.

In the longitudinal Amsterdam Growth and Health study of 235 teenagers (aged 11–17 years) over a 4 year period, V_{O_2max} increased more in boys than in girls (Kemper & Verschuur, 1987). V_{O_2max} (ml kg^{-1} body weight) remained constant in boys (59 ml kg^{-1}) but fell from 50 to 45 ml kg^{-1} in girls, partly attributable to the increase in body fat of the girls. However, values per kilogram of FFM were constant in boys (70 ml kg^{-1} FFM) but still showed a fall in girls (68 to 63 ml kg^{-1} FFM). Constant V_{O_2max} (ml kg^{-1} body weight) was not, however, found in longitudinal studies in Canada, Germany and Norway (Kemper, 1992) although the finding of a greater fall in boys than girls is consistent. The cross-sectional data show a constancy in boys aged 6–18 years at 50 ml kg^{-1} (Bailey, Malina & Mirwald, 1986) although some studies show a slight fall after adolescence. Peak velocity in the Dutch study coincided with peak height velocity, demonstrating no discrepancy between structural and functional growth in these teenagers as far as V_{O_2max} was concerned.

Binkhorst *et al.* (1985) took an allometric approach to comparing the V_{O_2max} of children of different sexes and ages. They set out to find the best descriptive formula of the allometric equation $V_{O_2max} = aM^b$, where M was body weight or FFM. Values of a and b were found by minimizing the correlation with sex, age, height, weight or FFM. The data from 271 children randomly selected from several sets of data were used. A single equation for FFM for both sexes was obtained:

$$V_{O_2max} = 0.048 \, FFM^{1.05},$$

indicating no sex difference once FFM was allowed for. This was not true for body weight and is at variance with the results of Davies, Barnes & Godfrey (1972b) where a sex difference in V_{O_2max} (ml kg^{-1} FFM) was found in European children. This disappeared when leg volume was the basis of comparison. In ninety-two 6–16-year-olds, lean leg volume explained the sex and age differences and accounted for 80% of the variation in V_{O_2max}. This is much more than in adults and may be another example of the range effect.

Children respond to vigorous intensive training programmes with an average increase of V_{O_2max} (ml kg^{-1}) of 8–10% (Krahenbuhl *et al.*, 1985). V_{O_2max} declines with age in adulthood both absolutely and relatively (Shephard, 1978). Because of the fat gain with age, the latter is greater than the former. V_{O_2max} begins to decline at about 20 years of age; by 65 years, it is 30–40% lower. In older subjects, V_{O_2max} is reported to be independent of body composition (Davies, 1972).

Daily work performance and productivity

Throughout much of the world, production depends on the physical effort of humans and animals. In humans, size can determine the amount of agricultural, industrial and domestic labour that can be performed. In terms of efficiency and energy conservation, small body size may have advantages, particularly in light tasks, but in every other respect large size is beneficial. Although the relationship is not strong, it is quite apparent in many studies. Spurr, Barac-Nieto & Maksud (1977) found significant correlations of productivity with height, weight and LBM in Columbian sugar-cane cutters pursuing self-paced, continuous work at 35% of their V_{O_2max}. The correlations with age and fat were not significant. Stepwise multiple regression analysis showed that V_{O_2max}, % body fat and height contributed significantly to the regression and explained 47% of the variance. Fitter, leaner and taller subjects had higher productivity. In contrast, Davies (1973) found no relation between the productivity of East African sugar-cane cutters and body size or composition variables. This was explained by poor motivation and chronic health problems, particularly parasitic infections. In a Third World industrial context, Satyanarayana *et al.* (1977) found a positive relation between weight, height and LBM and productivity in low-intensity work. After removing the effects of height, the advantage of bigger workers persisted.

In many occupations even where the work is physically heavy, skill may be more important than size. In Sweden, wood cutters with high productivity did not differ from average-output workers in height, weight, limb circumferences or muscle strength. The only difference was in aerobic capacity, so that a given task was less demanding, and they were more efficient, in terms of wood cut per unit of energy expenditure (Hansson, 1965).

Findings and applications

Anthropometric indices may explain significant amounts of the variance in some types of performance and work capacity in groups of individuals. However, even with adjustment for body size, age and sex, large individual differences are observed. Why is size not as important as might be expected? All performance variables are multifactorial in origin, and determinism is to be avoided. Why do the facts not fit the dimensional theory? Work capacity and strength should be proportional to L^2, but this is not so in children or adults (Asmussen, 1973; Astrand & Rodahl, 1977; Shephard, 1988). Dimensional analysis of the body assumes a cubic relation between length and volume (that is, the body is a sphere or series of spheres), whereas it is better described as a series of truncated cones. Such analysis further assumes that bodies are of similar densities. These assumptions of geometric and compositional similarity may not be correct. Biological adaptation, training, psychology and maturation may operate to alter the simple relations. Power and ratio scaling may have a place in comparing different species but there are usually more suitable approaches for human children and adults.

There are a number of other possible explanations for the mis-match of strength and size and changes in strength and size. Improved motor unit recruitment may play a role in strength gain without hypertrophy or in the supernormal strength shown by children or small adults lifting, for example, cars off accident victims. The normal inhibitory impulses that prevent muscles exerting forces that would damage bones and tendons may themselves be inhibited. More muscle fibres may be recruited or firing of nerves better synchronized to facilitate contraction. Thus, neural and psychological factors can influence strength and its measurement. However, in well-motivated subjects, the maximum voluntary isometric force produced is not different from that elicited by supramaximal stimulation (Maughan, 1986). Shephard (1988) considers that tests of muscle strength have yielded little more information about work capacity that that provided by a determination of body weight. Other reasons for the poor correlations of strength and CSA could be the high day-to-day variability (10–20%) in tests of muscle strength (Astrand & Rodahl, 1977).

Which indices of size or composition should be used? The answer will depend on the types of performance and the resources available. For example, for limb strength, muscle CSA or volume by serial computed tomography would be ideal, but a good enough estimate can usually be obtained by anthropometry with corrections for the subcutaneous adipose tissue and bone volume and the non-circularity of the limb (Heymsfield *et al.*, 1982).

What is probably as important as the choice of index is the method of standardization. Ratio and exponent scores, as per kilogram weight, per kilogram LBM or per kilogram$^{0.75}$ have been used widely in the study of energetics. To adjust a score for sizes differences, e.g. weight, LBM, CSA, muscle mass or limb volume, by dividing to give a per kilogram weight, etc. score is fallacious and may be misleading (Tanner, 1949; Katch, 1972). It cannot be assumed that weight has been allowed for and that the new score is independent of weight. The use of a ratio adjustment assumes a direct proportionality, $Y = kX$, between the two variables (which rarely exists), i.e. that the line that best fits the data passes through the origin and implies a correlation of $r = 1$. Instead, performance and size variables usually covary according to $Y = a + bX$, where b is the regression coefficient of performance on size. Usually, the intercept term, a, is positive and significantly different from zero with the effect that V_{O_2} kg^{-1} is negatively associated with weight (bigger individuals appear to perform less well than expected and smaller individuals better than expected).

In correlational analysis, the ratio standard may produce spurious correlations. Kleiber (1950) has argued for the use of ratio standards such as V_{O_2} kg^{-1} as being inherently meaningful biologically, and that if a theoretical regression equation does not fit the data as well as an empirical regression equation it would still be preferable scientifically to use the theoretical curve. This rests on the assumption that animals and individuals are comparable geometrically and of similar composition. As the ratio approach is simple and clear, it has been most widely and misleadingly used.

The recommended procedures for adjusting performance variables for size and composition differences are also simple but are not often performed. Firstly, Tanner (1964) has used bivariate plots to illustrate regional differences in muscular development and skeletal dimensions and proportions in Olympic athletes. Alternatively, to allow for the effects of weight in correlation analysis, partial correlations can be used. Thirdly, in some circumstances, logarithmic or power standards can be used (Katch, 1973; Davies, Cole & Lucas, 1989). Finally, individual size adjusted scores can be easily obtained from

$$\hat{Y} = Y - b(X - \bar{X}),$$

where $\hat{Y}$ is the adjusted performance score, Y is the observed score, b is the regression coefficient of Y on X, X is the individual size score, and $\bar{X}$ is the group mean size score. The procedure is described by Katch & Katch (1974). This requires moderately large samples but results in the most valid adjustment. It can be used for standardization to a reference size or weight. In men, these might be height 1.7 m, weight 65 kg, FFM 60 kg; in women, 1.55 m, 55 kg and 45 kg, respectively.

The value of removing the variance in performance due to size can be in highlighting the role of other factors and in that way furthering understanding of the processes involved. For example, standardizing for size differences has allowed the effects of physical activity on V_{O_2max} and ventilatory capacity to be illustrated (Cotes, Reed & Mortimore, 1982).

Estimation of performance and selection of workers on the basis of size is widely used in many parts of the world, but it is inexact on an individual basis. Although anthropometry goes some way towards explaining inter-individual variation, there will always be group anomalies. In many countries the small rural children outperform their larger urban counter-parts. Size differences can be outweighed by other factors such as activity or fitness differences.

References

American College of Sports Medicine (1990). The recommended quantity and quality of exercise for developing and maintaining cardiorespiratory and muscular fitness in healthy adults. *Medicine and Science in Exercise and Sports* **22**, 265–274.

Asmussen, E. (1973). Growth in muscular strength and power. In: *Physical Activity: Human Growth and Development*, ed. G. L. Rarick, pp. 60–79. New York: Academic Press.

Astrand, P.-O. & Rodahl, K. (1977). *Textbook of Work Physiology*. 2nd edition. New York: McGraw Hill.

Bailey, D.A., Malina, R. M. & Mirwald, R. L. (1986). Physical activity and growth of the child. In: *Human Growth*, vol. 2, 2nd edition, ed. F. Falkner & J. M. Tanner, pp. 147–70. New York: Plenum Press.

Beall, C. M. & Goldstein, M. C. (1988). Sociocultural influences on the working capacity of elderly Nepali men. In: *Capacity for Work in the Tropics*, ed. K. J. Collins & D. F. Roberts, pp. 215–26. Cambridge University Press.

Binkhorst, R. A., Vant Hof, M. A., Saris, W. H. M. & Noordeloos, A. (1985). Max-O_2 reference values for children in relation to body mass. In: *Children and Exercise XI*, ed. R. A. Binkhorst, H. C. G. Kemper & W. H. M. Saris, pp. 170–4. Champaign, Illinois: Human Kinetics Publishers.

Caiozzo, V. J. & Kyle, C. R. (1980). The effect of external loading upon power output in stair climbing. *European Journal of Applied Physiology* **44**, 217–22.

Cameron, N., Mirwald, R. L. & Bailey, D. A. (1980). Standards for the assessment of normal absolute maximal aerobic power. In: *Kinanthropometry*, vol. 2, ed. M. Ostyn, G. Beunen & J. Simon, pp. 349–59. Baltimore: University Park Press.

Cotes, J. E., Reed, J. W. & Mortimore, I. L. (1982). Determinants of capacity for physical work. In: *Energy and Effort*, ed. G. A. Harrison, pp. 39–64. London: Taylor & Francis.

Cureton, K., Bishop, P., Hutchinson, P., Newland, H., Vickery, S. & Zwiren, L. (1986). Sex difference in maximal oxygen uptake; effect of equating haemoglobin concentration. *European Journal of Applied Physiology* **54**, 656–60.

Davies, C. T. M. (1971). Human power output in exercise of short duration in relation to body size and composition. *Ergonomics* **14**, 245–56.

Davies, C. T. M. (1972). Maximum aerobic power in relation to body composition in healthy, sedentary adults. *Human Biology* **44**, 127–39.

Davies, C. T. M. (1973). The relationship of maximum aerobic power output to productivity and absenteeism of East African sugar cane workers. *British Journal of Industrial Medicine* **30**, 146–54.

Davies, C. T. M., Barnes, C., Fox, R. H., Ojikutu, R. O. & Samueloff, A. S. (1972a) Ethnic differences in physical working capacity. *Journal of Applied Physiology* **23**, 726–32.

Davies, C. T. M., Barnes, C. & Godfrey, S. (1972b). Body composition and maximum exercise performance in children. *Human Biology* **44**, 195–214.

Davies, C. T. M., Mbelwa, D., Crockford, G. & Weiner, J. S. (1973). Exercise tolerance and body composition in male and female Africans age 18–30 years. *Human Biology* **45**, 31–40.

Davies, C. T. M. & Van Haaren, J. P. M. (1973). Maximal aerobic power and body composition in healthy East African older male and female subjects. *American Journal of Physical Anthropology* **39**, 395–401.

Davies, P. S. W., Cole, T. J. & Lucas, A. (1989). Adjusting energy expenditure for body weight in early infancy. *European Journal of Clinical Nutrition* **43**, 641–45.

Faulkner, J. A. & White, T. P. (1990). Adaptations of skeletal muscle to physical activity. In: *Exercise, Fitness and Health: a consensus of current knowledge*, ed. C. Bouchard, R. J. Shephard, T. Stephens, J. R. Sutton, & B. D. McPherson, pp. 265–79. Champaign, Illinois: Human Kinetics Books.

Gould, S. J. (1984). *The Mismeasure of Man*. London: Penguin Books.

Hansson, J. E. (1965). The relationship between individual characteristics of the worker and output of work in logging operations. *Studia Forestalia Svegica* **29**, 68–77.

Heymsfield, S. B., McManus, C., Smith, J., Stevens, V. & Nixon, D. W. (1982). Anthropometric measurement of muscle mass: revised equations for calculating bone-free arm muscle area. *American Journal of Clinical Nutrition* **36**, 680–90.

Ikai, M. & Fukunaga, T. (1968). Calculation of muscle strength per unit cross-sectional area of human muscle by means of ultrasonic measurement. *Internationale Zeitschrift für angewande Physiologie einschlieblich Arbeitsphysiologie* **26**, 26–32.

Katch, V. (1972). Correlational v ratio adjustments of body weight in exercise-oxygen studies. *Ergonomics* **15**, 671–80.

Katch, V. L. (1973). Use of the oxygen/body weight ratio in correlational analyses: spurious correlations and statistical considerations. *Medicine and Science in Sports* **5**, 253–7.

Katch, V. L. & Katch, F. I. (1974). Use of weight-adjusted oxygen uptake scores that avoid spurious correlations. *Research Quarterly* **45**, 447–51.

Kemper, H. C. G. (1992). Physical development and childhood activity. In: *Physical Activity and Health*, ed. N. G. Norgan, pp. 84–100. Cambridge University Press.

Kemper, H. C. G. & Verschuur, R. (1985). Motor performance fitness tests. In: *Growth, Health and Fitness of Teenagers*, ed. H. C. G. Kemper, pp. 96–106. Basel: Karger.

Kemper, H. C. G. & Verschuur, R. (1987). Longitudinal study of maximal aerobic power in teenagers. *Annals of Human Biology* **14**, 435–44.

Kleiber, M. (1950). Physiological meaning of regression equations. *Journal of Applied Physiology* **2**, 417–23.

Kitagawa, K., Suzuki, M. & Miyashita, M. (1980). Anaerobic power output of young obese men: comparison of non-obese men and the role of excess fat. *European Journal of Applied Physiology* **43**, 229–34.

Krahenbuhl, G. S., Skinner, G. S. & Kohrt, W. M. (1985). Developmental aspects of maximal aerobic power in children. *Exercise and Sports Science Reviews* **13**, 503–38.

Malina, R. M. (1975). Anthropometric correlates of strength and motor performance. *Exercise and Sports Science Reviews* **3**, 249–74.

Malina, R. M. (1986). Growth of muscle tissue and muscle mass. In: *Human Growth*, Vol. 2, 2nd edition, ed. F. Falkner & J. M. Tanner, pp. 77–99. New York: Plenum Press.

Malina, R. M. & Bouchard, C. (1991). *Growth, Maturation and Physical Activity*. Champaign, Illinois: Human Kinetics Books.

Maughan, R. J. (1986). Muscle structure and strength in man. In: *Kinanthropometry*, vol. 3, ed. T. Reilly, J. Watkins & J. Borms, London; E & F N Spon.

Maughan, R. J., Watson, J. S. & Weir, J. (1983a). Strength and cross-sectional area of human skeletal muscle. *Journal of Physiology* **338**, 37–49.

Maughan, R. J., Watson, J. S. & Weir, J. (1983b). Relationship between muscle strength and muscle cross-sectional area in male sprinters and endurance runners. *European Journal of Applied Physiology* **50**, 309–18.

Parker, D. F., Round, J. M., Sacco, P. & Jones, D. A. (1990). A cross-sectional survey of upper and lower limb strength in boys and girls during adolescence. *Annals of Human Biology* **17**, 199–211.

Pheasant, S. (1986). *Bodyspace: anthropometry, ergonomics and design*. London: Taylor & Francis.

Satyanarayana, K., Naidu, A. N., Chatterjee, B. & Rao, B. S. N. (1977). Body size and work output. *American Journal of Clinical Nutrition* **30**, 322–5.

Schantz, P., Randall-Fox, E., Hutchinson, W., Tyden, A. & Astrand, P.-O. (1983). Muscle fibre type distribution, muscle cross-sectional area and maximal voluntary strength in humans. *Acta Physiologica Scandinavica* **117**, 219–26.

Shephard, R. J. (1978). *Human Physiological Work Capacity*. Cambridge University Press.

Shephard, R. J. (1988). Work capacity: methodology in a tropical environment. In: *Capacity for Work in the Tropics*, ed. K. J. Collins & D. F. Roberts, pp. 1–30. Cambridge University Press.

Sparling, P. D. (1980). A meta-analysis of studies comparing maximal oxygen uptake in men and women. *Research Quarterly in Exercise and Sport* **51**, 542–52.

Sparling, P. D. & Cureton, K. J. (1983). Biological determinants of the sex difference in 12-min run performance. *Medicine and Science in Sports and Exercise* **15**, 218–23.

Spurr, G. B., Barac-Nieto, M. & Maksud, M. G. (1977). Productivity and maximal oxygen consumption in sugar cane cutters. *American Journal of Clinical Nutrition* **30**, 316–21.

Tanner, J. M. (1949). Fallacy of per-weight and per-surface area standards, and their relation to spurious correlation. *Journal of Applied Physiology* **2**, 1–15.

Tanner, J. M. (1962). *Growth at Adolescence.* 2nd edition. Oxford: Blackwell Scientific Publications.

Tanner, J. M. (1964). *The Physique of the Olympic Athlete.* London: George Allen & Unwin.

Wells, C. L. (1985). *Women, Sport and Performance.* Champaign, Illinois: Human Kinetics Publishers, Inc.

Wilmore, J. H. (1974). Alterations in strength, body composition and anthropometric measurements consequent to a 10-week weight training program. *Medicine and Science in Sports* **6**, 133–8.

11 *Anthropometry, strength and motor fitness*

ROBERT M. MALINA

Introduction

Body size, proportions, physique and composition are factors which influence physical fitness. Historically, stature and weight, both indicators of overall body size, have been used extensively with age and sex in efforts to identify some optimum combination of these variables for classifying children, youth and young adults in a variety of physical activities. Skinfold thicknesses are routinely used to estimate body composition, and are now included in physical fitness test batteries. Body size, specifically body weight, is the standard frame of reference for expressing physiological parameters, such as $\dot{V}_{O_2max}$. Hence, anthropometry is central to the study of physical fitness in the general population and in special populations, including elite athletes and those chronically stressed by undernutrition.

The present chapter considers the anthropometric correlates of physical fitness, and builds upon an earlier review (Malina, 1975). It is limited largely to samples of well-nourished children and youth, but also considers related data for disadvantaged and undernourished samples. Fatness as a factor affecting fitness is considered separately, as is the possibility of an optimal body size for physical fitness and performance.

Fitness and performance

Performance is viewed in the context of standardized strength and motor tasks, which were historically defined as the components of physical fitness. More recently, however, the definition of fitness has taken a health-related perspective, in which fitness is operationalized as cardiorespiratory endurance, abdominal muscular strength and endurance, lower back flexibility, and fatness (Malina, 1991). Hence, the terms health-related fitness and motor fitness are used. The concept of fitness continues to evolve as apparent in the morphological, muscular, motor, cardiorespiratory and metabolic components of physical and physiological fitness offered by Bouchard & Shephard (1993).

160

Guidelines and limitations
Basic statistics in studies relating anthropometry to performance and fitness are zero-order and partial correlation coefficients. The following are offered as a guide in interpreting correlations: below 0.30, low; 0.30 to 0.60, moderate; 0.60 to 0.85, moderately high; over 0.85, high. The statistical significance of correlation coefficients is to a large extent related to sample size and the range of the two variables being correlated. This is especially apparent in studies reporting low, significant correlations in large samples. On the other hand, the biological or functional significance of the apparent relation or lack of relation also needs consideration. In addition to correlational analyses, several multivariate approaches to anthropometry and performance are considered.

Body size and fitness-related performance
Correlational analyses
Correlations between stature and weight and performance on a variety of motor tasks are generally low to moderate in children and youths 4–18 years of age (Table 11.1) and are of limited predictive utility. Correlations do not differ by sex, race or socioeconomic status. Items in which the body is projected (dashes and jumps) show, but not consistently, negative correlations with body weight. Items in which the body is raised (pull-ups) or supported (flexed arm hang) off the ground by the arms show consistently negative correlations with body weight, some of which reach into the moderate range. In contrast, correlations of stature and weight with a variety of strength tasks are higher than those for motor fitness and generally fall in the moderate range (Table 11.2). Thus, the taller and heavier individual tends to be stronger. As for motor fitness, correlations do not differ by sex, race or socioeconomic status.

Correlational studies in young adult males and females, usually college students, yield results similar to those observed in children and youths. Stature and weight are, in general, poorly related to motor fitness and moderately related to several strength tests. The latter correlations range from +0.27 to +0.66 (Malina, 1975).

Given the association among age, stature and weight, second-order partial correlations between body size and performance in children aged 4–11 years are summarized in Table 11.3. Correlations do not differ between boys and girls or among children of different racial, socioeconomic and nutritional backgrounds. The partial correlations are variable, but several trends are apparent. Although not shown in the table, age is positively related to strength and motor fitness even

Table 11.1. *Zero order correlations between stature and weight and motor fitness in children and youth 4–18 years of age*

Merrett (1992): sexes combined except as indicated

	4 years		5 years	
	Stature	Weight	Stature	Weight
20 yard dash[1]	−0.28	−0.56	0.45	0.28
standing long jump	0.09	0.00	0.33	0.13
scramble (agility)[1]	−0.34	−0.48	0.16	0.22
static balance	−0.13	−0.18	0.38	0.15
distance throw				
boys	0.46	0.44	0.17	−0.04
girls	−0.01	0.04	0.34	−0.18

Seils (1951)

	Boys 7.6 ± 0.5 years		Girls 7.5 ± 0.4 years	
	Stature	Weight	Stature	Weight
40 yard dash[1]	0.06	−0.08	0.05	−0.06
standing long jump	0.13	−0.06	−0.21	−0.27
sidestepping (agility)	−0.10	−0.02	−0.23	−0.13
static balance	−0.03	−0.07	−0.05	−0.06
distance throw	0.02	−0.11	−0.03	−0.00

Rarick & Oyster (1964)

	Boys 8.3 ± 0.7 years	
	Stature	Weight
30 yard dash[1]	0.19	0.07
standing long jump	0.26	0.08
throwing velocity	0.49	0.35

Rocha Ferreira *et al.* (1991): 8-year-old Brazilian children, low socioeconomic status

	Boys		Girls	
	Stature	Weight	Stature	Weight
50 m dash[1]	0.21	0.12	0.14	−0.03
standing long jump	0.03	−0.01	0.12	−0.09
shuttle run[1] (agility)	0.20	0.09	0.31	0.13
distance run (9 min)	0.11	−0.06	0.02	−0.24

(*Continued*)

when stature and weight are controlled, which emphasizes the role of neuromuscular maturation and experience in the performance of strength and motor tasks. On the other hand, after controlling for age and stature, body weight tends to have a negative influence on performance,

Table 11.1 (*cont.*)

R. M. Malina (unpublished data): ranges of age-specific correlations for American Black and White children 6–11 years of age

	Boys		Girls	
	Stature	Weight	Stature	Weight
35 yard dash[1]	−0.33 to 0.34	−0.56 to 0.21	−0.28 to 0.60	−0.32 to 0.68
standing long jump	−0.27 to 0.41	−0.39 to 0.39	−0.12 to 0.57	−0.34 to 0.41
distance throw	0.03 to 0.49	−0.03 to 0.46	−0.15 to 0.52	−0.11 to 0.60

Espenschade (1963): ranges of age-specific correlations for children 10–17 years of age

	Boys		Girls	
	Stature	Weight	Stature	Weight
50 yard dash[2]	−0.35 to 0.18	−0.14 to 0.30	−0.13 to 0.02	0.04 to 0.24
standing long jump	0.04 to 0.34	−0.13 to 0.14	0.05 to 0.22	−0.03 to −0.22
distance throw	0.02 to 0.44	0.04 to 0.31	0.04 to 0.31	0.02 to 0.29
pull-up	−0.24 to 0.01	−0.35 to −0.10		
knee push-up			−0.22 to 0.00	−0.22 to −0.03
sit-up	−0.04 to 0.06	−0.13 to −0.05	−0.09 to 0.07	−0.18 to 0.10

Montoye *et al.* (1972): ranges of age-specific correlations for children 9–18 years of age

	Boys		Girls	
	Stature	Weight	Stature	Weight
50 yard dash[2]	−0.41 to 0.01	−0.11 to 0.26	−0.26 to 0.08	0.09 to 0.45
standing long jump	−0.02 to 0.42	−0.30 to 0.22	−0.02 to 0.34	−0.35 to 0.02
shuttle run[2]	−0.31 to 0.10	−0.08 to 0.37	−0.20 to 0.07	−0.04 to 0.40
600 yard run[2]	−0.36 to 0.12	−0.04 to 0.46	−0.11 to 0.10	0.23 to 0.52
softball throw	0.19 to 0.45	0.05 to 0.36	−0.05 to 0.38	−0.05 to 0.31
pull-ups	−0.34 to 0.04	−0.50 to −0.15	—	—
flexed arm hang	—	—	−0.26 to 0.08	−0.47 to −0.35
sit-ups	−0.09 to 0.23	−0.30 to 0.02	−0.18 to 0.04	−0.33 to −0.08
trunk flexion flexibility	−0.17 to 0.11	−0.09 to 0.18	−0.11 to 0.05	−0.19 to 0.03

[1]Signs for timed running events have been inverted because the lower time is the better performance.
[2]It is not certain in these studies whether the signs for timed running events have been inverted. They are reported as in the specific reports.

especially in those tasks in which the body is projected, while after controlling for age and body weight, correlations between stature and performance tend to be positive.

Data on the relation between other anthropometric dimensions (except skinfold thicknesses; see below) are extremely limited, and the

Table 11.2. *Zero order correlations between stature and weight and static strength in children 4–11 years of age*

Gabbard & Patterson (1980): sexes combined, ages 3–5 years

	Stature	Weight
right and left grip	−0.38 to 0.15	−0.34 to 0.33

Merrett (1992): sexes combined, ages 4–5 years

	Stature	Weight
right and left grip	0.12 to 0.46	0.05 to 0.29

Rarick & Oyster (1964): boys aged 8.3 ± 0.7 years

	Stature	Weight
wrist flexion	0.68	0.63
elbow flexion	0.74	0.71
shoulder medial rotation	0.40	0.43
shoulder adduction	0.53	0.54
ankle extension	0.72	0.73
knee extension	0.73	0.67
hip flexion	0.53	0.48
hip extension	0.66	0.61

Rocha Ferreira *et al.* (1991): 8-year-old Brazilian children, low socioeconomic status

	Boys		Girls	
	Stature	Weight	Stature	Weight
grip	0.47	0.48	0.52	0.31

R. M. Malina (unpublished data): ranges of age-specific correlations for American Black and White children 6–11 years of age

	Boys		Girls	
	Stature	Weight	Stature	Weight
right grip	0.26 to 0.76	0.34 to 0.79	0.01 to 0.75	0.16 to 0.77
left grip	0.22 to 0.82	0.24 to 0.91	−0.23 to 0.54	0.06 to 0.76
push	0.03 to 0.67	0.16 to 0.73	−0.01 to 0.72	0.24 to 0.60
pull	−0.10 to 0.53	0.17 to 0.73	0.08 to 0.72	0.15 to 0.77

available correlations are similar to those for stature and weight. For example, correlations between leg length and performance on a variety of motor tasks range from −0.10 to +0.39 for individuals 6 years through college age (Malina, 1975). These values are similar to those for stature. On the other hand, limb circumferences correlate with strength approximately at the same level as body weight, e.g. +0.46 to +0.62 for forearm

Table 11.3. *Second order partial correlations between motor fitness and body size: stature controlling for age and weight (S.AW) and weight controlling for age and stature (W.AS)*

Merrett (1992): sexes combined except as indicated

	4 years		5 years	
	S.AW	W.AS	S.AW	W.AS
20 yard dash[1]	0.65	−0.76	0.27	−0.08
standing long jump	−0.03	−0.01	0.25	−0.13
scramble (agility)[1]	−0.24	−0.17	−0.07	0.18
static balance	0.05	−0.12	0.49	−0.28
distance throw				
boys	0.03	0.13	0.53	−0.53
girls	−0.52	0.44	0.38	−0.46
right grip strength	0.10	−0.09	0.45	−0.13
left grip strength	0.13	−0.02	0.23	−0.09

Seils (1951)

	Boys 7.6 ± 0.5 years		Girls 7.5 ± 0.4 years	
	S.AW	W.AS	S.AW	W.AS
40 yard dash[1]	−0.04	−0.04	0.16	−0.17
standing long jump	0.16	−0.20	0.15	−0.29
sidestepping (agility)	−0.25	0.07	−0.24	0.08
static balance	−0.01	−0.13	0.03	−0.08
distance throw	0.05	−0.15	−0.10	0.08

Rarick & Oyster (1964): boys aged 8.3 ± 0.7 years

	S.AW	W.AS
30 yard dash[1]	0.12	−0.12
standing long jump	0.30	−0.27
throwing velocity	0.23	−0.14
strength:		
wrist flexion	0.28	0.12
elbow flexion	0.30	0.21
shoulder medial rotation	0.09	0.18
shoulder adduction	0.06	0.19
ankle extension	0.21	0.35
knee extension	0.36	0.11
hip flexion	0.17	0.03
hip extension	0.24	0.11

(*Continued*)

Table 11.3 (*cont.*)

Rocha Ferreira *et al.* (1991): 8-year-old Brazilian children, low socioeconomic status

	Boys		Girls	
	S.AW	W.AS	S.AW	W.AS
50 m dash[1]	0.14	−0.07	0.18	−0.13
standing long jump	0.07	−0.06	0.24	−0.22
shuttle run[1] (agility)	0.19	−0.12	0.28	−0.07
distance run (9 min)	0.27	−0.26	0.24	−0.31
grip strength	0.14	0.19	0.42	−0.03

R. M. Malina (unpublished data): American Black and White children aged 6–11 years

	Boys		Girls	
	S.AW	W.AS	S.AW	W.AS
35 yard dash[1]	0.20	−0.24	0.18	−0.05
standing long jump	0.35	−0.42	0.31	−0.31
distance throw	0.31	−0.09	0.04	0.06
grip strength	0.32	0.29	0.16	0.25
push strength	0.05	0.29	−0.06	0.28
pull strength	0.07	0.30	−0.02	0.29

Malina & Buschang (1985): chronically undernourished indigenous children aged 6–15 years from southern Mexico

	Boys		Girls	
	S.AW	W.AS	S.AW	W.AS
35 yard dash[1]	0.26	−0.19	0.32	−0.17
standing long jump	0.24	−0.04	0.21	0.01
distance throw:				
< 9 years	0.18	0.04	0.35	−0.06
≥ 9 years	0.23	0.24	0.23	0.01
right grip strength	0.13	0.28	0.26	0.30
left grip strength	0.07	0.39	0.22	0.37

[1]Signs for timed running events have been inverted because the lower time is the better performance.

circumference and grip strength and +0.51 to +0.62 for corrected arm circumference and grip strength in boys and girls 6–12 years of age (Malina, 1975). Correlations between grip, elbow flexor and elbow extensor strength and forearm and arm girth range from +0.19 to +0.70 in adult males (Roberts, Provins & Morton, 1959).

Multivariate analyses

Results of stepwise regression with age, stature and weight and performance on a variety of fitness test items not only emphasize the importance
of age and body size, but also indicate variation with sex and performance
task. In children aged 9–18 years, age, stature and weight account for a
similar percentage of variation in trunk flexibility and abdominal strength
in boys and girls (5–18%). However, in the other measures (shoulder
strength (pull-ups for boys, flexed arm hang for girls), standing long
jump, shuttle run, 50 yard dash, softball throw, 600 yard run), age,
stature and weight account for more of the variance in the performances
of boys (33–61%) than of girls (18–36%) (Montoye, Frantz & Kozar,
1972). This would seem to emphasize the need to consider other anthropometric dimensions and perhaps cultural variables in explaining variation in performance, especially in girls.

To examine additional variation in motor fitness and strength that
may be explained by other anthropometric dimensions, multiple regression analyses were used with 4–5-year-old well-nourished children
(Merrett, 1992), 8-year-old Brazilian children of low socioeconomic
status (Rocha Ferreira, 1987), and 6–15-year-old chronically undernourished indigenous schoolchildren in southern Mexico (Malina &
Buschang, 1985). In these analyses, the residuals of several anthropometric dimensions, e.g. segment lengths, skeletal breadths, limb circumferences, and skinfolds, based on the combined effects of age, stature
and weight, were regressed on strength and motor fitness. In the three
samples from different health and nutritional backgrounds, few variables add significantly to describing the remaining variation in strength
and motor performance after age, stature and weight are controlled.
Subcutaneous fatness, however, tends to exert a negative influence on
the performance of adequately nourished, impoverished and undernourished children. It appears, nevertheless, that body size *per se* is the
significant factor influencing the strength and motor fitness of children
at these ages.

In a different approach, 15 anthropometric dimensions were reduced
via principal component analysis, and multiple regression was applied to
the relation between performance and the principal components in
children aged 6–10 years (Malina & Moriyama, 1991). Four principal
components accounted for about 90% of the variance in anthropometric
characteristics. Only two had eigenvalues of 1 or more, the first related to
body mass with an emphasis on subcutaneous fat (66–76% of the
variance) and the second to skeletal length (11–16%). The third and
fourth components, with eigenvalues less than 1, related to skeletal

robustness and relative muscularity (6–9%). It is of interest, however, that the latter two components, which accounted for a relatively small percentage of variation in anthropometric dimensions, with few exceptions, accounted for a greater percentage of the variance in four measures of static strength and a ball throw for distance (a measure of power and coordination). The first two components, which accounted for the majority of variance in anthropometric dimensions, accounted for more of the variance in a dash and jump, both events in which the body must be moved through space.

Although anthropometric dimensions account for a substantial portion of variation in performance, a considerable amount is not accounted for by the dimensions included in the analyses. This suggests that other variables (morphological, maturational and social), should be included in such analyses. For example, among boys 8–11 years old, age, stature and weight accounted for 10–44% of the variance in performance on a youth fitness test: pull-ups, sit-ups, shuttle run, standing long jump, 50 yard dash, softball throw, 600 yard run (Cureton, Boileau & Lohman, 1975). When body composition measures (body density, potassium concentration, skinfolds) were added, the percentage of variation accounted for increased significantly in all test items except sit-ups.

Since strength and motor fitness are influenced by motivational and other factors in the cultural environment, it is appropriate to include such variables in multivariate analyses, particularly in the context of examining sex differences in performance and fitness. For example, among 5-year-old children, only anthropometric variables predict the throwing performance of boys, while a combination of anthropometric and family environmental variables predict throwing performance of girls (Nelson *et al.*, 1986).

Fatness and fitness
Fatness per se
There is much concern about the relative fatness and unfitness of children and youths; fatness generally exerts a negative influence upon fitness. Correlations between fatness, most often measured as skinfold thicknesses, and motor fitness are consistently negative and low to moderate during childhood (Table 11.4) and adolescence (Table 11.5). The negative relation is more apparent in those events requiring the projection (jumps), rapid movement (dashes, shuttle runs) and lifting (leg lifts) of the body and the support of the body off the ground (flexed arm hang). Subcutaneous fatness is also negatively related to cardiorespiratory fitness as reflected in the pulse rate recovery to a standard step test.

Table 11.4. *Ranges of age-specific correlations between triceps, subscapular and mid-axillary skinfold thicknesses and performance in American Black and White children aged 6–11 years*

	Boys	Girls
35 yard dash[1]	−0.56 to 0.13	−0.39 to 0.31
standing long jump	−0.58 to −0.05	−0.61 to −0.14
distance throw	−0.35 to 0.19	−0.60 to 0.30
right grip strength	−0.03 to 0.60	−0.06 to 0.85
left grip strength	−0.12 to 0.57	−0.21 to 0.72
push strength	0.00 to 0.58	−0.18 to 0.45
pull strength	−0.02 to 0.58	−0.14 to 0.56

Source: R. M. Malina, unpublished data.
[1]Signs for timed running events have been inverted because the lower time is the better performance.

Table 11.5. *Ranges of age-specific correlations between the sum of four skinfolds and motor fitness tests in Belgian males aged 12–20 years*

Test (fitness factor)	*r*	Partial *r* controlling for stature and weight
stick balance (eye-hand coordination)	0.00 to −0.07	0.00 to −0.07
plate tapping (speed of limb movement)	0.00 to −0.06	0.00 to −0.11
sit and reach (flexibility)	0.00 to −0.13	−0.15 to −0.25
vertical jump (explosive strength)	−0.18 to −0.37	−0.28 to −0.40
arm pull (static strength)	0.00 to 0.21	−0.28 to −0.40
bent arm hang (functional strength)	−0.28 to −0.44	−0.13 to −0.30
leg lifts (trunk strength)	0.00 to −0.26	−0.17 to −0.33
shuttle run (running speed)	0.00 to −0.27	−0.18 to −0.32
pulse rate after exercise (pulse recovery)	0.00 to −0.28	0.00 to −0.21

Source: Adapted from Beunen *et al.* (1983).

On the other hand, skinfold thicknesses are essentially unrelated or positively related to performance tasks involving projection or balance of an object (distance throw, stick balance), speed of arm movement (plate tapping), and flexibility of the lower back (sit and reach). In the case of the ball throw for distance, the positive correlation reflects the larger size of fatter children (Malina, Skrabanek & Little, 1989). Although data are less extensive, correlations of similar magnitude are apparent when estimates of total body fat mass or relative fatness are used (Malina, 1992).

In an analysis of health-related fitness tests in children 6–16 years of age, the sum of the triceps and subscapular skinfolds (a component of the health-related fitness test) is inversely related to distance run and sit-up ($r = 0.11$ to -0.18) performance and is not related to the sit and reach test (r -0.00 and $+0.05$). Given the low correlations, the amount of variance accounted for is small (Pate, Slentz & Katz, 1989). The relation between skinfolds and the distance run and sit-ups in this sample is linear in girls and curvilinear in boys; thus, the fattest boys perform disproportionately worse than the leanest boys.

Similar trends are apparent among college males, i.e. the correlations between skinfold thicknesses and performance on a variety of tasks are negative and low to moderate, -0.58 to -0.26 (Kireilis & Cureton, 1947; Clarke, 1957). The influence of fatness on physical fitness of college men, based on scaled scores for seven items of motor and health-related fitness (50 m dash, shuttle run, standing long jump, 1000 m run, pull-ups, sit-ups, and sit and reach) is shown in Fig. 11.1. Fitness scores decrease linearly with an increase in fatness (Welon, Jurynec & Sliwa, 1988), which contrasts with the curvilinear relation suggested for the distance run and sit-ups in boys 6–16 years old (Pate *et al.*, 1989).

In contrast to motor fitness items, correlations between skinfold thicknesses and measures of static strength are generally positive (Tables 11.4 and 11.5). The positive relation reflects the larger body size of fatter children (Malina *et al.*, 1989; Beunen *et al.*, 1982) when stature and weight are controlled in adolescent males, correlations between arm pull strength and fatness are negative (Table 11.5).

Extremes of fatness or leanness

It is at the extremes of fatness that its negative consequences on physical performance and fitness are most apparent. This is shown in Fig. 11.2, which compares the motor fitness scores of the fattest 5% and leanest 5% of boys in each age group based upon the sum of four skinfolds (Beunen *et al.*, 1983). With the exception of static strength (arm pull), speed of arm movement (plate tapping) and the stick balance, the fattest boys attain, on average, significantly poorer results on motor fitness (shuttle run, vertical jump) and health-related fitness (sit and reach, flexibility; leg lifts, abdominal strength; flexed arm hang, muscular endurance; and pulse recovery after a one-minute step test, cardiorespiratory endurance).

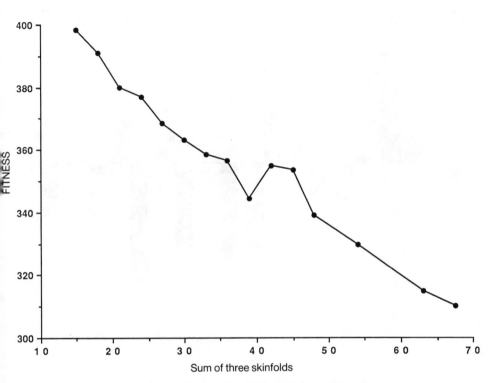

Fig. 11.1. Dependence of physical fitness (composite score based on seven tests, see text) on subcutaneous fatness (sum of three skinfold thicknesses) in young adult males (redrawn after Welon *et al.*, 1988).

Relative fat distribution

There is also the possibility that relative fat distribution is a significant factor related to physical performance and fitness. Among boys 8–11 years old, those with relatively more subcutaneous fat on the trunk (upper quartile of the distribution of the T/E ratio, the ratio of the sum of two trunk skinfolds [subscapular and midaxillary] to the sum of two extremity skinfolds [triceps and medial calf]) are not only heavier and fatter, but do not perform as well in running, jumping and throwing tasks as do boys with relatively less trunk fat (Malina & Pena Reyes, 1993). The two groups do not differ in muscular strength. When strength and motor fitness are expressed per unit body weight, thus allowing for the size differences between the groups, performance differences between boys in the upper and lower quartiles of the T/E ratio are more apparent. These results thus suggest that more centrally distributed subcutaneous

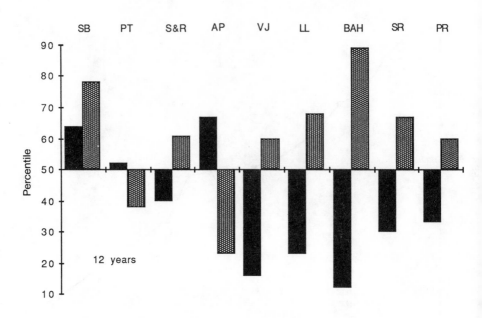

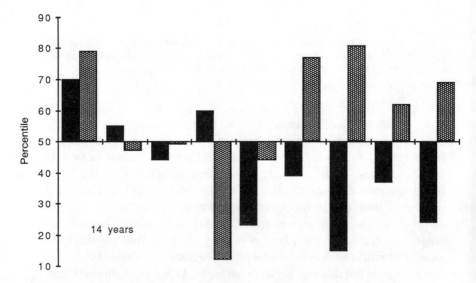

Fig. 11.2. Motor fitness of the fattest 5% and the leanest 5% of Belgian boys at 12, 14, 16 and 18 years of age plotted relative to Belgian reference data. SB, stick balance; PT, plate tapping; S&R, sit and reach; AP, arm pull; VJ, vertical jump; LL, leg lifts; BAH, bent arm hang; SR, shuttle run; PR, pulse recovery (redrawn from Beunen *et al.*, 1983).

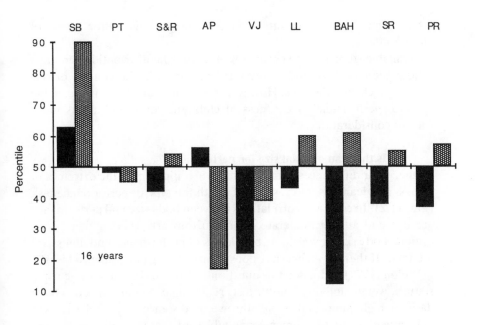

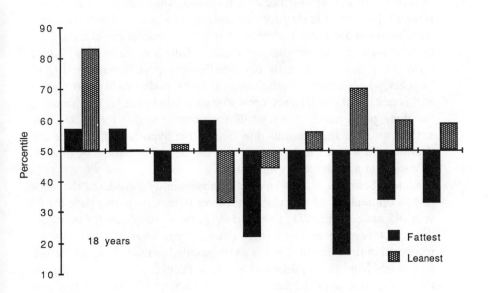

Fig. 11.2 (*cont.*)

fat may have a negative effect on the strength and motor fitness of children.

Available studies of the correlates of relative fat distribution generally follow adult models, addressing fat distribution in the context of risk factors for chronic diseases. However, functional correlates, if any, in the physical performance and fitness of children, youth and adults merit further consideration.

Is there an optimal size for performance?

Rather clear differences in motor fitness are apparent at the extremes of fatness and leanness, but results vary with the type of performance task (Fig. 11.2). In contrast, correlations between body size and performance are low and at best moderate. One can thus ask whether there is an optimal body size at which the best levels of performance and fitness are attained. If there is such a size, does it vary among performance tasks?

Welon (1979) addressed this question in boys 10–18 years of age using stature, weight and three motor tests requiring power and speed: a 60 m dash, a high jump and a ball throw for distance. Optimal size was determined from two-dimensional tables of stature and weight, i.e. stature and weight at which best performance was attained. Age-for-age from 10–18 years, the statures and weights at which best performances were attained are taller and heavier than the general population. The optimal statures and weights are rather similar for the run and jump; however, both are larger in the distance throw, especially between 10 and 14 years, which emphasizes the role of absolute body size in performance of this task. At the older ages, optimal statures do not differ much among the three performance tasks, while the optimal weight for throwing is slightly greater. These results thus suggest the hypothesis that there are statures and weights that are optimal for the performances of boys in running, jumping and throwing tasks.

Welon, Sekita & Sławinska (1981) subsequently considered the stability of optimal sizes for performance over time. Comparing data for 17 year old males from 1951, 1966 and 1978, the optimal size for performance in three power tasks (high jump, long jump and ball throw) increased in the same magnitude as the secular increase in mean stature and weight from 1951 and 1966 (Fig. 11.3). From 1966 to 1978, however, the optimal size for performance remained stable, while mean stature and weight continued to increase. These observations would seem to suggest that optimal size for performance in these speed and power tasks are more related to functional requirements of the tasks without regard to

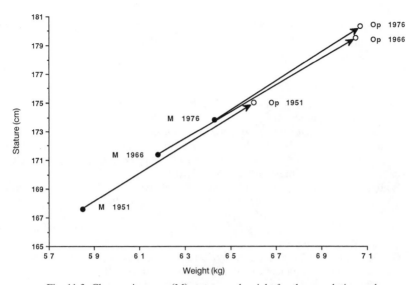

Fig. 11.3. Changes in mean (M) stature and weight for the population and optimal (Op) stature and weight for performance in 17-year-old Polish males in 1951, 1966 and 1978 (redrawn after Welon (1979) and Welon *et al.* (1981)).

body size. In contrast to these observations for 17-year-old males, the increase in optimal size for performance in the same tasks from 1951 to 1966 in 14-year-old boys was considerably greater than the secular increase in mean stature and weight (Welon, 1979). More recent data for 14-year-old boys were not available.

The differences in secular gains in optimal size for performance and mean size in 14- and 17-year-old males from 1951 to 1966 perhaps reflect maturity-associated variation during male adolescence. The optimal size is perhaps attained by early-maturing 14-year-old boys, who are generally better performers and who are larger than their age peers (Malina & Bouchard, 1991). However, at 17 years of age, there is some catch-up by average and late-maturing boys.

It would be interesting to extend the concept of optimal size for performance to females, specifically adolescents in whom performances tend to plateau. The concept merits application to different fitness test batteries because some have called for tests that are not influenced by body size and maturity status, and to chronically nutritionally stressed populations who are characterized by reduced body size.

The observations of Welon (1979) also permit, to some extent, a functional interpretation of secular changes in body size. Secular increases in performance are rather proportional to increases in body size, but not all populations show secular improvements in performance in conjunction with increases in size (Malina, 1978).

References

Beunen, G., Malina, R. M., Ostyn, M., Renson, R., Simons, J. & Van Gerven, D. (1982). Fatness and skeletal maturity of Belgian boys 12 through 17 years of age. *American Journal of Physical Anthropology* **59**, 387–92.

Beunen, G., Malina, R. M., Ostyn, M., Renson, R., Simons, J. & Van Gerven, D. (1983). Fatness, growth and motor fitness of Belgian boys 12 through 20 years of age. *Human Biology* **55**, 599–613.

Bouchard, C. & Shephard, R. J. (1993). Physical activity, fitness and health: A model and key concepts. In: *Proceedings of the International Consensus Symposium on Physical Activity, Fitness and Health, 1992*, ed. C. Bouchard, R. J. Shephard & T. Stephens, Champaign, Illinois: Human Kinetics Publishers. (In press.)

Clarke, H. H. (1957). Relationship of strength and anthropometric measures to physical performances involving the trunk and legs. *Research Quarterly* **28**, 223–33.

Cureton, K. J., Boileau, R. A. & Lohman, T. G. (1975). Relationship between body composition measures and AAHPER test performances in young boys. *Research Quarterly* **46**, 218–29.

Espenschade, A. S. (1963). Restudy of relationships between physical performances of school children and age, height, and weight. *Research Quarterly* **34**, 144–53.

Gabbard, C. P. & Patterson, P. E. (1980). Relationship and comparison of selected anthropometric measures to muscular endurance and strength in children aged 3–5 years. *Annals of Human Biology* **7**, 583–6.

Kireilis, R. W. & Cureton, T. K. (1947). The relationships of external fat to physical education activities and fitness tests. *Research Quarterly* **18**, 123–34.

Malina, R. M. (1975). Anthropometric correlates of strength and motor performance. *Exercise and Sport Sciences Reviews* **3**, 249–74.

Malina, R. M. (1978). Secular changes in growth, maturation, and physical performance. *Exercise and Sport Sciences Reviews* **6**, 203–55.

Malina, R. M. (1991). Fitness and performance: Adult health and the culture of youth. In: *New Possibilities, New Paradigms?* (American Academy of Physical Education Papers No. 24), ed. R. J. Park & H. M. Eckert, pp. 30–8. Champaign, Illinois: Human Kinetics Publishers.

Malina, R. M. (1992). Physique and body composition: Effects on performance and effects of training, semistarvation, and overtraining. In: *Eating, Body Weight and Performance in Athletes: Disorders of Modern Society*, ed. K. D. Brownell, J. Rodin & J. H. Wilmore, pp. 94–111. Philadelphia: Lea & Febiger.

Malina, R. M. & Bouchard, C. (1991). *Growth, Maturation, and Physical Activity*. Champaign, Illinois: Human Kinetics Publishers.

Malina, R. M. & Buschang, P. H. (1985). Growth, strength and motor performance of Zapotec children, Oaxaca, Mexico. *Human Biology* **57**, 163–81.

Malina, R. M. & Moriyama, M. (1991). Growth and motor performance of Black and White children 6–10 years of age: A multivariate analysis. *American Journal of Human Biology* **3**, 599–611.

Malina, R. M. & Pena Reyes, M. E. (1993). Relative fat distribution - Relationship to skeletal maturation, growth status, and performance. *American Journal of Human Biology* (in press).

Malina, R. M., Skrabanek, M. F. & Little, B. B. (1989). Growth and maturity status of Black and White children classified as obese by different criteria. *American Journal of Human Biology* **1**, 193–9.

Merrett, D. M. S. (1992). Anthropometric Correlates of Motor Performance in Preschool Children. Master's thesis, University of Texas at Austin.

Montoye, H. J., Frantz, M. E. & Kozar, A. J. (1972). The value of age, height and weight in establishing standards of fitness for children. *Journal of Sports Medicine and Physical Fitness* **12**, 174–9.

Nelson, J. K., Thomas, J. R., Nelson, K. R. & Abraham, P. C. (1986). Gender differences in children's throwing performance: Biology and environment. *Research Quarterly for Exercise and Sport* **57**, 280–7.

Pate, R. R., Slentz, C. A. & Katz, D. P. (1989). Relationships between skinfold thickness and performance of health-related fitness test items. *Research Quarterly for Exercise and Sport* **60**, 183–9.

Rarick, G. L. & Oyster, N. (1964). Physical maturity, muscular strength, and motor performance of young school-age boys. *Research Quarterly* **35**, 523–31.

Roberts, D. F., Provins, K. A. & Morton, R. J. (1959). Arm strength and body dimensions. *Human Biology* **31**, 334–43.

Rocha Ferreira, M. B. (1987). Growth, physical performance and psychological characteristics of eight year old Brazilian school children from low socieconomic background. Doctoral dissertation, University of Texas at Austin.

Rocha Ferreira, M. B., Malina, R. M. & Rocha, L. L. (1991). Anthropometric, functional and psychological characteristics of eight-year-old Brazilian children from low socioeconomic status. In *Human Growth, Physical Fitness and Nutrition*, ed. R. J. Shephard & J. Parizkova, pp. 109–18. Basel: S. Karger.

Seils, L. G. (1951). The relationship between measures of physical growth and gross motor performance of primary-grade school children. *Research Quarterly* **22**, 244–60.

Welon, Z. (1979). The relationship of secular increase in size to physical ability. *Studies in Physical Anthropology* **5**, 13–20.

Welon, Z., Jurynec, R. & Śliwa, W. (1988). Ciężar należny mężczyzn. *Matieraly i Prace Antropologiczne* **109**, 53–71.

Welon, Z., Sekita, B. & Sławinska, T. (1981). Secular increase in body size and physical ability. *Studies in Physical Anthropology* **7**, 13–18.

12 *Anthropometry in the US armed forces*

CLAIRE C. GORDON AND KARL E. FRIEDL

Military anthropometry in the United States has a long history, beginning at least as early as the Civil War, when such variables as stature, weight, and the body mass index (BMI) were utilized to identify recruits likely to be malnourished, tuberculous, or otherwise unfit for military duty (Ordronaux, 1863). The Civil War surveys also encouraged extensive investigation of the relationships between anthropometry and ancestry, birthplace, physiological measures, disease prevalence, and physical anomalies (Gould, 1869; Baxter, 1875). During World War I (WWI), stature, weight, BMI, pubic height, and chest circumference were utilized as indicators of fitness for load-carrying, marching, and fighting (Davenport & Love, 1921). Indeed, the nature and validity of relations between anthropometry and soldier health and physical performance continue to be a primary focus of military research, and they form the basis of many anthropometric standards for the selection and retention of individual military personnel (Friedl, 1992).

Whereas anthropometric standards for accession, retention, and occupational assignment are by nature applied to the individual soldier, it is the anthropometric variation of military populations as a whole that must be considered in the design and sizing of clothing, protective equipment, workstations, and other military hardware. The first US military survey to specifically address clothing sizing was conducted on approximately 100 000 separatees (soldiers discharged from service) at the end of WWI (Davenport & Love, 1921). By the end of World War II (WWII), gross incompatibilities between body size distributions and the workstations of major military hardware systems (such as the gun turrets of the B-17 bomber aircraft) had fuelled the application of anthropometry in the ever-growing field of human engineering (Brues, 1992). Periodic anthropometric surveys of US military personnel have been undertaken ever

178

Table 12.1. *Anthropometric surveys of US military populations*

Year	Sample	Population	Source
1861–65	1 232 256	volunteers	Gould (1869)
1863–65	501 068	draftees	Baxter (1875)
1971–18	1 961 692	draftees	Davenport & Love (1921)
1919	103 909	separatees	Davenport & Love (1921)
1946	105 062	Army men	Newman & White (1951)
1946	8 859	Army women	Randall & Munro (1949)
1950	4 063	Air Force flyers	Hertzberg *et al.* (1954)
1964	1 549	Navy flyers	Gifford *et al.* (1965)
1966	6 682	Army men	White & Churchill (1971)
1966	2 008	Marines	White & Churchill (1978)
1967	2 420	Air Force flyers	Grunhofer & Kroh (1975)
1968	1 905	Air Force women	Clauser *et al.* (1972)
1970	1 482	Army Aviators	Churchill *et al.* (1971)
1977	1 331	Army women	Churchill *et al.* (1977)
1988	5 506	Army men	Gordon *et al.* (1989)
1988	3 491	Army women	Gordon *et al.* (1989)

since (see Table 12.1). Concise historical overviews of these are provided by Churchill & McConville (1976) and White (1978); comprehensive descriptions of post-WWII research are available in Air Force (Robinette & Fowler, 1988) and Army (Bell, Donelson & Wolfson, 1991) annotated bibliographies.

Why 'military' anthropometry?

The application of anthropometry to fitness and human engineering problems is not necessarily unique to the military. However, military populations themselves are unique since they are neither biological populations nor random samples of the biological populations represented in the US and its territories. Recruiting strategies interact with a host of sociological variables such as socioeconomic status, education, and social attitudes to influence those who 'immigrate' into the military. Regulations governing body size, occupational assignment, and career progression further influence military age, gender, and height–weight distributions. Thus, studies of anthropometric variation over time and space, and relationships between anthropometric variables and measures of health and performance, must address complex interactions between biological and social factors that influence the dependent variables of interest. In fact, the distributions of such demographic variables as age, gender, and race are so influential in determining anthropometric distributions that demographic shifts alone can render an anthropometric database obsolete (Bradtmiller, Rhatnaparkhi & Tebbetts, 1986; Gordon *et al.*, 1989), and may be more important than the secular trends of individual biological populations in that regard (Greiner & Gordon, 1990).

Other aspects of military anthropometry are also unique. Because research results are implemented in military regulations and/or materiel (equipment) specifications that directly affect the safety, performance, and careers of large numbers of individuals, measurement validity, reliability and precision are crucial. Measurement validity is determined by the closeness of the approximation between the anthropometric variable and the epidemiological or engineering factor it represents in the application at hand. Crotch height, for example, is valid for clothing design but inappropriate as a substitute for trochanteric height in a man-model or functional leg length in a workstation design. Regrettably, many classical anthropometric dimensions are simply not valid for military application, making standardization of measurement techniques with academia difficult despite significant efforts such as the Airlie Consensus Conference (Lohman, Roche & Martorell, 1988). Because a dimension appropriate for one military application may be invalid in another, multipurpose military surveys have of necessity included large numbers of dimensions, and these have been carefully selected and meticulously defined to enhance their validity for military applications (Clauser *et al.*, 1986a,b).

Relatively stringent controls on data reliability and parameter estimate precision are also required, owing to the unique role of military anthropometry in military policy-making, specifications, and regulations. Data reliability is enhanced through extensive landmarking (drawing anatomical landmarks on the body using surgical markers), frequent test–retest, and on-site computerized data entry and editing (Clauser *et al.*, 1988; Churchill, Bradtmiller & Gordon, 1988; Gordon & Bradtmiller, 1992). Parameter estimate precision is ensured through 'worst case' power calculations for relevant statistics and relatively complex sampling strategies and subject acquisition procedures to ensure that demographic and occupational subgroups are appropriately represented (Gordon *et al.*, 1989). The prohibitive cost of these large sample sizes has led military anthropologists to explore a variety of alternatives to random and stratified random sampling for certain applications (Churchill & McConville, 1976). Demographically and/or anthropometrically matched subsamples of existing databases are also utilized to limit the need for new data collection (Bradtmiller, McConville & Clauser, 1985; Annis & McConville, 1990b).

Table 12.2. *Height standards for military accessions*

Service	Males	Females
USA	60–80 in	58–80 in
USAF	60–80 in	58–80 in
USN	60–78 in	58–78 in
USMC	60–78 in	58–78 in

NHANES II (Najjar & Rowland, 1987) 1st–99th percentiles: 62.6 – 75.6 in (males); 57.6 – 69.7 in (females).

Military anthropometry and the individual: personnel selection
Anthropometry is used intensively in military personnel selection for accession, retention, and occupational training. In general, height restrictions are intended primarily to exclude unusually large or small individuals for whom protective equipment will be difficult to obtain; occupation-specific restrictions ensure equipment compatibility for hardware systems with limited accommodation potential; and weight-for-height and percentage body fat restrictions are applied to ensure acceptable levels of fitness.

Accession standards
The current US Army height standards are: 60–80 inches for men (152.4–203.2 cm) and 58–80 in for women (147.3–203.2 cm), but even these standards can be waived (AR 40-501, 1989). As can be seen in Table 12.2, the height limits are similar for the three main services, but the Marine Corps has a more restrictive upper height limit (72 in; 182.9 cm) for women. Comparison with NHANESII data (Najjar & Rowland, 1987) suggests that none of these standards eliminates more than 2% of the civilian population.

Accession standards for the services also include weight–height and/or body fat restrictions. For most of this century, weight standards were used by the US military to exclude underweight men, but this application reversed with the use of weight standards for weight control, following public criticism in the mid-1970s that military personnel tended to be overly fat and appeared to be unprepared to defend the nation (Friedl, 1992). Body weight standards were then established which screened for overweight instead of underweight using weight-for-height limits that approximated a body mass index (wt/ht^2) maximum (Laurence, 1988).

Until 1991, restrictive weight standards for women excluded 29% of the general population from entering the US Army (based on the NHANESII data), while only 3% of males were excluded. Based on a medical definition of overweight (at 120% of the young population average), few women allowed to enlist were overweight but a considerable portion of men were (Laurence, 1988). In a 1983 sample, these overweight men were found to have a significantly higher rate of attrition from the military, for reasons other than enforcement of weight standards. Men who were underweight (under 80% of the population average) also had a higher attrition rate, producing a U-shaped curve for 36-month attrition. Buddin (1989) later found that changes in Army basic training attenuated the higher attrition of overweight men, although it still remained higher than average. Buddin (1989) also found that lax enforcement of the weight entry standards allowed many women 5–10 lb (2.3–4.5 kg) above their standard to enter the Army anyway, and that these women did not demonstrate a higher attrition rate. More recently, in a large sample of US Army recruits followed through basic training and the first six months after basic training, overweight women were found to have a lower attrition than the 'within standards' weight women when body fat was equal (Friedl *et al.*, 1989).

At the upper ranges of body mass index, men show a decrease in aerobic capacity but an increase in lift capacity compared with the average (Fig. 12.1). A similar relationship exists for women. Thus, absolute weight standards tend to exclude some of the strongest individuals and suggest a serious flaw in military selection since various studies have demonstrated that the majority of military tasks involve lifting and carrying (Robertson & Trent, 1985; Vogel *et al.*, 1980). In the same data set, body fat has no correlation with lift capacity, suggesting that a body fat standard would not inadvertently eliminate strong individuals from the military.

Because the use of weight or BMI alone discriminated against well-muscled individuals, the weight regulations were not rigorously enforced and it was left to the subjective assessment of a physician to determine if an overweight soldier was also obese. President Carter asked for research and recommendations to improve the fitness and long-range health of the military (Department of Defense, 1981). This led to a 1983 directive that all services would use circumference-based anthropometric regression equations to estimate body fat, as the US Marines were already doing (Wright, Dotson & Davis, 1980, 1981). Regression-estimated percentage body fat thus replaced subjective assessments, with recommended standards of 20 and 26% body fat for men and women, respectively.

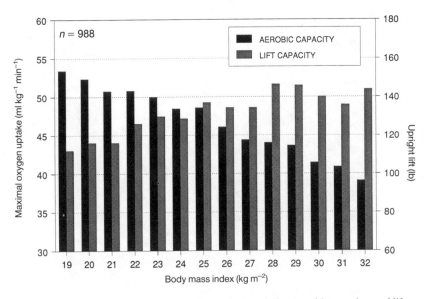

Fig. 12.1. The relationship between body mass index, aerobic capacity, and lift capacity for 988 Army males.

Since 1983, the services have each continued to modify their entry standards; the US Navy and Army now include body fat measures in their exclusion criteria. Based upon the 1989 study by Friedl and colleagues, which reports individual success of men and women in achieving their retention standards six months after the end of basic training, the Army allows male accessions 4% body fat over the retention standards to which they will be later held; Army accession standards for women are the same as retention standards.

Retention standards
Retention standards require that every individual on military active duty be weighed and/or measured for body fat at least once per year to ensure that they fall below the prescribed upper limits of percentage body fat. Individuals not meeting these standards are given a first-time opportunity to come within standards, and subsequent failures to meet the standards culminate in elimination from the military. As can be seen in Table 12.3, each of the services set different fat standards in relation to their own objectives for military appearance, health considerations, and physical fitness requirements. However, the ultimate goal of each and the driving force behind the Department of Defense Directive mandating a weight

Table 12.3. *Relative fat limits (%) for US military*

Males	USAF	USA	USN	USMC
17–20 yrs	20	20	26	18
21–27 yrs	20	22	26	18
28–29 yrs	20	24	26	18
30–39 yrs	26	24	26	18
40+ yrs	26	26	26	18
Females				
17–20 yrs	28	30	36	26
21–27 yrs	28	32	36	26
28–29 yrs	28	34	36	26
30–39 yrs	34	34	36	26
40+ yrs	34	36	36	26

control programme for all services is to discourage overeating and encourage exercise (Kryswicki, Consolazio & Johnson, 1970).

The services have also developed different predictive equations, which are presented in Table 12.4. These have been periodically revised since 1983; three sets of male and female circumference equations are currently in use. Each of these equations is based on studies of US Military populations, with a best-fit multiple regression analysis to determine which of the most convenient and reproducible anthropometric measurements in the hands of lay observers are the best predictors of body fat measured by hydrostatic weighing. The striking similarity of the three male equations, in contrast to the disparity between female equations, reinforces the perception that male body fat is relatively well predicted by an abdominal girth, while the greater variety of fat sites available in women makes standardization of predictive equations rather more difficult (Vogel & Friedl, 1992).

Methods which are technically more sophisticated than circumference measurements have been repeatedly proposed for adoption by the military. So far, however, no *expedient* method has surfaced which substantially improves upon anthropometric estimations of fatness. Standards based upon body circumferences also correlate well with the objectives of the military services' weight control programmes. Abdominal circumference, for example, is the primary offender of military appearance, the primary site of excess fat deposition in overfed and underexercised individuals, and the site most associated with adverse health risks (Larsson *et al.*, 1984; Terry *et al.*, 1991). Used in the

Table 12.4. *Predictive equations currently in use by US military*

All measurements are in cm and kg; abd1 is defined at the natural waist; abd2 is defined at the navel.

US Air Force and Navy[2]
men: density = $(-0.191 \times \log[\text{abd2-neck}]) + (0.155 \times \log[\text{height}]) + 1.032$.
 $n = 602; r = 0.90$, see = 3.52.
women: density = $(-0.350 \times \log[\text{abd1} + \text{hip-neck}]) + (0.221 \times \log[\text{height}]) + 1.296$.
 $n = 214, r = 0.85$, see = 3.72

US Army[2]
men: % fat = $(76.5 \times \log[\text{abd2-neck}]) - (68.7 \times \log[\text{height}]) + 43.7$.
 $n = 1126, r = 0.82$, see = 4.02.
women: % fat = $(105.3 \times \log[\text{weight}]) - (0.200 \times \text{wrist}) - (0.533 \times \text{neck}) - (1.574 \times$
 $\text{forearm}) + (0.173 \times \text{hip}) - (0.515 \times \text{height}) - 35.6$.
 $n = 266, r = 0.82$, see = 3.60.

US Marine Corps[3]
men: % fat = $(0.740 \times \text{abd2}) - (1.249 \times \text{neck}) + 40.985$.
 $n = 279, r = 0.81$, see = 3.67.
women: % fat = $(1.051 \times \text{biceps}) - (1.522 \times \text{forearm}) - (0.879 \times \text{neck}) + (0.326 \times$
 $\text{abd2}) + (0.597 \times \text{thigh}) + 0.707$.
 $n = 181, r = 0.73$, see = 4.11.

[1]Hogdon & Beckett, 1984a,b; % body fat = $100 \times (4.95/\text{density} - 4.50)$.
[2]Vogel *et al.* (1988).
[3]Wright, Dotson & Davis (1980, 1981).

dichotomous determination of who is or is not maintaining a fit appearance and a reasonable level of physical fitness, the circumferential estimations of body fat provide a suitable screening tool (Hodgdon, Fitzgerald & Vogel, 1990; Conway, Cronan & Peterson, 1989).

Ongoing research for soldier selection
Current approaches to identification of overfat service members rely on the reference method of hydrostatic weighing. Individuals with large body mass, those who perform regular intensive weight-bearing exercise, and Black Americans are likely to be underestimated for body fat because of the assumptions implicit in this method; other groups may be overestimated. The resulting anthropometric equations may be none the less equitable estimates of body fat because they are independent of bone mass, and particularly if they are initially developed from test populations for which the assumptions for hydrostatically determined body fat are generally valid (Friedl & Vogel, 1991). However, ethnic and racial differences in regional fat distribution would be expected to affect anthropometric equations, especially the female equations, which in-

volve estimation of more than one principal site of fat deposition (Seidell *et al.*, 1990; Zillikens & Conway, 1990; Vogel & Friedl, 1992). Studies are currently under way which re-examine the current equations across a range of body sizes and across the three principal racial or ethnic groups represented in the US Army: Blacks, Hispanics, and non-Hispanic Whites. These are being compared to a four-compartment model of fat estimation which includes hydrostatic weighing, total body water, and bone mineral measurements (Friedl *et al.*, 1992).

Since the predictive equations for body fat are used to follow individuals for success in achieving their fat standards within a relatively short period of time (3–18 months, depending on the service), the equations are currently under evaluation for their ability to predict small changes in fatness. An Army–Navy collaborative study will attempt to establish a single anthropometric equation for all military services which suitably classifies fatness in women before and after eight weeks of exercise-induced fat weight loss, taking into account objective measures of aerobic fitness, strength, and health status.

Another improvement in soldier selection standards under consideration is anthropometrically based assessment of fat-free mass to ensure the adequacy of muscular strength of future male and female recruits. Minimum standards of weight or fat-free weight could be effectively tabled against maximum allowances of body fat so that greater relative body fat is allowed for individuals with greater amounts of metabolically more active fat-free mass. Additional research into the development of such a standard is required.

Occupational assignment

In addition to standards for accession and retention, certain military occupations have unique anthropometric standards to ensure full compatibility with available military hardware and/or unique military duties. Table 12.5 summarizes prevailing occupation-specific anthropometric restrictions for the US Army.

Equipment compatibility is the most common reason for anthropometric restriction, and aircraft-specific restrictions on pilot anthropometry are a classic example of this. Safe operation of aircraft requires that the pilot have appropriate 'over the nose' visual field, proper canopy and ejection path clearances, and functional reach capability for all hand- and foot-operated controls. In practice, the design of cockpit geometries that provide wide ranges of multivariate accommodation is difficult. Furthermore, since low vertical profiles are needed to minimize wind drag and battlefield detectability, engineering trade-offs are likely to result in

Table 12.5. Occupation-specific anthropometric standards

Occupation	Restrictions	Justification
Diver	Height: 66–76 in (168–193 cm)	Limited size range for diving suits
Pilot	Crotch height: ≥75 cm	Workspace limitations
	Span: ≥164 cm	
	Sitting height: ≥102 cm	
	Weight: ≤230 lb (104 kg)	
MANPADS/PMS	Height: ≥64 in (162 cm)	Must carry Stinger missile
Crew member	Height: ≥68 in (173 cm) (men)	Body size larger than population average
Military police	≥64 in (162 cm) (women)	
Tank crewman (M48–M60, M1)	Height: ≥73 in (185 cm)	Workspace limitations

Sources: AR 40-501 (1989) and AR 611-201 (1990).

Table 12.6. *Anthropometric standards for military aviators*

	Restrictions
USAF	
Flying Class II	Height: 64–76 in (162–193 cm)
Flying trainees	Height: 64–76 in (162–193 cm)
	Sitting height: 34–39 in (86–99 cm)
USA	
General	Crotch height ≥75 cm
	Span ≥164 cm
	Sitting height ≤102 cm
	Weight ≤230 lb (104 kg)
OV1 Mohawk	Weight ≤220 lb (100 kg)
OH58 Kiowa	Sitting height ≤95 cm
USN	
General	Height:
	men ≥62 in (157 cm)
	women ≥ 58 in (147 cm)
	Sitting height: 32–41 in (81–104 cm)
	Buttock–leg length: 36–50 in (91–127 cm)
	Buttock–knee length: 22–28 in (56–71 cm)
	Functional reach ≥28 in (71 cm)
Aircraft with ejection seats	Weight: 132–218 lb (60–99 kg)

Sources: Chase (1990); NR 15-34 (1991); AFR 160-43 (1987).

limited workstation space, and it is likely that anthropometric restrictions on military pilots and armoured vehicle crews will continue in the foreseeable future.

Table 12.6 summarizes anthropometric restrictions on US military aviators. Differences in pilot restrictions among the services arise because different aircraft often have different anthropometric accommodation ranges and because there are different philosophies regarding the training of individuals who may fit some, but not all, of the aircraft in their service's inventory. Research to identify the anthropometric limitations of contemporary aircraft continues in all three US services and their allies (Schopper & Cote, 1984; Cote & Schopper, 1984; Schopper, 1986; Turner, 1986; Rose & Erickson, 1988; Farr & Buescher, 1989; Rothwell & Pigeau, 1990; G. F. Zehner, personal communication), although there is considerable debate regarding the best application of such information. Retrofits of aircraft (physical modification of in-service aircraft) are prohibitively expensive, but extensive anthropometric restrictions may also be unacceptable, particularly if reasonable percentages of the female population are to be accommodated (see Advisory Group for Aerospace Research and Development, 1990, for discussion).

Anthropometric restriction to ensure adequate occupational performance is much less common in the US military, primarily because of the relatively weak relations between body dimensions and objective measures of performance such as strength and endurance (Ayoub & Mital, 1989). At present, the only occupation in which anthropometric standards relate to anticipated performance is military police. Height minima for Army military police are set at approximately 1 in (2.5 cm) above the male and female means so that they will appear larger than most soldiers in crowd control situations. An earlier standard setting a minimum height of 66 in (167.6 cm) and minimum weight of 149 lb (67.7 kg) for firefighters is in the process of being rescinded. The Army concluded that few individuals can hold the large fire hoses alone, regardless of body size, and the restriction unnecessarily excludes most women.

Military anthropometry and the population: materiel system design and sizing

The anthropometric distributions of military populations play a central role in the development and fielding of their materiel (clothing and equipment) systems. Anthropometry influences everything from dress uniforms to boots, body armour, respirators, backpacks, field kitchens, tentage, and the crewstation geometries of jeeps, submarines, helicopters, and tactical aircraft. In general, military designers attempt to accommodate the largest percentage of soldiers possible within standard sizing systems and workstation adjustabilities. The goal for clothing and individual equipment is to achieve maximum accommodation with the fewest sizes possible in order to simplify military logistics and cost to the taxpayer. For military transportation and weapons systems the goal is maximum accommodation with minimum workstation space and weight in order to optimize fuel efficiency, increase speed, and minimize detectability by radar or other surveillance techniques. As will be apparent in the discussions below, the constant need to optimize fit and accommodation while minimizing cost, space, and weight has driven military anthropologists to utilize relatively sophisticated statistical methods in their applications of anthropometry.

Materiel system specifications

All military systems begin their development with a 'requirements document' that describes the system and provides performance specifi-

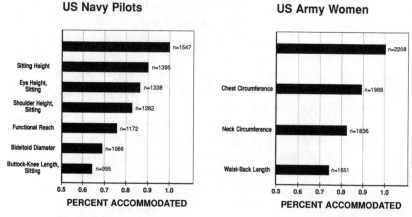

Fig. 12.2. Sequential reduction in population accommodation with
simultaneous 5th–95th percentile accommodation requirements for multiple
dimensions.

cations that must be met for its intended implementation. Initial specifications for systems with human interfaces state the body size range(s)
over which a system must be operative, and thus indirectly determine the
percentage of the user population that will be accommodated. Tradition-
ally, such 'accommodation requirements' take the form of a boilerplate
line such as 'must accommodate the 5th through 95th percentile soldier',
and their intent is to provide operational support for the central 90% of
the military population without customized fitting. Unfortunately such
simple language leaves in doubt which body dimensions are to be
accommodated across the 5th–95th percentile range, and implies the
existence of mythical people whose body dimensions are all 5th percentile
or all 95th percentile, at either end of the range to be accommodated
(Churchill, 1978; Robinette & McConville, 1981; Annis & McConville,
1990a).

Furthermore, although accommodation of 90% of the population is the
goal, simultaneous 5th–95th percentile accommodation for more than
one dimension inevitably leads to less than 90% overall accommodation
because body dimensions are not perfectly correlated with one another
(Moroney and Smith, 1972). Figure 12.2 illustrates this problem. With
three key sizing dimensions for a dress shirt, simultaneous 5th–95th
percentile ranges capture only 75% of the Army female population; with
six key crewstation dimensions, simultaneous 5th–95th percentile ranges
capture only 64% of the Naval aviator population (Moroney & Smith,
1972). In general, the rate of multivariate accommodation degradation

varies as a function of the correlations between body dimensions, and considerable US and allied military research has focused on computerized estimation of multivariate accommodation rates (Bittner, 1976; Hendy, 1990; Rothwell & Pigeau, 1990). Percentile-based specifications are particularly problematic in workstation applications because these geometries are usually determined by at least four or five anthropometric dimensions that may be poorly correlated with one another, and because the most extreme cases for accommodation may not be uniformly the largest and smallest for all their dimensions, but rather combinations of large and small extremes (Roebuck, Kroemer & Thomson, 1975; Bittner *et al.*, 1987; Hendy, 1990; Zehner, Meindl & Hudson, 1992).

In order to ensure that the extreme values used to specify accommodation requirements result in the intended rates of accommodation, both the Navy and Air Force have explicitly discouraged the use of percentiles in specifications (Arnoff, 1987; Zehner *et al.*, 1992), and the most recent update to MIL-STD-1472D (1991), *Human Engineering Design Criteria for Military Systems*, carries a strong caution against the use of univariate percentiles when more than one key design dimension is involved. Instead, it is recommended that principal components (PC) analysis be applied to reduce the dimensionality of the multivariate space; then the anthropometric data are plotted in the new PC space and a 90, 95, or 98% accommodation circle (2 components) or sphere/ellipsoid (3 compartments) is fitted to the target population (Robinson, Robinette & Zehner, 1992; Meindl, Zehner & Hudson, 1993). Mid-quadrant points on this accommodation surface (see Fig. 12.3) represent the extreme body sizes and proportions present in the population, and these are transformed back into percentiles or actual population values for each extreme case.

The results of such multivariate analyses can be included in specifications as matrices of 'test cases' and subsequently input as government-furnished parameters for computerized man-models and design aids. The dimensionality of the multivariate space, and therefore the number of extreme cases required in each specification, varies with the number and diversity of body dimensions that are considered critical to the design and is thus somewhat subjective. The CADRE manikin series includes 17 cases (Bittner *et al.*, 1987), whereas the United States Air Force (USAF) workstation series contains either 8 or 14 depending upon the number of body dimensions to be specified (Zehner *et al.*, 1992). The assumption underlying these procedures is that accommodation of extreme body proportions on the surface of the multivariate accommodation envelope will ensure accommodation for all those in the population who are less extreme (Meindl *et al.*, 1993).

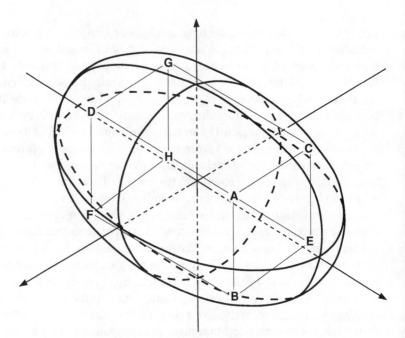

Fig. 12.3. Mid-quadrant points on a three-dimensional accommodation surface (after Fig. 3. in Meindl *et al.*, 1993).

Anthropometric sizing of clothing and individual equipment

Anthropometric data are routinely utilized in the sizing of clothing and individual equipment (CIE) in all three services. The universal goal in military sizing is to meet the accommodation requirement with the fewest number of sizes possible while maintaining a quality of fit that maximizes safety and performance. Although individual services take slightly different approaches in achieving this goal, they share a common, well-established process that involves five fundamental steps: (i) selection of key sizing dimensions for labelling and issuing the item; (ii) determination of the number of sizes needed to accommodate the target population, and the anthropometric limits for each size category; (iii) calculation of nude design values to be used in drafting and grading patterns or moulds for each size category; (iv) creation of prototype garments and verification of garment proportions and limits of fit using military test subjects; and (v) estimation of the population proportions falling into each size category in the system (McConville, 1978; McConville, Robinette & White, 1981).

All anthropometric sizing presupposes the availability of a database that includes the required body dimensions, measured on a sample of individuals that is representative of the target population. In practice, anthropometric surveys are so costly that representative databases are often constructed from existing ones by stratified random sampling in which age, gender, race, and sometimes height and weight distributions in the target group are matched (Bradtmiller *et al.*, 1985; Gordon *et al.*, 1989; Annis & McConville, 1990b).

With an appropriate database in hand, garment design and purpose are used to determine which dimensions are critical to functional fit and to select one or two key dimensions for sizing and issuing. Key sizing dimensions should sort the user population into subgroups whose members are similar to one another in those body dimensions most important to garment fit and function. Usually, correlation coefficients or principal components analysis are used to identify promising key dimensions, and these can be compared for efficiency using the average 'within-size standard deviation (SZ-SD)' as a measure of within-size homogeneity for critical body dimensions (Gordon, 1986; Robinette & Annis, 1986). Good key dimensions are highly correlated with other dimensions critical to garment fit and have relatively low SZ-SDs for these as well. In practice, military sizing systems rarely utilize more than two key dimensions, owing to the geometric progression in number of sizes that ensues (Roebuck *et al.*, 1975); often, the statistically optimum key dimension is not selected because its reliability is too low for implementation by non-specialists who may be issuing equipment. In most sizing systems, one dimension is selected to control linear variation and a second dimension controls circumferential variation.

After key dimensions are selected, the number of sizes needed to meet the accommodation requirements is determined. Obviously with more sizes in a sizing system, the within-size variation for critical body dimensions will be smaller, and a better garment fit will be possible. However, one rapidly reaches a point beyond which increasing the number of sizes does not substantially reduce body size variability within size categories. This is usually visible on plots of the SZ-SD against number of sizes, given fixed accommodation limits. In practice, garment design and function greatly influence the magnitude of acceptable within-size variation, and often the SZ-SDs of successful sizing systems for similar garment types are used as guidelines.

Once a sizing system structure such as that in Fig. 12.4 is outlined, nude design values for each size category are calculated for all critical body dimensions. Design values are used by the clothing designer or engineer for creating the patterns, models, or moulds used to manufacture the

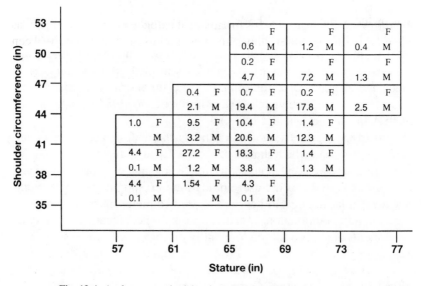

Fig. 12.4. Anthropometric sizing for a US Army field coat. F, percentage of females; M, percentage of males.

developmental item. Multiple regressions using key dimensions as independent variables and critical dimensions as dependent variables are ordinarily used to generate design values because regression estimates can be combined without distorting normal body proportions (McConville & Churchill, 1976; Robinette & McConville, 1981). Depending upon the snugness of fit desired, one can design for mid-size individuals by entering mid-size key dimension values in the regression, design for the largest individuals by regressing on the maximum within-size values of the key dimensions, or design to various extremes by regressing on mid-size values and adding or subtracting multiples of the average within-size standard deviation or standard error of the estimate (Robinette & Annis, 1986; Robinette, Mellian & Ervin, 1990). Statistics calculated directly from size category subgroups are rarely used to set design values because anthropometric variables are not usually normally distributed within size subgroups (McConville *et al.*, 1981).

Using anthropometric design values, master patterns are drafted for a size category near the centre of the sizing system, prototypes are made, and a small-scale fitting trial is conducted to verify master pattern proportions. When master pattern dimensions are finalized, the pattern is graded into other sizes and lengths in the system, usually using a computerized pattern grading system. Dimensional increments ('grade rules') between sizes and lengths are a simple matter to calculate either as the difference in design values for adjacent categories or more directly as the product of regression slopes and key dimension differences between size categories. Prototype garments are then made for a full-scale fitting trial involving substantial numbers of subjects in all size categories. Full-scale fitting trials permit fine tuning of grade rules and verify the limits of fit for each size category before the garments are subjected to operational trials in the field.

The methods used in generating nude design values for pattern drafting and model or mould making are really a specialized case of creating proportional man-models. Thus anthropometric design values can also be used in specifications for dressforms and manikins so that clothing designers can drape as well as draft patterns, and they are quite compatible with the latest in computer-aided design and computer-aided pattern grading technologies. Mathematical man-models based upon height–weight regressions are also used to generate specifications for the external dimensions of ejection 'dummies' used in biodynamic simulations and testing of escape systems (Tri-Service Aeromedical Research Panel, 1988).

The estimation of population proportions for each size category, commonly called 'tariffing', is the final step in the anthropometric sizing process. Population proportions are ordinarily estimated by sorting an appropriate anthropometric database using the key dimension limits for each size category. Tariffs indicate the relative frequency with which each size category should be purchased; they are ordinarily estimated for males and females separately (see Figure 12.4) and subsequently weighted according to the prevailing gender ratio in the target population. Tariffs are used by military procurement officials to structure multimillion-dollar contracts with civilian garment manufacturers, by stock managers at the Central Initial Issue Facilities supplying major training centres, and by supply sergeants at the individual unit level.

Whereas population-wide tariffs work well for large-scale manufacturing contracts, they are often unable to predict accurately the numbers of each size needed at training centres because of age biases in the soldiers processed and at smaller unit levels because of age, gender, and race biases that result from sampling error and the secondary effects of rank and occupational requirements inherent in the unit's military mission. Since contemporary combat scenarios involve rapid deployments that rely upon pre-positioned pallets of equipment, unit-specific tariffing plays a critical role in military logistical support. Tariffs must be accurate in order to ensure sufficient numbers of the sizes needed in critical equipment such as chemical protective overgarments, body armour, and boots.

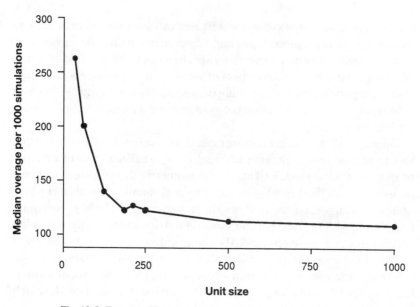

Fig. 12.5. Excess uniforms needed as a function of the number of soldiers to be fitted in a single event.

Ongoing research by the US Army is addressing the statistical limitations of unit-specific tariffing through statistical simulations with its 1988 database in which randomly sampled units of various size and gender composition are issued uniforms based upon prevailing Army sizing systems and tariffs. The size category with the largest relative shortfall is then used to estimate the number of uniforms needed (expressed as a percentage of the number of soldiers in the unit) to ensure that everyone gets an adequately fitted uniform at a single issuing event. Preliminary results for a combat uniform coat are presented in Fig. 12.5. Such functions can be used by Army logisticians in assessing the feasibility and cost of pre-positioning equipment for various organizational levels.

Anthropometry and workstation design

Anthropometry is also critical to the design of crewstations in aircraft, armoured vehicles, and ships, not to mention artillery firing stations, field kitchens and field hospitals. Applied anthropometry in these systems is intended to optimize the man–machine interfaces that are critical to mission performance. Since most major military hardware systems are developed under civilian contract, the methods used in applying anthropometric data to workstation geometry derivation can vary considerably, and many details of design development are proprietary. Nevertheless, a general approach is shared by all human engineers in workstation design, and this involves task identification, dimension selection, geometry derivation, workstation testing and validation, and accommodation mapping (Roebuck *et al.*, 1975; McConville, 1978).

Task identification involves enumeration of critical tasks that must be performed at the workstation, and defining the man–machine interfaces that influence task success and safety. Aircraft pilots, for example, require appropriate visual fields, must be able to actuate all hand and foot controls, must have adequate canopy, instrument panel, and emergency egress clearances, and must be supported in safe and comfortable postures for extended missions and emergency operations (MIL-STD-1333B, 1976). These operational requirements automatically indicate a set of key anthropometric variables that will 'drive' the workstation geometry. Commonly used key workstation dimensions include: seated eye height, functional (arm) reach, seated acromion height, buttock–knee length, and seated knee or popliteal height (Kennedy, 1986; MIL-STD-1333B, 1976; Hendy, 1990; Rothwell & Pigeau, 1990; Zehner *et al.*, 1992). As in CIE applications, a limited set of key dimensions is explicitly accommodated in the design process, and a more extensive set of dimensions critical to system function may be addressed indirectly through various statistical estimation techniques.

Application of key dimensions in the design process is considerably more complex in workstations than in clothing because the whole body must be accommodated within a single design and because the anthropometric 'worst case' models usually do not involve uniformly large or small individuals, but rather individuals with extreme body proportions (for example, a pilot with short trunk and long legs). Derivation of a seated workstation with vision requirements usually starts with seated eye height being used to determine the range of seat adjustability required to position all operators in the target population on the operational sight lines. Then functional reach and acromial height are used to orient and locate instrument panels within the operator's reach throughout the range of seat adjustment. Foot-operated controls and the inferior edge of the instrument panel are located using buttock–knee length and knee or popliteal heights. Once these fundamental aspects of geometry are determined, head, knee, and emergency egress clearances are ensured. The order in which these steps are undertaken varies as a function of task priorities and other design constraints, and may also vary as a function of the actual method used to arrive at design values.

Several approaches are used to derive anthropometric design values for input into workstation models, but most human engineering specialists agree that combinations of worst-case proportions are desirable (Roebuck *et al.*, 1975; Hendy, 1990; Zehner *et al.*, 1992). Early USAF geometries were based upon 'extreme' regression estimates such as the minimum reach expected for the 1st and 99th percentile sitting eye heights (Kennedy, 1986). Most recently, the USAF recommends a principal components approach that reduces the key and critical anthropometric variable space to two or three dimensions, and then identifies extreme body proportions as mid-quadrant points on a 90% accommodation circle or sphere in that space (Robinson *et al.*, 1992; Zehner *et al.*, 1992). The United States Navy (USN) also bases its design requirements upon combinations of extreme body proportions presented as matrices of test cases (Arnoff, 1987).

Validation of military workstation geometries used to rely heavily upon task simulation by clothed subjects in full-scale 'mock-ups'. Today, however, early design concepts can be created within computer-aided design (CAD) environments and tested against three-dimensional man-models such as Combiman, Boeman, Sammie, and Jack (see Rothwell, 1985, 1989; Kroemer *et al.*, 1989; Paquette, 1990 for reviews). In fact, computer programs that simulate cockpit 'checks' on critical tasks can now be run so quickly that iterative testing using whole populations of individuals (real surveys or randomly generated populations) is feasible. These results can be readily incorporated into the design process itself, or used to 'map' the anthropometric accommodation envelope for systems already in the field (Bittner, Morissey & Moroney, 1975; Hendy, Anderson & Drumm, 1984; Rothwell & Pigeau, 1990). Although simulated fit-testing with computerized man-models should never replace full-scale human factors evaluations or individual pilot-cockpit checks because of their limitations in replicating realistic body postures and dimensions of the clothed or equipped operator (Rothwell, 1989), the integration of mathematical man-models and CAD technology is already revolutionizing military workstation design.

Sex and racial heterogeneity in design and sizing

Anthropometry plays a crucial role in quantifying the diversity of body sizes and shapes that attend the gender and racial heterogeneity present in US military populations. Most military systems were designed based upon male data, and initial efforts at gender-integrated protective equipment involved simply scaling down the male patterns into smaller sizes and lengths (Gordon, 1986; Reeps, Pheeny & Brady, 1990). Since the body proportions of women differ significantly from those of men (Robinette, Churchill & McConville, 1979) the scaled-down clothing and equipment does not fit women well (Woodward *et al.*, 1981; Reeps *et al.*, 1990). Similarly, most (if not all) contemporary military aircraft were designed for men, and their anthropometric accommodation envelopes may exclude large percentages of women (Schopper, 1986; Coblentz, Mollard & Ignazi, 1990; Rothwell & Pigeau, 1990; Turner, 1990).

Military research on gender differences in body size and proportion has explored both the nature and magnitude of male–female differences in general (Robinette *et al.*, 1979) and after controlling for potential key sizing dimensions (McConville *et al.*, 1981; Schafer & Bates, 1988). The results of these studies suggest that gender-integrated sizing programmes may be possible for two-piece field uniforms and some field equipment, but are unlikely to be successful in dress uniforms or in one-piece coveralls.

Gender-integrated sizing involves several unique aspects (Gordon, 1986). The best key dimensions are those that maximize the separation of men and women into separate size categories, thus minimizing the within-size variation due to sexual dimorphism. With optimal key dimensions, there is usually a region of larger sizes worn primarily by men; a region of smaller sizes worn primarily by women; and a central region of gender overlap where sizes will be worn by both men and women (see Figure 12.4, for example). Since computerized pattern grading systems operate with a great deal of interpolation between landmarks, certain aspects of master pattern shape and proportion are carried automatically through-out the sizing system. Thus preparation of a single master pattern in a central, gender-integrated size and subsequent grading of the pattern into male- and female-specific regions of the sizing system compromises fit for individuals in gender-specific areas where pattern proportions are unique. Separate master patterns are therefore drafted for each region: male regression equations are used to specify design values for the upper region; female regression equations are used for the lower region. In the central region, both male and female regression estimates are calculated, and when they are quite different, the more extreme value, regardless of gender, is selected. Computation of separate regression equations and design values for each gender is a critical feature of this approach because pooling the genders will result in equations that describe neither gender well, and if the database reflected the prevailing 89% male composition of the Army, for example, the anthropometric variation attributable to the female minority would have little impact upon parameter estimates. Similar approaches can be taken in workstation design, beginning with the multivariate accommodation specifications that might arise from separate male and female analyses, with selection of the most extreme midquadrant points, regardless of gender (Meindl *et al.*, 1993).

Variation in body size and shape attributable to population differences is equally important in military anthropometry. However, until recently there were insufficient *human engineering* data on military minority groups to assess the extent to which racial variation need be accommodated in military systems and to address anthropometric design solutions. Recent research by the US Army, however, clearly indicates that racial minority groups differ sufficiently in body size alone so as to be differentially disaccommodated by materiel systems designed against Army-wide summary statistics (Walker, 1991). These results suggest that race-specific anthropometric distributions should be considered at both the accommodation requirement and engineering design value stages of materiel system development for those dimensions known to be 'race-sensitive' (see Clauser *et al.*, 1986a,b for a discussion). Race-specific parameter estimates can be incorporated relatively easily into the sizing and workstation procedures outlined above. In fact, Navy women's uniform patterns (Robinette *et al.*, 1990) and Air Force face-forms (Annis, 1985) already incorporate some design values set solely by minority groups with more extreme distributions than the population as a whole. Racial differences in torso vs. limb lengths may be critical to workstation geometries, and these can be addressed by deriving multivariate accommodation criteria separately for different racial groups and then choosing the most extreme of the extreme midquadrant points derived (Meindl *et al.*, 1993).

Secular trends

Because some military systems take decades to field, and many are in use for decades, secular trends in body size are an important issue in military anthropometry. Most research is geared to projecting body size distributions in the 20 to 30 year future, and these projections are sometimes substituted for contemporary values when a new system is developed. The study of secular trends in military populations is tricky because they are not biological populations *per se*, but rather the result of 'immigration' by civilians from many different biological populations, each of which may have its own rate of change. Military secular trends are thus the result of at least three fairly independent factors: (i) secular trends occurring in biological populations; (ii) changes in social attitudes, military recruitment strategies, and accession standards that influence who 'immigrates' into the military; and (iii) changes in physical fitness

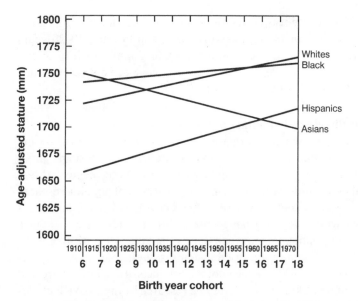

Fig. 12.6. Race-specific secular trends in stature for US Army males. The equations for the lines are as follows. Whites, $y = 1700 + 3.71\,x$, see = 5.11, $r = 0.847$; Blacks, $y = 1732 + 1.46\,x$, see = 5.86, r = 0.480; Hispanics, $y = 1626 + 5.08\,x$, see = 6.72, $r = 0.823$; Asians, $y = 1779 - 4.88\,x$, see = 10.27, $t = -0.623$; for all equations, $p = 0.000$.

requirements that directly influence the anthropometric parameters of members of the military (Greiner & Gordon, 1990, 1991, 1992).

Secular trends in body size are usually estimated from age-corrected data derived from temporally sequential studies on the 'same' population. Until recently, this has also been the approach used in military studies of secular trends, despite the questionable continuity of military populations in a biological sense. The biologically heterogeneous nature of the US military is relatively easily accommodated in secular trend models by estimating trends for individual racial groups (see Fig. 12.6) and weighing these estimates according to demographic projections when predictions are desired (Greiner & Gordon, 1990). However, body size predictions for future military populations are extremely sensitive to differences in age and race composition, and the factors influencing demographic composition are often unpredictable and temporally unstable. Even within-race estimates exhibit temporal perturbations such as the negative secular trend for stature in Asian soldiers. This trend reflects a shift in the origins of Asian soldiers from predominantly American-born Japanese to predominantly foreign-born Filipino (Greiner & Gordon, 1992). The instability of cultural factors influencing the composition of military populations thus makes projections more than 10–20 years into the future tenuous at best, and for some groups, such as Army women, it has made interpretation of even race-specific secular trends extremely difficult (Greiner & Gordon, 1991).

New directions in military anthropometry

New technologies such as helmet-mounted information displays and multilayered, modular, protective clothing demand increasingly more close-fitting materiel systems. In response to these needs, three-dimensional morphometry has become a critical area of ongoing research in military anthropometry. Current work by the USAF on three-dimensional surface digitizing has focused on scans of the head and face to improve the fit of helmets, oxygen masks, and the integration of night vision goggles and helmet-mounted visual displays. The USAF Cyberware scans include 130 000 surface points. Subjects are scanned bare and with helmets and masks in place. Ongoing research by the USAF includes automation of landmark identification, software to facilitate storage and manipulation of the huge databases produced by scanning technologies, and multivariate statistical methods to identify extreme body sizes and shapes in populations of head and face scans. The application of surface and tissue scanning technologies to ergonomic man-model enfleshment, casualty reduction models, and materiel system design and models, and materiel system design and sizing, promises to be a critical area of basic research for all US services in the coming decades.

Acknowledgements

The authors gratefully acknowledge Mr David Rose at the Naval Air Warfare Center, Mr Gregory Zehner at the Air Force Systems Command Armstrong Laboratory, and Mr James Annis at Anthropology Research Project, Inc., for their support in obtaining recent and/or unpublished policy and research documents. Ms Nancy Bell of Geocenters, Inc. provided extensive bibliographic assistance. Mr Steve Smith, also on the staff of Geocenters, executed the figures. Valuable editorial comments were made by Mrs Jane Johnson, US Army Natick R, D, & E Center.

References

Advisory Group for Aerospace Research & Development (1990). *Recruiting, Selection, Training, and Military Operations of Female Aircrew*. (AGARD Conference Proceedings No. 491.) Neuilly-Sur-Seine: North Atlantic Treaty Organization.

Air Force Regulation 160-43(C4) (1987). *Medical Examination and Medical Standards*. Washington, DC: Department of the Air Force.

Annis, J. F. (1985). *The Development of an Integrated Seven Size System for Full Face Respirators*. Appendix C in Air Force Contract F33615-82-C-0510 Final Report. Air Force Aerospace Medical Research Laboratory, Wright-Patterson AFB, Ohio.

Annis, J. F. & McConville, J. T. (1990a). Application of anthropometric data in sizing and design. In: *Advances in Industrial Ergonomics and Safety*, vol. 2, ed. B. Das, pp. 309–14. Philadelphia: Taylor & Francis.

Annis, J. F. & McConville, J. T. (1990b). *Sizing Systems for Close Fitting Nuclear, Biological, and Chemical Undergarments*. Final Report Contract Serial Number W7714-9-5989/1-ST. Department of National Defence, Defence Research Establishment, Ottawa, Ontario, Canada.

Army Regulation 40-501 (1989). *Standards of Medical Fitness*. Washington, DC: Headquarters, Department of the Army.

Army Regulation 611-20 (1990) *Enlisted Career Management Fields and Military Occupational Specialties*. Washington, DC: Headquarters, Department of the Army.

Arnoff, H. (1987). Human engineering policy revisions in the Naval Air Systems Command programs. Memorandum, Naval Air Systems Command, Department of the Navy, Washington, DC.

Ayoub, M. M. & Mital, A. (1989). *Manual Materials Handling*. London: Taylor & Francis.

Baxter, J. H. (1875). *Statistics, Medical and Anthropological, of the Provost-Marshal-General's Bureau, Derived from the Records of the Examination for Military Service in the Armies of the United States During the Late War of the Rebellion*. Washington, DC: Government Printing Office.

Bell, N., Donelson, S. M. & Wolfson, E. (1991). *An Annotated Bibliography of U.S. Army Natick Anthropology (1947–1991)*. (Technical Report NATICK/TR-91/044.) US Army Natick Research, Development & Engineering Center, Natick, Massachusetts.

Bittner, A. C. (1976). *Computerized Accommodated Percentage Evaluation: Review and Prospectus*. (Technical Publication TP-76-46.) Pacific Missile Test Center, Point Mugu, California.

Bittner, A. C., Morissey, S. J. & Moroney, W. F. (1975). *Demonstration of an Approach to Evaluate Cockpit/Aircrew Anthropometric Compatibility: Advanced Harrier (AV-16A) Analysis*. (Technical Publication TP-75-31.) Pacific Missile Test Center, Point Mugu, California.

Bittner, A. C., Glenn, F. A., Harris, R. M., Iavecchia, H. P. & Wherry, R. J., (1987). CADRE: a family of manikins for workstation design. In: *Trends in Ergonomics/Human Factors* vol. 4, ed. S. S. Asfour, pp. 733–40. North-Holland: Elsevier Science Publishers.

Bradtmiller, B., McConville, J. T. & Clauser, C. E. (1985). *Evaluation of a statistical matching procedure*. (Contract #DAAK60-84-C-0086, Task IV Final Report.) US Army Natick Research, Development & Engineering Center, Natick, Massachusetts.

Bradtmiller, B., Rhatnaparkhi, J. & Tebbetts, I. (1986). *Demographic and Anthropometric Assessment of a U.S. Army Anthropometric Data Base*. (Technical Report NATICK/TR-86/004.) US Army Natick Research, Development & Engineering Center, Natick, Massachusetts.

Brues, A. M. (1992). Applied physical anthropology in the Army Air Force and the development of the ball turret. *Anthropology Newsletter* **33**, 3.

Buddin, R. (1989). *Weight Problems and Attrition of High-Quality Military Recruits*. Santa Monica, California: The RAND Corporation, N-2847-FMP.

Chase, N. B. (1990). Memorandum for All Flight Surgeons, Subject: APL 11-90 Aviation Anthropometry, dated 18 April 1990. Headquarters US Army Aeromedical Center, Fort Rucker, Alabama.

Churchill, E. (1978). Statistical considerations in man-machine designs. In: *Anthropometric Source Book*, vol. 1 (*Anthropometry for Designers*) chapter 9 pp. IX-1–62. (NASA Reference Publication 1024.) Washington, DC: National Aeronautics and Space Administration.

Churchill, E. & McConville, J. T. (1976). *Sampling and Data Gathering Strategies for Future USAF Anthropometry*. (Technical Report AMRL-TR-74-102.) USAF Aerospace Medical Research Laboratory, Wright-Patterson AFB, Ohio.

Churchill, E., McConville, J. T., Laubach, L. L. & White, R. M. (1971). *Anthropometry of U.S. Army Aviators - 1970*. (Technical Report 72-52-CE.) US Army Natick Laboratories, Natick, Massachusetts.

Churchill, E., Churchill, T., McConville, J. T. & White, R. M. (1977). *Anthropometry of Women of the U.S. Army - 1977; Report No. 2, the Basic Univariate Statistics*. (Technical Report NATICK/TR-77/024.) US Army Natick Research and Development Command, Natick, Massachusetts.

Churchill, T. D., Bradtmiller, B. & Gordon, C. C. (1988). *Computer Software Used in U.S. Army Anthropometric Survey 1987-1988*. (Technical Report NATICK/TR-88/045.) US Army Natick Research, Development & Engineering Center, Natick, Massachusetts.

Clauser, C. E., Tucker, P. E., McConville, J. T., Churchill, E., Laubach, L. & Reardon, J. (1972). *Anthropometry of Air Force Women*. (Technical Report AMRL-TR-70-5.) Aerospace Medical Research Laboratory, Wright-Patterson AFB, Ohio.

Clauser, C. E., McConville, J. T., Gordon, C. C. & Tebbetts, I. O. (1986a). *Selection of Dimensions for an Anthropometric Data Base*, vol. 1 (*Rationale, Summary, & Conclusions*). (Technical Report NATICK/TR-86/053.) US Army Natick Research, Development & Engineering Center, Natick, Massachusetts.

Clauser, C. E., McConville, J. T., Gordon, C. C. & Tebbetts, I. O. (1986b). *Selection of Dimensions for an Anthropometric Data Base*, vol. 2 (Dimension Evaluation Sheets). (Technical Report NATICK/TR-86/054.) US Army Natick Research, Development & Engineering Center, Natick, Massachusetts.

Clauser, C. E., Tebbetts, I., Bradtmiller, B., McConville, J. & Gordon, C. (1988). *Measurer's Handbook - U.S. Army Anthropometric Survey, 1987–1988*. (Technical Report NATICK/TR-88/043). US Army Natick Research, Development & Engineering Center, Natick, Massachusetts.

Coblentz, A., Mollard, R. & Ignazi, G. (1990). Normes anthropometriques et selection des personnels navigants feminins francais. In: *AGARD Conference*

Proceedings No. 491 (Recruiting, Selection, Training and Military Operations of Female Aircrew), pp. 16-1 – 16-11. Neuilly-Sur-Seine: North Atlantic Treaty Organization.

Conway, T. L., Cronan, T. A. & Peterson, K. A. (1989). Circumference-estimated percent body fat vs. weight-height indices: relationships to physical fitness. *Aviation, Space, and Environmental Medicine* **60**, 433–7.

Cote, D. O. & Schopper, A. W. (1984). *Anthropometric Cockpit Compatibility Assessment of U.S. Army Aircraft for Large and Small Personnel Wearing a Cold Weather, Armored Vest, Chemical Defense Protective Clothing Configuration.* (USAARL Report No. 81-11.) US Army Aeromedical Research Laboratory, Fort Rucker, Alabama.

Davenport, C. B. & Love, A. G. (1921). *The Medical Department of the United States Army in the World War*, vol. 15 (Statistics), part 1 (Army Anthropology). Washington, DC: US Government Printing Office.

Department of Defense (1981). *Study of the Military Services Physical Fitness.* Washington, DC: Office of the Assistant Secretary of Defense for Manpower, Reserve Affairs and Logistics, April 3, 1981.

Farr, W. D. & Buescher, T. M. (1989). U.S. Army anthropometric standards for rotary-wing aviators in the light observation helicopter. *Aviation, Space, and Environmental Medicine* **60** (suppl. 7), A74-6.

Friedl, K. E. (1992). Body composition and military performance: origins of the Army standards. In: *Body Composition and Military Performance*, ed. B. M. Marriott & J. Grumstrup-Scott, pp. 31–55. Washington, DC: National Academy of Sciences.

Friedl, K. E. & Vogel, J. A. (1991). Looking for a few good generalized body-fat equations. *American Journal of Clinical Nutrition* **53**, 795–6.

Friedl, K. E., Vogel, J. A., Bovee, M. W. & Jones, B. H. (1989). *Assessment of Body Weight Standards in Male and Female Army Recruits.* (Technical Report T15-90.) US Army Research Institute of Environmental Medicine, Natick, Massachusetts.

Friedl, K. E., De Luca, J. P., Marchitelli, L. J. & Vogel, J. A. (1992). Reliability of body-fat estimations from a four-compartment model by using density, body water, and bone mineral measurements. *American Journal of Clinical Nutrition* **55**, 764–70.

Gifford, E. C., Provost, J. R. & Lazo, J. (1965). *Anthropometry of Naval Aviators – 1964.* (Report NAEC-ACEL-533.) Aerospace Crew Equipment Laboratory, US Naval Air Engineering Center, Philadelphia, Pennsylvania.

Gordon, C. C. (1986). Anthropometric sizing and fit testing of a single battledress uniform for U.S. Army men and women. In: *Performance of Protective Clothing* (ASTM STP 900), ed. R. L. Barker & G. C. Coletta, pp. 581–92. Philadelphia: American Society for Testing and Materials.

Gordon, C. C. & Bradtmiller, B. (1992). Interobserver error in a large scale anthropometric survey. *American Journal of Human Biology* **4**, 253–63.

Gordon, C. C., Bradtmiller, B., Churchill, T., Clauser, C. E., McConville, J. T., Tebbetts, I. O. & Walker, R. A. (1989). *1988 Anthropometric Survey of U.S. Army Personnel: Methods and Summary Statistics.* (Technical Report NATICK/TR-89/044.) US Army Natick Research, Development & Engineering Center, Natick, Massachusetts.

Gould, B. A. (1869). *Investigations in the Military and Anthropological Statistics of American Soldiers.* New York: Hurd and Houghton. (Reprinted in 1979 by Arno Press, New York.)

Greiner, T. M. & Gordon, C. C. (1990). *An Assessment of Long-Term Changes in Anthropometric Dimensions: Secular Trends of U.S. Army Males.* (Technical Report NATICK/TR-91/006.) Natick Research, Development & Engineering Center, Natick, Massachusetts.

Greiner, T. M. & Gordon, C. C. (1991). Biocultural influences in the analysis of secular trends. Paper presented at the 90th Annual Meeting of the American Anthropological Association, Chicago, Illinois, 20–24 November 1991.

Greiner, T. M. & Gordon, C. C. (1992). Secular trends of 22 body dimensions in four racial/cultural groups of American males. *American Journal of Human Biology* **4**, 235–46.

Grunhofer, H. & Kroh, G. (1975). *A Review of Anthropometric Data of German Air Force and United States Air Force Flying Personnel 1967–1968.* (Technical Report AGARD-AG-205.) Neuilly-Sur-Seine: North Atlantic Treaty Organization.

Hendy, K. C. (1990). Aircrew/cockpit compatibility: a multivariate problem seeking a multivariate solution. In: *AGARD Conference Proceedings No. 491 (Recruiting, Selection, Training & Military Operations of Female Aircrew)*, pp. 15-1 – 15-8. Neuilly-Sur-Seine: North Atlantic Treaty Organization.

Hendy, K. C., Anderson, K. W. & Drumm, D. M. (1984). *A Graphic Anthropometric Aid for Seating and Workplace Design.* (Technical Report AR-003-023.) Department of Defence Aeronautical Research Laboratories, Melbourne, Australia.

Hertzberg, H. T. E., Daniels, G. S. & Churchill, E. (1954). *Anthropometry of Flying Personnel – 1950.* (Technical Report WADC TR-52-321.) Aeromedical Laboratory, Wright Air Development Center, Wright-Patterson AFB, Ohio.

Hodgdon, J. A. & Fitzgerald, P. I. (1987). Validity of impedance predictions at various levels of fatness. *Human Biology* **59**, 281–98.

Hodgdon, J. A., Fitzgerald, P. I. & Vogel, J. A. (1990). *Relationships between body fat and appearance ratings of U.S. soldiers.* (Technical Report T12-90.) US Army Research Institute of Environmental Medicine, Natick, Massachusetts.

Kennedy, K. W. (1986). *The Derivation of Low Profile and Variable Cockpit Geometries to Achieve 1st to 99th Percentile Accommodation.* (Technical Report AAMRL-TR-86-016.) Armstrong Aerospace Medical Research Laboratory, Wright-Patterson AFB, Ohio.

Kroemer, K. H. E., Snook, S. H., Meadows, S. K. & Deutsch, S. (eds) (1989). *Ergonomic Models of Anthropometry, Human Biomechanics, and Operator-Equipment Interfaces: Proceedings of a Workshop.* Washington, DC: National Academy Press.

Kryswicki, H. J., Consolazio, C. F. & Johnson, H. L. (1970). Alterations in exercise and body composition with age. In: *Proceedings of the Eighth International Congress on Nutrition, Prague, September 1969*, ed. J. Masek, K. Osancova & D. P. Cuthbertson, pp. 522–6. Amsterdam: *Excerpta Medica International*, Series No. 213.

Larsson, B., Svardsuud, K., Wilhelmsen, L., Bjorntorp, P. & Tibblin, G. (1984). Abdominal adipose tissue distribution, obesity, and risk of cardiovascular disease and death: 13-year follow up of participants in the study of men born in 1913. *British Medical Journal* **288**, 1401–4.

Laurence, M. T. (1988). *Enlistment Height/Weight Standards and Attrition from the Military*. (Technical Report, April 1988.) Defense Manpower Data Center, Arlington, Virginia.

Lohman, T. G., Roche, A. F. & Martorell, R. (1988). *Anthropometric Standardization Reference Manual*. Champaign, Illinois: Human Kinetics Books.

Lukaski, H. C. (1987). Bioelectrical impedance analysis. In: *Nutrition '87*, ed. O. A. Levander, pp. 78–81. Bethesda, Maryland: American Institute of Nutrition.

McConville, J. T. (1978). Anthropometry in sizing and design. In: *Anthropometric Source Book*, vol. 1 (*Anthropometry for Designers*) (NASA Reference Publication 1024), chapter 8, pp. VIII-1–23. Washington, DC: National Aeronautics and Space Administration.

McConville, J. T. & Churchill, E. (1976). *Statistical Concepts in Design*. (Technical Report AMRL-TR-76-29.) Aerospace Medical Research Laboratory, Wright-Patterson AFB, Ohio.

McConville, J. T., Robinette, K. M. & White, R. M. (1981). *An Investigation of Integrated Sizing for U.S. Army Men and Women*. (Technical Report NATICK/TR-81/033.) US Army Natick Research and Development Laboratories, Natick, Massachusetts.

Meindl, R. S., Zehner, G. F. & Hudson, J. A. (1993). *A Multivariate Anthropometric Method for Crewstation Design: Unabridged*. (Technical Report.) Armstrong Laboratory, Air Force Systems Command, Wright-Patterson AFB, Ohio.

MIL-STD-1333B (1976). *Aircrew Station Geometry for Military Aircraft*. Washington, DC: Department of Defense.

MIL-STD-1472D (1991). *Human Engineering Design Criteria for Military Systems, Equipment and Facilities*. Redstone Arsenal: US Army Missile Command.

Moroney, W. F. & Smith, M. J. (1972). *Empirical Reduction in Potential User Population as the Result of Imposed Multivariate Anthropometric Limits*. (Technical Report NAMRL-1164.) Naval Aerospace Medical Research Laboratory, Pensacola, Florida.

Najjar, M. & Rowland, M. (1987). *Anthropometric Reference Data and Prevalence of Overweight, United States, 1976–80*. (Vital & Health Statistics, Series 11, No. 238, Public Health Service.) Washington, DC: US Government Printing Office.

Navy Regulation 15-34 (1991). *Medical Examinations*. Washington, DC: Department of the Navy.

Newman, R. W. & White, R. M. (1951). *Reference Anthropometry of Army Men*. (Environmental Protection Section Report No. 180.) US Army Quartermaster Climatic Research Laboratory, Lawrence, Massachusetts.

Ordronaux, J. (1863). *Manual of Instructions for Military Surgeons on the Examination of Recruits and Discharge of Soldiers*. New York: Van Nostrand.

Paquette, S. P. (1990). *Human and Analogue Models for Computer-Aided Design and Engineering Applications*. (Technical Report NATICK/TR-90/054.) US Army Natick Research, Development & Engineering Center, Natick, Massachusetts.

Randall, F. E. & Munro, E. H. (1949). *Anthropometric Nomograph of Army Women*. (Environmental Protection Section Report No. 1458.) U.S. Army Quartermaster Climatic Research Laboratory, Lawrence, Massachusetts.

Reeps, S. M., Pheeny, H. T. & Brady, J. A. (1990). Accommodation of female aircrew in USN protective flight clothing and equipment. In: AGARD Conference Proceedings No. 491 (*Recruiting, Selection, Training and Military Operations of Female Aircrew*), pp. 22-1 – 22-7. Neuilly-Sur-Seine: North Atlantic Treaty Organization.

Robertson, D. W. & Trent, T. T. (1985). *Documentation of Muscularly Demanding Job Tasks and Validation of an Occupational Strength Test Battery (STB)*. (Report No. 86-1. Naval Personnel Research and Development Center, San Diego, California.

Robinette, K. M. & Annis, J. F. (1986). *A Nine-Size System for Chemical Defense Gloves*. (Technical Report AAMRL-TR-86-029.) Armstrong Aerospace Medical Research Laboratory, Wright-Patterson, AFB, Ohio.

Robinette, K. M. & Churchill, T. (1979). *Design Criteria for Characterizing Individuals in the Extreme Upper and Lower Body Size Ranges*. (Technical Report AMRL-TR-79-33.) USAF Aerospace Medical Research Laboratory, Wright-Patterson AFB, Ohio.

Robinette, K. M., Churchill, T. & McConville, J. T. (1979) *A Comparison of Male and Female Body Sizes and Proportions*. (Technical Report AMRL-TR-79-69.) Aerospace Medical Research Laboratory, Wright-Patterson AFB, Ohio.

Robinette, K. M. & Fowler, J. (1988). *Annotated Bibliography of United States Air Force Engineering Anthropometry – 1946 to 1988*. (Technical Report AAMRL-TR-88-013.) Armstrong Aerospace Medical Research Laboratory, Wright-Patterson AFB, Ohio.

Robinette, K. M. & McConville, J. T. (1981). *An Alternative to Percentile Models*. (SAE Technical Paper No. 810217). Warrendale: Society of Automotive Engineers.

Robinette, K. M., Mellian, S. A. & Ervin, C. A. (1990). *Development of Sizing Systems for Navy Women's Uniforms*. (Technical Report NCTRF 183.) Navy Clothing & Textile Research Facility, Natick, Massachusetts.

Robinson, J. C., Robinette, K. M. & Zehner, G. F. (1992). *User's Guide to Accessing the Center for Anthropometric Research Data Anthropometric Data Base*, 2nd Edition. (Technical Report AL-TR-1992-0036.) Armstrong Laboratory, Air Force Systems Command, Wright-Patterson AFB, Ohio.

Roebuck, J. A., Kroemer, K. H. E. & Thomson, W. G. (1975). *Engineering Anthropometry Methods*. New York: John Wiley & Sons.

Rose, D. A. & Erickson, R. T. (1988). *Naval Aviator Anthropometric and Aviation Life Support System Equipment Cockpit Incompatibilities*. (Technical Report NADC-88120-60.) Naval Air Development Center, Warminster, Pennsylvania.

Rothwell, P. L. (1985). Use of man-modelling CAD systems by the ergonomist. In: *People and Computers: Designing the Interface*, ed. P. Johnson & S. Cook, pp. 199–208. New York: Cambridge University Press.

Rothwell, P. L. (1989). Representation of man using CAD technology: user beware. In: *Applications of Human Performance Models to System Design*, ed.

G. R. McMillan, D. Beevis, E. Salas, M. H. Strub, R. Sutton & L. V. Bread, pp. 365–72. New York: Plenum Press.

Rothwell, P. L. & Pigeau, R. A. (1990). Anthropometric accommodation of females in Canadian Forces aircraft crew stations. In: *AGARD Conference Proceedings No. 491 (Recruiting, Selection, Training & Military Operations of Female Aircrew)*, pp. 18-1 – 18-13. Neuilly-Sur-Seine: North Atlantic Treaty Organization.

Schafer, E. & Bates, B. T. (1988). *Anthropometric Comparisons Between Body Measurements of Men and Women*. (Technical Report TR-88-020). Armstrong Aerospace Medical Research Laboratory, Wright-Patterson AFB, Ohio.

Schopper, A. W. (1986). *Proportions of Overall U.S. Army Male and Female Populations Eligible for Flying Duty: Impact of Linear Anthropometric Screening Requirements*. (USAARL Report No. 86-14.) US Army Aeromedical Research Laboratory, Fort Rucker, Alabama.

Schopper, A. W. & Cote, D. O. (1984). *Anthropometric Cockpit Compatibility Assessment of U.S. Army Aircraft for Large and Small Personnel Wearing a Training, Warm-Weather Clothing Configuration*. (USAARL Report No. 84-10.) US Army Aeromedical Research Laboratory, Fort Rucker, Alabama.

Seidell, J. C., Cigolini, M., Chrozewska, J., Ellsinger, B. M., Di Brase, G., Bjorntorp, P., Hautvast, J. G. A., Contaldo, F., Szostak, V. & Scuro, L. A. (1990). Androgenicity in relation to body fat distribution and metabolism in 38-year-old women – the European fat distribution study. *Journal of Clinical Epidemiology* **43**, 21–34.

Terry, R. B., Stefanick, M. L., Haskell, W. L. & Wood, P. D. (1991). Contributions of regional adipose tissue depots to plasma lipoprotein concentrations in overweight men and women: possible protective effects of thigh fat. *Metabolism* **40**, 733–40.

Tri-Service Aeromedical Research Panel (1988). *Anthropometry and Mass Distribution for Human Analogues*, vol. I (*Military Male Aviators*). (USAARL Report 88-5. US Army Aeromedical Research Laboratory, Fort Rucker, Alabama.

Turner, G. M. (1986). *Aircrew Size Limitations – RAF Policy and Procedures*. (Aircrew Equipment Group Report No. 525.) Royal Air Force Institute of Aviation Medicine, Farnborough, United Kingdom.

Turner, G. M. (1990). The application of USAF female anthropometric data to identify problems with the introduction of female aircrew into the Royal Air Force. In: *AGARD Conference Proceedings No. 491 (Recruiting, Selection, Training & Military Operations of Female Aircrew)*, pp. 17-1 – 17-3. Neuilly-Sur-Seine: North Atlantic Treaty Organization.

Vogel, J. A. & Friedl, K. E. (1992). Body fat assessment in women: special considerations. *Sports Medicine* **13**, 245–69.

Vogel, J. A., Wright, J. E., Patton, J. F., Sharp, D. S., Dawson, J. & Eschenback, M. P. (1980). *A System for Establishing Occupationally-Related Gender-Free Physical Fitness Standards*. (Technical Report No. T5/80.) US Army Research Institute of Environmental Medicine, Natick, Massachusetts.

Walker, R. A. (1991). The impact of racial variation on human engineering design criteria. Paper presented at the 90th Annual Meeting of the American Anthropological Association, Chicago, Illinois, 20–24 November 1991.

White, R. M. (1978). *United States Army Anthropometry: 1946–1977.* (Technical Report NATICK/TR-79/007.) US Army Natick Research & Development Command, Natick, Massachusetts.

White, R. M. & Churchill, E. (1971). *The Body Size of Soldiers: U.S. Army Anthropometry – 1966.* (Technical Report 72-51-CE.) US Army Natick Laboratories, Natick, Massachusetts.

Woodward, A. A., Corona, B. M., Thomas, M. L. & Bachovchin, V. L. (1981). *Sizing and Fitting Evaluation of Battledress Uniforms for Female Soldiers.* (Technical Memorandum 7-81, DA Project No. 1G74713L40.) US Army Human Engineering Laboratory, Aberdeen Proving Ground, Maryland.

Wright, H. W., Dotson, C. O. & Davis, P. O. (1980). An investigation of assessment techniques for body composition of women Marines. *U.S. Navy Medicine* **71**, 15–26.

Wright, H. W., Dotson, C. O. & Davis, P. O. (1981). A simple technique for measurement of percent body fat in man. *U.S. Navy Medicine* **72**, 23–7.

Zehner, G. F., Meindl, R. S. & Hudson, J. A. (1992). *A Multivariate Anthropometric Method for Crewstation Design: Abridged.* (Technical Report.) Armstrong Laboratory, Air Force Systems Command, Wright-Patterson AFB, Ohio.

Zehner, G. F. (personal communication). A technical report describing anthropometric limitations of contemporary USAF aircraft is in preparation by G. F. Zehner and K. W. Kennedy at the Armstrong Laboratory, Air Force Systems Command, Wright-Patterson A.F.B., Ohio.

Zillikens, M. C. & Conway, J. M. (1990). Anthropometry in Blacks: applicability of generalized skinfold equations and differences in fat patterning between Blacks and Whites. *American Journal of Clinical Nutrition* **52**, 45–51.

Index

211